The New Arab Social Order

Also of Interest

OPEC, the Gulf, and the World Petroleum Market, Fereidun Fesharaki

Libya: The Experience of Oil, J. A. Allen

The United Arab Emirates: Unity in Fragmentation, Ali Mohammed Khalifa

Food, Development, and Politics in the Middle East, Marvin Weinbaum

OPEC: Twenty Years and Beyond, edited by Ragaei El Mallakh

About the Book and Author

The New Arab Social Order:
A Study of the Social Impact of Oil Wealth
Saad Eddin Ibrahim

The skyrocketing Arab oil revenues of the 1970s have triggered tremendous socioeconomic forces in the Arab world. Observers have extensively studied the financial and geopolitical aspects of Arab oil, but generally have ignored the human and social repercussions stimulated by the oil wealth. This book challenges the commonly accepted view of the impact of manpower movements across the Arab "wealth divide," looking at the new social formations, class structures, value systems, and social cleavages that have been emerging in both rich and poor Arab countries. Dr. Ibrahim posits that these developments add up to a silent social revolution and are quite possibly a prelude to more overt tension, conflict, and political turmoil.

Saad Eddin Ibrahim is professor of sociology at The American University in Cairo and head of Arab affairs at Al-Ahram Center for Political and Strategic Studies. He is the author of numerous publications, including *Kissinger and the Middle East* (1975) and *Trends of Arab Public Opinion Toward Arab Unity* (1980).

The New Arab Social Order

A Study of the Social Impact of Oil Wealth

Saad Eddin Ibrahim

Westview Press • Boulder, Colorado
Croom Helm • London, England

This volume is included in Westview's Special Studies on the Middle East.

Published in 1982 in the United States of America by
  Westview Press, Inc.
  5500 Central Avenue
  Boulder, Colorado 80301
  Frederick A. Praeger, President and Publisher

Published in 1982 in Great Britain by
  Croom Helm Ltd
  2–10 St Johns Road
  London SW11

Library of Congress Catalog Card Number: 81-16191
ISBN (U.S.): 0-86531-314-8
ISBN (U.K.): 0-7099-1305-2

Printed and bound in the United States of America

Contents

Tables and Figures

Figures

Acknowledgments

The bulk of this study was written during 1980 while I was a visiting professor at the University of California at Los Angeles (UCLA). The atmosphere provided by the Gustave Von Grunebaum Center for Near Eastern Studies and the light teaching load demanded by the Sociology Department made it possible to do most of the library research and writing.

This study is a spin-off of a larger research project on the poor and rich Arab states coordinated by Professor Malcolm Kerr of UCLA and Professor Sayed Yassin, director of Al-Ahram's Center for Political and Strategic Studies in Cairo. Their encouragement throughout and their valuable comments on an earlier draft were instrumental in completing this work and improving its quality.

In the summer of 1980 a workshop for participants on the Poor and Rich Arab States Project was held at UCLA. Professors G. Amin, N. Ayubi, H. Beblawi, P. Jaber, F. El-Gindi, and G. Sabagh attended the workshop, along with the two project coordinators. Their close scrutiny and sharp criticism of the first draft were quite helpful in upgrading this study.

Other friends, colleagues, and students were exposed to the ideas and arguments made in this study in one form or another. In a graduate study seminar at UCLA offered jointly by my friend Ali Dessouki and me, the main arguments of this book were presented in their embryonic form. The students, along with professors N. Ayubi, N. Keddie, and G. Sabagh, who were regular attendants of the seminar, gave these arguments their first merciless test. Professor Afaf L. El-Sayed Marsot of UCLA also read the first draft and made several encouraging comments, which were much needed by that time.

Mrs. Lindy Ayubi and Mrs. Elizabeth Absoud struggled through earlier drafts of the manuscript, checked and corrected my irresponsible spelling of countless words, and typed the first and final drafts, respectively. My long-time graduate assistants, Jehan Attia and Nemat Guenera, patiently checked the notes and prepared the bibliography.

Finally, my wife and former student, Dr. Barbara Lethem Ibrahim, who is my sharpest critic, made it possible for me to complete this work. Her gracious absence with full responsibility for the children for three months during the summer of 1980 was much appreciated.

Saad Eddin Ibrahim

1
Introduction

Social orders reproduce themselves with every new generation. But with each reproduction, varying degrees of alteration or even mutation take place. The Arab social order is no exception. Since the traumatic rediscovery of the West by the Arabs at the end of the eighteenth century and the subsequent Western penetration into the Arab homeland, four big waves of social change have left their deep impacts on the Arab social structure. The colonial experience, modern science and technology, the national struggle for emancipation, and oil are the hallmarks of the four tidal waves and their chain-reaction effects in the transformation of Arab society.[1] Every Arab generation since the 1800s has experienced the collapse of one or more aspects of the premodern social order and the gestation, difficult labor, and occasional Cesarian birth of a new one. There have been many false pregnancies and several miscarriages. But through it all, the old structures never disappeared; they lay there, albeit in a crumpled or twisted form, but have continued to coexist with new or with caricatures of modern structures. The continuous interplay between elements of the old and the new has given the Arab World a permanent state of "transition" for the last two centuries. Every generation believed it was the bearer of the burdens of "transition," and occasionally felt trapped or victimized by it.

The Arab social order in the 1980s is a product of previous orders intersecting with regional and global events of the last two decades. The symbolic point of its emergence may date back to the Arab defeat of 1967, to the death of Nasser in 1970, or to the Arab sense of "triumph" in their fourth war with Israel in 1973.[2] But whatever the hypothetical conception point of the new order, oil has been its underlying factor. As a salient substructural force, oil has not only altered the global reaction between the Arabs and the rest of the world, but has also triggered manifest as well as latent forces of change in the inter-Arab equation, within each Arab society, and inside most men and women of the Arab World. To be sure, oil had been affecting the social landscape in a score of producing countries for the previous three decades. But it is in the last ten years that the oil-related social changes have been phenomenally accelerated within those countries and have spilled over dramatically into neighboring countries. In this sense, it is justified to speak of one Arab social order; the chain of causation begins in some countries and ends up in others, and vice versa.

It would be an oversimplification to attribute all features of the new Arab social order to oil. But it is not an exaggeration to contend that oil is the most important single factor in giving this order its unique characteristics. In this sense, we submit that oil in its own right has triggered as many qualitative and quantitative changes as each of the three previous waves: colonialism, introduction of science and technology, and national struggle for liberation.

The new Arab social order we propose to analyze here is still emerging; it is in a continuous state of flux. Thus the word "order" should not imply "orderly," "congruency," or "harmony." If anything, early indications point to marked tension, conflict, and inconsistencies in the new Arab social order. It is an "order," nevertheless, insofar as its elements are linked to and affect one another. This new order may be held together by fear or trust, love or hate, national unifiers or subcultural diversifiers; or by a combination of all. But it is held together by constant internal motion even if it seems to outsiders to be immobile.

When we assert that oil has been a major determinant of the new social order it should of course be realized that we are talking not simply about oil as a "raw material." It is all the facets of this strategic substance; i.e., as energy source, technology, money, geopolitics, and manpower. The interaction among all these facets on one hand, and the existing social structures on the other, has produced a host of social-cultural changes that we are subsuming under the label "new order." It includes the emergence of new social formations (e.g., classes, status groups), new demographic allocations and dislocations, new values and normative systems, new behavioral patterns, and new lines of conflict.

Like all societal configurations, the new Arab social order has its images—outward manifestations of substructural dynamics. We start, in Chapter 2, with some of these images: then we trace them back to the major social forces at work in contemporary Arab society. Three of these images (the mechanized nomad, the lumpen capitalist-entrepreneur, and the *"kafil"*) are from the oil-rich Arab countries. Three others (the Egyptian peasant in Arabia, the veiled medical student, and the angry Muslim militant) are primarily from non-oil countries. All six images exist everywhere in the Arab World; but some are more pronounced in oil countries and some are more preponderant in non-oil countries. The major societal dynamics to which these images and other new sociocultural products are traceable may be summed up in one phrase: movement of manpower and money across country borders caused by oil. The volume and pattern of this movement are analyzed in Chapter 3.

Egypt and Saudi Arabia will be our focal points of reference. They epitomize the salient features of the new Arab social order. One, Egypt, is overpopulated, poor, with surplus labor, a tremendous capacity to absorb capital of which there is very little, and with fairly well-developed manpower and social institutions. The other, Saudi Arabia, is underpopulated, with labor shortage, limited capacity to absorb capital of which there is plenty, and with underdeveloped manpower and only the embryonic genesis of modern institutions. The two countries in many ways represent opposite ends of one bipolar social order in the Arab World at present. In Chapters 4 and 5 we discuss the causes and consequences of labor exportation from Egypt and labor importation to Saudi Arabia, respectively.

The Arab World has had several revolutions in this century. Some have been loud with sounds and fury. Others have been silent. Loud or silent, a revolution is primarily defined by its impact. Oil and movement of manpower and money across country lines is one of the Arab World's silent revolutions. Its impact is the birth of a new Arab social order. A major feature of that order is a new stratification system among the Arab states and within each state. The novel phenomenon of a "country-class" in the Arab World is discussed in Chapter 6. The new inter-Arab stratification system has, in turn, generated new links and interdependence among the poor, the middle, the rich, and the super-rich Arab states. Such links, we argue in Chapter 6, give the Arab World a level of socioeconomic unity unprecedented since the zenith of the Arab-Islamic Empire of the eighth century A.D. But the quality of this unity is a far cry from what Arab Nationalists have dreamt of in this twentieth century.

In the final chapter, Chapter 7, we discuss some of the political bottlenecks in the new Arab order. We argue that the phenomenal growth of oil wealth has not been accompanied by structural socioeconomic-political development. Inter-Arab and intra-Arab inequalities, as well as growing dependence relations with more advanced countries, especially in the West, are generating tremendous tension in the new Arab order.

Images of the New Social Order

Arab society has known three major modes of living: desert, countryside, and town. One way of gauging social change is to monitor over time what happens in each of these three modes of living. The six images of change we sketch below cover the spectrum of Arab human ecology. The first image, the mechanized Bedouin, is central to the present-day desert mode of living. The two images of lumpen capitalists, as well as the veiled medical student and the angry Muslim militant, are typically urban images. The Egyptian peasant outside the Nile Valley is an outgrowth of the rural mode of living.

Each of the six images is symptomatic of structural changes in Arab society. A change is defined here as "structural" if it entails qualitative rather than merely quantitative alteration in values, norms, attitudes, relations, or behavioral patterns.[1]

The Mechanized Bedouin

Nomadism is one of the oldest life-styles in the Arab World.[2] The fact that over 80 percent of the area is desert, arid, and with very little rainfall gave rise to nomadic pastoral life for a segment of Arab population—the Bedouins. All the country states of the Arab World have a Bedouin component in their population. But it is in Saudi Arabia, the Gulf States, southwestern Iraq, the Syrian desert, Libya, Sudan, and Somalia that Bedouin population exceeds 10 percent of the total. The 1977 Saudi census estimates their number at about 1.9 million or 25 percent of the kingdom's total official population.

The main social organization of the Bedouins is made up of the tribe (*kabila*) and its subsegments (*ʿashirah, batn,* and *fakhz*). Their habitat is the desert, their shelter is animal-hair tents, and their means of sustenance are camel or sheep herds. Their value system emphasizes primordial loyalty to the kinship group, communalism, courage, and hospitality. In sum, the traditional image of the nomadic Bedouin for the last few millenia has been a tent, a herd, a horse, a sword, a primordial value system, and constant roaming in the desert. This combination of elements made for a successful system of adaptation to a harsh environment. It also set the Bedouin life-style aside in sharp distinction from the two sedentary life-styles of Arab society, the rural and the urban.

This nomadic life-style, which had resisted any marked alteration for thousands of years, is now undergoing major changes. In the early days of oil exploration in the late 1930s, Bedouins began to work first as guides for American oil companies and then as unskilled laborers. Some of them were trained to drive and maintain trucks. Some began to purchase secondhand pickup trucks from the Arabian-American Oil Company (ARAMCO).[3] It was a new status symbol for the few during the 1950s and 1960s. But in the last ten years the truck and other types of motor vehicles have become a "tent-hold" item. Now they are the functional equivalent of baggage camels and horses. Trucks are used to haul water, to transport flocks of sheep from one grazing site to another, and to oversee camel herding over a wide expanse of desert.

The motor vehicle has had a tremendous effect on the life of the Bedouins. It has opened up new cultural and economic vistas to the nomads. Now they go to cities more often; they listen to the radio all the time while roaming the desert; and they deal with car agents, mechanics, electricians, and gasoline dealers.

The increasing use of trucks in the desert has been accompanied by other equally dramatic changes in the infrastructure basic to the exploitation of the desert. Both government and oil companies developed underground water resources by drilling deep wells. As a result, the nomad's patterns of grazing and time cycles have markedly changed. Now they can stay longer, especially in the summer, in one site close to waterheads. They have also learned to share water sources with other tribes, since the wells are not tribally dug or owned. These two developments have inspired the government to offer the nomads educational, social, and health services during the summer season. The services delivery program is known as the Summer Campaign and has expanded steadily since 1977 to cover the entire kingdom. The government is planting, and in fact building into the Summer Campaigns, the seeds of sedentarization of the Saudi Bedouins. The location of the school, the mosque, and the clinic around a deep water well gives the nomadic tribes a point of reference and an incentive to settle. Other enticements are constantly offered.[4]

Underlying the interest of the government in settling the nomads is the serious shortage of manpower in Saudi Arabia—a problem that is discussed in more than one place in this volume. The Saudi nomadic

Bedouins and the Saudi women are the two major untapped sources of badly needed indigenous manpower. While it may be quite a time before the puritanical Saudi mores allow the tapping of womanpower, the nomads are readily accessible.

Efforts to incorporate nomads into modern sectors of the Saudi society have succeeded in only two areas: working in the oil fields and enlisting in the Saudi National Guard.[5] In both cases, however, the individual Bedouin remains strongly committed to his tribe and to its nomadic life-style. He shuttles back and forth between the two subcultures for some years, then often gets married, retires from the modern sector, and settles back into the nomadic life-style along with the rest of his clan or tribe. Of course, some may opt for permanent sedentary life, but this is still the exception.

Reverting back to a nomadic life-style, however, is not going back to traditional nomadism. The tent, the camel, the sheep, the horse, and the sword are all still there. But cascading over them are the truck, the radio, and the machine gun. The Bedouins still move around the vast Arabian desert. But they linger longer at each site; and when they decide to move from one site to another it is now much faster. The herd is still the Bedouins' major economic base—for milk, meat, hair, transport, and as a medium of exchange. But now it is supplemented by cash money from wages and salaries obtained from working in the oil fields or as national guardsmen. The traditional Bedouin diet of milk, dates, and meat has been supplemented by Uncle Ben's Converted Rice and canned food.

Oil and the wealth spilling over from it have affected the Bedouins in still another way. Camels are now bred as luxury and sport items. The Royal Family and the Saudi upper stratum have gone heavily into camel racing in recent years. The Bedouins have, in turn, made a sizeable profit from the new sport. A good race camel may sell for as much as $15,000.

The Saudi Bedouins, like other groups in the Arab World, have been touched deeply by oil and its chain effects. We noted here some of the obvious consequences. No doubt there are other consequences that remain latent. Also, like other groups, the Bedouins are silently struggling to preserve a way of life in the face of new technologies, new modes of production, and new economic forces. In this dialectical interplay, the outcome evolves as a synthesis of sorts. Thus modern technology, symbolized by the motor vehicle, is used to preserve a traditional way of life: herding and roaming the desert. Likewise, a traditional means of sustenance, the camel, has turned from an imperative for survival into a means of luxury sport. Cash provides a link between the desert grazing sites and the city's modern sports arena.

In his reaction to modern occupations, the Bedouin again has been selective. When asked by this researcher about which occupations they would like to see their children engaged in (other than herding), the majority picked military ones—with air force pilots at the top of the list. Commanding things or people appeals to the Bedouins. We suspect that their choice is not without relevance to their traditional value system. If courage, chivalry, and constant moving are part of the Bedouins' normative system, then commanding an air force supersonic fighter seems to come very close. Commanding a tank, an armored vehicle, or a truck, still reflects the same normative system. Little wonder, therefore, that most of the Bedouins who opted for modern occupations ended up in the Saudi Army, National Guard, or as truck drivers. In this sense, the Bedouins have avoided the sharp dichotomous choices which may otherwise negate one another. Phrased differently, the Bedouins have picked from the arsenal of modernity those items that could be wed to, or even enhance, their traditions. This is not to suggest that such synthesis has always been smooth or without its share of strain. There are signs of increased divorce, alcoholism, and drug use among the younger generation of Bedouins who shuttle back and forth between the two subcultures. There is also a growing restlessness and defiance of traditional authority. But all of these signs are still too limited in scope and frequency to draw any firm conclusions.

Lumpen Capitalists: The Saudi Entrepreneur[6]

Another image of a changing social order in the Arab World is that of the new Saudi entrepreneur. Most oil countries—mainly Saudi Arabia and Kuwait—have had a traditional commercial class equivalent to the Bazarries in Iran and the Khan Khalili merchants in Egypt. Unlike Iran under the Shah, these traditional merchants in Arab oil countries are thriving, having expanded their activities and diversified their merchandise. But along with them a new class of entrepreneurs has evolved. Their frame of reference is international and they deal with governments and multinational corporations. Their activities do not fit readily into the customary categories of entrepreneurs under modern capitalism, nor in those of traditional merchants. These new Saudi entrepreneurs are not fruitfully productive; nor are they completely parasitic. But they could be anything in between. Unlike the typical Western counterpart, the Saudi entrepreneur does not take any risk and loses hardly any of his capital. In fact he may undertake his role without much or any capital to start with. Nevertheless he is always assured of making a profit.

Abdullah is a typical new Saudi entrepreneur.[7] His profile and mode of operation are illustrative of the entire class. A native of one of central Najd's tribes, Abdullah completed his secondary education in Saudi

Arabia. He was to go to Egypt for his college education in the early 1960s. But deteriorating relations between the kingdom and Nasser's Egypt resulted in his being sent to the United States instead. After a crash course in English in Texas, Abdullah enrolled in one of the West Coast universities where he obtained a B.A. in social science. He returned to Saudi Arabia and served for two years as a civil servant, then was sent back to the United States to obtain an M.A. degree in planning and public administration. Upon completing this mission he joined the then newly established Ministry of Planning. Along with other Western-educated Saudi technocrats, he presided over the drawing up of the first two five-year plans for the kingdom's social and economic development. Soon after, Abdullah resigned from his government post; at the age of 34 he started a "private company." This undertaking was a "conglomerate" right from the beginning. Its first brochure indicated that the company dealt with and intended to engage in import-export; feasibility studies for private and public institutions; consulting in engineering management and social services delivery systems; construction of roads, public buildings, housing, power and water stations; and building of hotels, hospitals, and supermarkets. In brief, there was hardly an area of "hard-" or "software" activities that was not covered by the company's charter. In less than five years of operation, Abdullah and his partners were all multimillionaires. The miracle of this phenomenal "success" becomes the more startling as we learn that the "conglomerate" began with the equivalent of $50,000 as capital, a four-room villa donated by one of the five partners as a temporary headquarters, a telephone, a telex hookup, two typists, and Abdullah as the only fulltime member out of the five. With this skeleton staff, the company handled several hundred million dollars' worth of government contracts. Their initial business included the building of primary schools, an airport, two feeder roads, welfare community centers, and seven huge studies for various ministries. All of the company's business in the first five years was with the Saudi government.

The story of Abdullah is that of several thousand Saudis who are seen at home in flying white robes, quite vigilant about the kingdom's traditions and Islamic rituals. They are the same jetsetters in Pierre Cardin business suits making multimillion-dollar deals in Paris, London, and New York or spending hundreds of thousands in gambling casinos in Monaco and Las Vegas.

The "secret" of success for the new Saudi entrepreneur is the accident of geology (oil), education, government service, and the economic boom in the 1970s. Since there is no risk, the only thing that differentiates one entrepreneur from another is his ability to assemble a "group" as partners in a private company. The ideal group consists of individuals who are blood relatives or close friends but who are strategically located in Saudi social and governmental structures.[8] Because the state is the number one spender, it follows that most profitable business must be transacted with the government. It helps if one or more of the partners is in the government and in on the planning of the next five years' projects. They would have valuable and advance information as well as easy access to former technocratic colleagues or even former subordinates who by that time would be making the decisions. It is also imperative for the group to have at least one high-ranking connection for political coverage in times of crisis. Most successful groups have a link with a member of the Royal Family.

The Saudi entrepreneur is masterful in the art of subcontracting. The indigenous Saudi partners do not actually do much beyond securing the big contracts. Every task called for by the latter, whether it is major or minor, is farmed out to subcontractors from the Arab World and more often from places as far off as South Korea and the United States. But in all cases, the Saudi entrepreneur ends up with a handsome profit. The profit is hard to evaluate in terms of a percentage "return on investment" for there is usually little or no seed capital invested to begin with.

This is not to suggest that the Saudi entrepreneur is entirely a parasite, reaping profit without work or appropriating the surplus value from some overexploited proletariat. In fact, he does perform a socioeconomic role which for lack of a better term we have called "lumpen capitalist."[9] He assembles partners and information. He establishes contacts with the outside world and secures political coverage inside Saudi Arabia. All these combined elements make for a bulldozer-like group to get things done in the Saudi environment. The latter contains a lot of rough, unpaved, and somewhat barren terrain in which only a bulldozer can operate.[10]

The new Saudi entrepreneur is a modern, educated individual reacting to the oil boom and to the tremendous wealth flowing from it. He deeply feels and perceives himself as performing a useful role in building Saudi Arabia. He may not argue the fact that he is overbuilding himself in the process, nor would he argue that his returns are a long way out of proportion with his actual performance.

He is a cultural broker par excellence as much as he is a business intermediary. He interprets the Saudi sociopolitical environment to the outside world and vice versa. The interpretation does not have to be accurate or objective but it always enhances the service of his vested interests. He realizes that the high premium on this cultural brokerage is temporary and will not last beyond the oil. Shrewdness and opportunism are the educated Saudis' responses to the glut of oil wealth.

Lumpen Capitalists: The Sponsor (*al-kafil*)[11]

A third image of the oil-based social order is that of *al-kafil*, literally meaning the sponsor. He is usually a native of an urban area of an under-populated oil-producing Arab country, i.e., Saudi Arabia, Kuwait, the United Arab Emirates, Qatar, or Libya. The combination of wealth, manpower shortage, and indigenous native fear of outsiders has coalesced to produce this most peculiar socioeconomic role—*al-kafil*.

Despite the Arab League economic agreements and labor charters,[12] most oil-rich Arab countries have enacted stringent migration and labor laws that blatantly discriminate against non-natives, including those from other Arab countries. With the exception of Iraq and Algeria, free travel (e.g., tourism) into oil-rich countries is not allowed. Travel has to be for work, official business, family visit, or pilgrimage (as in the case of Saudi Arabia). For all those seeking employment, there should be a contract and/or a sponsor as a prerequisite for obtaining visa, residence, and work permit. When the employer is the state, it acts as an impersonal organizational sponsor. But it is in the private and informal sectors that the class of individual sponsors emerges full-blown as a novelty of oil-based societies.

Abu-Hamad[13] is a typical example of the *kafil*. I encountered him during a mission for a UN agency in Saudi Arabia. Abu-Hamad was an official driver for that agency's office in Riyadh. The ostensible goal of the mission was to help in the upgrading of native Saudi manpower through literacy and vocational training programs. It was not unnatural, therefore, to strike up a conversation with the mission's driver on the subject of education. This was made easier by Abu-Hamad, who was quite inquisitive and an eager conversant with his guests. Abu-Hamad, as it turned out, was an illiterate in his late 40s, a third generation sedentarized Bedouin, married, and with five children, all of whom were in school. One of the interesting things about him was his belief in the value of education for his children but not at all for himself. As we presented him with the prospect of our opening accelerated adult literacy classes and asked him if he would join some evenings every week, his response was an emphatic but argumentative, "No." For one thing, Abu-Hamad was quite busy and satisfied with his life. He pointed out that he had inquired about how much money each person in the UN mission was making and had learned, to his satisfaction, that the head of the mission with

a Ph.D. (at least 20 years of formal education) and several years of experience was making less money than he was earning himself from
various sources. It turned out that Abu-Hamad was a *kafil*. Chauffeuring
a UN car was just something to do, since driving was the only skill he
had. The salary he received from it was a minute part of his total income.
The bulk of his earnings was derived from two grocery stores, a toy
store, a garage, a barbershop, and a tailoring shop, but he was neither
able to perform nor willing to learn any of the skills involved in these
enterprises. He hired others to do the work. To be more precise, others
may have approached him to be their *kafil*.

A non-Saudi cannot, by law, initiate or fully own a business in Saudi
Arabia. Thus a Syrian tailor or an Egyptian mechanic wishing to open a
shop must find a Saudi sponsor as a partner. Abu-Hamad was a partner
to or a full owner-employer of Egyptians, Palestinians, Syrians,
Lebanese, Yemenis, and Pakistanis. These other nationals put up the
capital, the skills, and the labor. He gave them only the legal coverage by
lending his fingerprint (later his signature) to contractual arrangements
to obtain licensing. In return, Abu-Hamad (a very pious and fair man)
was getting 50 percent of the profit. He and those sponsored by him
(*makfulin*) were quite happy with the arrangement. Other more greedy
kafils may appropriate as much as 80 percent of the profit for the same
legal coverage.

The institution of the *kafil* has several other variations. In one activist
version, a *kafil* may travel around the neighboring countries, recruit people of various skills, and set them up in appropriate enterprises as
employees of his or as partners. A *kafil* may simply import labor and
then retail it out to other local employers for a percentage of their wages.
In the least activist version, a *kafil* may lend his signature to enable
potential workers from other countries to come to Saudi Arabia. They
would be on their own until they found employment, and would then
pay their *kafil* a fee.

The *kafil*, of course, has some vague legal responsibility vis-à-vis both
the government and the sponsored (*al-makful*). He may be held account-
able for the public behavior of those sponsored by him. The *kafil* often
keeps with him the passport and all traveling documents of those individuals whom he sponsors. Thus they cannot travel in or out of the
country or work for anyone else without his consent. In other words, the
kafil not only extracts a substantial profit from the sponsored ones, but
he also controls them almost completely while they are in his country.

In its stark and extreme form, this "human trade" comes very close to
what might be called "temporary slavery." The local legal codes are entirely on the side of the *kafil*. He has the right to terminate the employ-

ment of, or partnership with a sponsored person at will. He can demand his deportation at any time. While these rights of a *kafil* are occasionally abused, the bulk of the transactions carried out under this institution are mutually beneficial, although far from being equal.

Like the other two images of the new social order, the *kafil* is a by-product of the changing substructure of the oil-rich Arab countries. The vast oil revenues, the skyrocketing public spending, the construction boom, the mounting demand for labor, and the limited supply of in-digenous manpower have made it imperative to import labor. But it is not free labor flow in response to strict supply and demand. A noneconomic variable intervenes in the process—the sociopolitical fear of being overwhelmed by outsiders. That fear reflects itself in migration, labor, business, and property laws, which lopsidedly favor the natives and discriminate against outsiders. It is this intricate chain of causation, triggered by oil, that has given rise to the *kafil*.

The *kafil* is a shrewd native with little or no formal education, re-sponding to his environment. In recent years, this environment has con-tained financial, human, and legal elements which he uses to his advan-tage. Not every native is a *kafil*; but enough in oil-rich countries are doing it to make them a distinct social formation. The *kafils*, like the new entrepreneurs discussed earlier, are performing a role and getting a substantial profit in the process. But since the role is not productively well defined, and since the profit is way out of proportion with any effort exerted by the *kafils*, we have also termed them as part of a "lumpen capitalist" group.

The Egyptian Peasant Outside the Nile Valley[14]

Moving over to the other side of the wealth divide in the Arab World, we also observe several images of the new social order. A visitor flying into Cairo's International Airport, say, from the mid-1970s on, is usually struck by the sight of thousands of Egyptian peasants crowding the place—arriving, departing, or mostly saying farewell to or welcoming relatives and friends. The visitor would readily observe that most of the village folk are using this mode of transportation for the first time. Their noise level, the amount and type of baggage, and the mixture of bewilderment and excitement indicate the peasants' unfamiliarity with the flying subculture. Most of the peasants are oil-country bound. Like other groups before them (high and medium level manpower), they are seeking work and fortune elsewhere outside the Nile Valley.

The migration of Egyptian peasants puts an end to a lingering stereotype of the Egyptians as the most sedentary of all Arabs. The stereotype was not so very inaccurate. Compared to their Syrian, Lebanese, Yemeni, Tunisian, Algerian, and Moroccan counterparts, Egyptians were indeed the least migratory Arabs. There were socio-ecological reasons for this oversedentarization of Egyptians, which we need not go into. Suffice it to say that like other hydraulic societies, Egyptians derived a reasonable subsistence livelihood from river-irrigated agricultural land in the Valley and the Delta. Over thousands of years, a symbiosis developed between man, land, river, and central authority. The continuity of this equilibrium was contingent upon the peasant's relationship to the land—as tiller and producer of value—some of which was to be appropriated by the central authority.[15]

The fact that Egypt's population has doubled several times in the last 200 years (from 5 million in 1800, to 10 in 1900, to 42 million in 1980) without any corresponding expansion of agricultural land (the latter grew only from 5 to 7 million acres in 200 years) meant a collapse of the millenial symbiosis. The mounting population pressure meant an increasing number of landless and poor peasants every year. The early reaction of the dispossessed was to stream into Egypt's urban areas; but in the last ten years, other younger generations of dispossessed Egyptians have discovered new outlets: the oil countries.

Serag is a typical case. Born in a Delta village to a small farmer as one of six children, he was sent to work for a village notable at the age of 8. He grew up close to the children of his employer, who were all at school. At the age of 18, he was drafted into the army and was caught up in the aftermath of the 1967 war. Serag was kept in the army until November 1974. He was one of those who crossed the Canal, and as an infantryman he participated in tank battles, using shoulder-carried antitank missile launchers. At the age of 26 he returned to the village, ready to get married and start a family. His former patron, the village notable, had died, and the household was scattered among heirs, most of them absentee. His own father had grown poorer and had sold the half acre he had once owned to pay for the marriages of two of the daughters. Serag left the village after two months and went to Alexandria, where one of the sons of his former employer was now living and teaching at the university. He asked the son to help him find a job; he offered to drive his car. While the son could have used a chauffeur, since he and his wife were working and had two school age children and possessed only one car, the young assistant professor could not afford Serag's salary and upkeep in the city. However, norms of hospitality, paternalism, and dictates of status prevented the son from turning his back on Serag. He let Serag work for him as a chauffeur at LE10 per month (about $15). Everyone was happy with the arrangement, since the assistant professor could now do extra work outside the university for additional income. Several months later, however, the arrangement was threatened as the professor learned that his request for secondment to the University of Riyadh had been approved and that he was to leave for Saudi Arabia within a few weeks. Serag implored the professor to take him too. The professor gave Serag a generous bonus and promised to find him a job in Saudi Arabia and then send for him. To Serag's surprise, within a few weeks he received a letter from the professor and a contract from a wealthy Saudi to work for him as a chauffeur.

Within ten days Serag got his travel papers and visa organized and was airborne for the first time in his life, bound for Saudi Arabia. He immediately started on his new job at SR500 a month (LE100; $150), in addition to free room and board. Serag was elated. He was saving virtually all his salary. In six months he was given three weeks off to go and visit his family. Arriving in the village in bright new clothes, carrying a radio-cassette combination for his elderly father and other assorted gifts for everyone in the family, Serag was the talk of the village for several weeks. People came in droves to greet him and possibly to make sure that what they had heard about his fortunes was really true. More important, many of the young well-wishers whispered in Serag's ear their hope of being helped by him to go to Saudi Arabia. Upon returning, Serag in fact began actively to seek employment for three of his brothers and his two brothers-in-law, and within the year he managed to secure contracts for all five of them. He then began to help other more distant friends and relatives.

In the summer of 1979, I enumerated the number of peasants from Serag's village who were in Saudi Arabia and the Gulf. The figure was 174—all aided by Serag in less than four years. Equally significant is the fact that other villagers began to seek to migrate to other Arab and non-Arab countries. The same enumeration in 1979 showed that about 150 persons from the same village were scattered among Lebanon, Jordan, Syria, and Iraq (their relatives did not know their exact locations)[16] and about 30 were reported to be in Libya. Six villagers were in Milan, Italy. All in all, about 360 peasants from the village were outside their habitat in the Nile Valley for the first time in their lives and possibly in the history of the village. Actually, except for the very few pilgrims every now and then, no one from that village is known ever to have left Egypt or, say, traveled in an airplane, until the early 1960s.

The case of Serag and his village is not uncommon among the other peasants of the 4,000 Egyptian villages. What these migrant workers do abroad is virtually any work they can find. Those among them who acquire skills while serving in the army end up with jobs that pay more—such as drivers, mechanics, electricians, or welders. Most of them, however, work in construction or service jobs. Surprisingly, very few are employed as farm workers in Saudi Arabia, where their Yemeni counterparts seem to have had an earlier start.

Virtually all peasants working abroad save money. The use pattern of their savings indicates that their money goes into marriage of self or close kin, gifts, purchase of land, building of new houses, and investing in tractors, flour mills, and irrigation pumps. Television sets, refrigerators, and gas stoves began to make their appearance in most villages immediately after their electrification. Many of the peasant migrants perceive their work sojourn as temporary. If the migrant is married, he leaves his wife and children in the village, either with his parents or in an independent household close to that of either his or her parents. He would send money periodically to his parents and his wife.

Many of these migrants have effected a marked change in the village class structure. In the 1950s and 1960s, education for the villagers was the fastest path of upward social mobility. Now it is migration to a rich Arab country that counts as the best mechanism. Many children of the poverty-stricken landless peasants are now well off, in the middle or upper-middle stratum of their village. They are intermarrying with families that, no more than ten or fifteen years ago, would only have hired them as farm workers, like young Serag.

The Veiled Medical Student

Another image that strikes the visitor to Cairo in the last decade is the sight of veiled and semiveiled women in the streets and public places. Especially noteworthy is the scene at the Kasr al-Aini Bridge on the Nile, between the Meridien Hotel and the Manial Palace. Here; dozens of young college women are seen crossing at the stop light on their way to Cairo University's Medical School. What is unusual about these women is the fact that quite a few of them are veiled.

For centuries the veil had come to symbolize the "oppression" of Muslim Arab women and their inferior status. In the early 1920s, a feminist leader, Hoda Sha'rawy, led a women's movement seeking greater equality.[17] One of its first acts of defiance was the unveiling—an act that came to symbolize their determination to be emancipated. The movement did succeed in modifying family and personal laws in 1927, obtaining more rights for women in education, the professions, and state employment.

The 1952 revolution pushed further the cause of women's rights, granting them the vote and the right to run for public office (in other words, political equality with men) in the 1956 constitution. By then the veil had nearly disappeared from major urban areas (it had never existed in rural areas on any noticeable scale). The march of women's emancipation still had a long way to go, but it was proceeding steadily. The number of girls enrolled in primary schools jumped from fewer than 300,000 in 1952 to over 1.6 million in 1976, a 530 percent increase. On the university level the increase was even more dramatic—from fewer than 10,000 in 1952 to more than 153,000 in 1976, an increase of more than 1500 percent in a quarter of a century. Women were appointed as cabinet members,[18] ambassadors, heads of corporations, and several were elected to the People's Assembly (Egypt's parliament).

Why then, all of a sudden, has the veil reappeared? And why especially among one of society's most educated sectors—urban college women? What does it mean for the cause of women's rights—does it represent a setback? Where does the whole phenomenon fit in the new emerging social order of the Arab World?

Ilham is a case in point.[19] At the age of 21 she was in her third year of medical school. Ilham is the second among five children born to a middle-class family in Mansoura, a Delta town. Her father was college educated, with a B.S. in accounting, and for twenty years has been a government employee in the Taxes Department (Internal Revenue). Her mother had only a few years of formal education. Ilham was the first female on both sides of her parents' families to go to college. When interviewed, she recounted her parents' eagerness and encouragement to excel in her studies at secondary school. She was always at the top of her class—something that inspired her and her parents to think of medical school and becoming a doctor. The first hurdle toward this goal was passing the statewide examination with high grades (*magmuʿa*). To most Egyptian families, the year of this examination is a long nightmare. If there is a son or daughter preparing for it, the whole household is often put on a "war footing." The state of top emergency is justified to most middle-class Egyptian families, since future career prospects of their children are contingent upon this single examination (*thanawiyya ʿamma*). Ilham made it with flying colors; her grades entitled her to the top medical school (that of Cairo University) in that year.[20] And even though she could have enrolled in the medical school at Mansoura University (her home town), she and her family opted for the best.

At the age of 18, Ilham moved to Cairo, full of excitement mixed with apprehension. This was her first experience of being on her own, away from her family. She secured a room in the women's dormitory at Cairo University. The mix of people she came across every day in the dormitory, the classroom, the bus, and in the street was quite bewildering.

Most of all she had a difficult time relating to some of her classmates, who seemed to have more money, better clothes, and broader experience. They knew more about life, sex, love, dating, and drinking. Some of them were heavily made up, smoked, and even went with men in their cars. Ilham reported that she was frightened as some of her classmates tried to draw her into their kind of circles. Until then, she was unveiled, wore modern clothes, had been a moviegoer with her family, and had read romantic novels. Nevertheless, the kind of life she was being enticed to join in Cairo sent waves of fear through her veins. She thought to herself that not only was she unable to do what the "other" women were doing, but in her heart she also condemned their behavior.

It was about the fourth month of her first year when she had an encounter that put her mind at rest. On the bus from Mansoura to Cairo, after the midyear recess, she sat next to another woman who was veiled. After a short while she noticed the veiled woman picking up a book to read—it was a college chemistry book. Ilham struck up a conversation with her seatmate. She was curious as to why the other was veiled if she was at college, sitting with men in the same classroom. Her companion told her that she was appalled by the behavior of some of the women in Cairo, disapproved of their display of expensive clothes and their disregard for "our values" and Islamic traditions. She insinuated to Ilham that some of these "decadent girls" might even be prostitutes, catering to wealthy tourists from oil countries. She knew some of them were from modest families and could not afford the kind of clothes they wore to school. Ilham was dumbfounded by these "revelations." Her traveling companion concluded by stating that she had decided to veil in order to set herself apart from the decadent crowd. Since her veiling, she prayed more regularly with some of her veiled friends and she studied much better. Ilham was very impressed. A week later she went back to Mansoura with all her modern, but modest, wardrobe and told her family of her decision to veil. Her parents, to her surprise, disapproved of the idea. Her two younger brothers protested vehemently that she would look odd and that they would be teased by their friends in the neighborhood. She finally settled the argument by tearfully sobbing that she did not want to be thought of as a prostitute to wealthy oil tourists in Cairo. Without really knowing for sure, she asserted that some of her classmates were just that, whereupon her parents and brothers fell silent, and concurred with her decision.

In her own account Ilham did not mention anything that was strictly political behind her decision to veil. But when asked about her views regarding some of the politically oriented religious groups on campus, she readily declared her support of their goals, i.e., the application of

Islamic *Shariʿa* to all spheres of life. She voted for their candidates in student elections and would marry one of them if proposed to. What about working outside the home? Yes, she would if her husband approved and if it did not conflict with her duty as a wife and mother.

Ilham and thousands like her in Egypt and elsewhere in the northern tier of the Arab World (Lebanon, Syria, Jordan, Tunisia, Morocco, Algeria) are enigmatic to outside observers, as well as to many of their fellow countrymen. For they are not old or middle-aged traditional women. They are young and highly educated. They are veiling by their own volition—and in many cases against their parents' wishes.[21] Is the veil a setback to modernity? Here we must submit that some of the Western social science categories do break down—or at least are rendered irrelevant. For if modernity means unveiling, fashionable clothes, mixing freely with the opposite sex, and dating, then Ilham and thousands like her would represent a setback to the cause of "modernity." If modernity, on the other hand, means learning of modern science, technology, and the humanities, and if it means commitment and preparation for a career outside the home, then Ilham and her like are quite "modern."

Here it may be useful to distinguish between imposed and volitional veiling; e.g., between, say, Saudi college women and their Egyptian counterparts. Educated women choosing to veil seem to be conveying a symbolic message, like anyone else who opts for a particular style or appearance.[22] They are asserting one or more of the following: an authentic identity vis-à-vis imitations of Western styles of life, disapproval of what seem to them decadent and corrupt practices in society, warding off costly effects of currently high inflation by avoiding conspicuous clothing, and establishing good (i.e., moral) reputations.

The veiled medical student represents a complicated response to a complicated world around her—a world over which she has no control. That world includes an influx of foreigners, oil wealth, expensive consumer goods, high inflation, and "alien" life-styles. Despite her superb achievements in examinations, she finds herself overwhelmed, estranged, and insignificant in a big, impersonal urban world. Clinging to a "heritage" seems to restore her feeling of worth, protect her against the unknown, and lessen the alienation she feels. In a curious way, like the Saudi Bedouins, Egyptian veiled medical students are quite selective vis-à-vis the "modernity bag." They take out of it science, technology, and commitment to professional careers. They leave out the rest. They feel and firmly believe that what they have selected is consistent with their "heritage," "Islamic tradition," and "authenticity (*asalah*)." It is their way of imposing a semblance of order on an otherwise chaotic world.

The Angry Muslim Militant

The male counterparts of the veiled college women are the young Muslim militants. This is an image mostly of college-educated, bearded, angry men. It is an image that has dominated the world's mass media since the Iranian revolution and especially since the seizure of the American Embassy and some fifty hostages in Tehran in November 1979. But insiders to the Arab and Middle East area had seen the genesis of this image much earlier. In Egypt, at least, it dates back to the aftermath of the 1967 defeat of Arab regimes at the hands of Israel. Many area observers sensed a resurgence of religiosity, which in the beginning was quite amorphous, mystical, retreatist, or superstitious.[23] Even Egypt's defeated regime sensed the phenomenon and attempted to exploit it to its own advantage.[24]

But as the decade of the sixties drew to an end, the amorphous religiosity was beginning to take shape, to harden at the edges, and to develop nuclear cores. We began to hear of organized Muslim groups on university campuses calling for the assertion of the Islamic faith and for exorcising Egypt and the Arab World of all imported ideologies and foreign influence. These beginnings coincided with Sadat's succession to power following the death of President Nasser. In the best traditions of Egyptian rulers, Sadat, too, sought to exploit this new spirit among the young. He needed some balancing popular base to counterweigh Nasserists and leftists, who were perceived as a serious challenge to his leadership. To him and his media, "imported ideology and influence" were synonymous with socialism and the Soviet Union. But little did Sadat know that these very Muslim groups would be even more hostile to his own ideological alternatives: the "Open Door Policy," accommodation with Israel, and alignment with the West and especially the United States.

The fact was driven home to the regime in a bloody coup d'etat attempt in April 1974, only six months after the October War, which was hailed as an Arab triumph. Sadat was still riding high in popularity and was being proclaimed by his media as the "redeemer-hero." The plot was carried out by a group known as the Islamic Liberation Organization and invariably called in the Arab media the Technical Military Academy Group (henceforth MA).[25] It was so called because their scheme for taking over started with occupation of the academy and seizure of its arsenal. The group was to march from there to the Arab Socialist Union (ASU), where President Sadat and the rest of Egypt's ruling elite were scheduled for a major state function. The attempt was foiled, but only after scores of militants, army, and security men had fallen dead and many more were injured.

From then on, the regime has been violently confronted by one Islamic group after another. Names of groups such as Al-Jihad (Holy War), Jund Allah (Soldiers of God), Jamaʿat al-Muslimin (the Muslim Group), and Jamaʿat al-Takfir w'al-Hijra (Repentance and Holy Flight, henceforth RHF), among others, began to be known to the public as they clashed with the authorities.[26] The spread of Islamic militancy was dramatically highlighted by the clash of July 1977, when the RHF group kidnapped and executed one of Sadat's former cabinet ministers for religious endowment (*al-Awqaf*), Sheikh Ahmad Hassan al-Dhahabi.[27] In the aftermath of gun battles, arrests, trials, and execution of its leaders, it was revealed that the RHF was 3,000 to 5,000 strong, tightly organized, and spread out all over the country.[28] Muslim candidates swept student elections in all of Egypt's universities after 1976,[29] a fact that prompted President Sadat to dissolve Egypt's student unions by a presidential decree in the summer of 1979.

The two Muslim publications *Al-Daʿwa* and *Al-Iʿtisam* have been widely read. After the virtual banning of all leftist publications, the two Muslim monthly magazines have been the only serious opposition papers—critical of Sadat's internal and external policies, especially of his peace treaty with Israel and his relationship with the United States and the deposed Shah of Iran.

Who are the Muslim militants? Why have they appeared at this point in time? Would they amount to anything similar to what happened in Iran? These and other relevant questions cannot be fully answered here. There are other detailed treatments of the subject.[30] Our interest is confined to sketching this emergent image of a new Arab social order.

Tallal is a bona fide Muslim militant.[31] He was one of the leading figures in one of the attempted coups d'etat. He was tried and sentenced to death along with other leading members of his group, but because of his young age (he was 21 years old at the time), his sentence was commuted to life imprisonment. He was interviewed along with other militants in prison between 1977 and 1979.

Tallal, the oldest of four children, was born in a small town to a small middle-class family. His father, a civil servant with a college education, was constantly trying his hand at poetry and novel writing but never achieved national fame. His mother had only a few years of education and was a devoted housewife. Both parents were born in a rural village, but the mother, more so than the father, retained her village manners and values. Tallal grew up in a house full of books and around friends of his father who traded political and literary ideas. But he acquired a strong dose of religion and tradition from his mother. As in most middle-class families, Tallal was continuously encouraged to achieve scholastically. In the *thanawiyya ʿamma* (the statewide examination at

the end of secondary school education), he obtained high grades, en-
abling him to enroll in the prestigious Faculty of Engineering at Alexandria University at the age of 17.

Tallal recalled that even though he was successful at studying, achieving was not his prime concern. When the 1967 defeat occurred, he was
only 15 years old, but he asserts that he was politically conscious and
was deeply shocked by the defeat. He remembers that he retreated to his
room for several days, oscillating between weeping, reflecting,
meditating, and sleeping, but hardly eating or talking to anyone. His
mother, worried about his state, urged him to take a bath, pray, and
read some Quran. He finally did, and to his surprise, felt an overwhelm-
ing sense of peace sweeping over him. He had read and memorized
Quranic verses for school homework before, but this time Tallal felt
quite different. The verses had a penetrating meaning that addressed
him, his crisis, and that of his nation directly. Tallal was a "reborn"
Muslim. He knew there and then that the Quran contained all the Truth,
and wondered why he and others had not realized that before. He kept
his discovery to himself for a while. Meanwhile his mother was quite
pleased with Tallal's emergence from his room, his strong appetite, and
his readiness to go out of the house again.

Tallal's first outing was ten days after the defeat. He went with his
father to a nearby city to attend a political rally in which one of Nasser's
top aides was to be the main speaker. Tallal recalls that he used to love
and believe in Nasser but that he was utterly bewildered when he heard
the speaker stating to the audience that the Arabs had not been defeated
in the war. The speaker asserted that the ultimate aim of Israel and
American imperialism was to depose Nasser or destroy him; and because
Nasser and other progressive regimes were still in power, the enemies'
conspiracy was foiled. Tallal did not believe the speaker and was plagued
by an instant doubt when the audience, including his father, applauded
the speaker. He remained bewildered for the next two years, taking his
comfort in praying and reading the Quran.

It was at Alexandria University, as a freshman, that Tallal's bewilderment came to an end. There, Tallal was living away from his family for
the first time. In the college mosque, the fellow next to him approached
him with the customary handshake following a prayer. In the process he
introduced himself and struck up a conversation with Tallal. This was
the beginning of Tallal's initiation into Islamic militancy, for he was invited by his fellow prayermate to attend a lecture on campus about the
struggle against Zionism. The speaker, it turned out, was a bearded
fellow student from a neighboring faculty. His approach to the topic ap-
pealed to Tallal—Zionism, Communism, and Capitalism are all enemies

of Islam and the Muslims; the only way to fight them back is to adhere to the Quran and the Sunna. The speaker recalled the brilliant fighting of the Muslim Brothers against the Jews in 1948, which (according to the speaker and Tallal's retelling of it) was the only effective effort to have almost rid the Palestinians of the "Jewish gangs," had it not been for the Arab governments' betrayal—especially that of Egypt, which stabbed the Muslim Brotherhood in the back while they were fighting. Everybody cheered and Tallal found himself this time applauding with the audience. He began to read avidly about the Muslim Brothers.

Tallal was recruited shortly after. His enthusiasm and devotion to the group made him, within a year, part of the inner core leadership. Their objective was to rid the Muslim World of all corrupt regimes, in order to reinstate the Islamic *Shariᶜa*. In 1974 they felt that Sadat had gone too far in selling out to the West and Israel, and something must be done about it. Thus they staged their coup, which, of course, did not succeed.

Tallal and many of his generation are quite angry at the present social order. Their outrage often takes the form of premature confrontation with the regime. Sometimes they realize that such confrontation will not bring the government down. But as they put it, "It is an outrage for God" (*ghadhbah lil-Allah*). For them it is "propaganda by deed," which can only lead to martyrdom or victory, and both are readily embraceable.

When the militants are persuaded to spell out their ideology, attitudes, and feelings, the listener comes away with an overall clear impression of what they are against but with only a vague, though colorful, impression of what they would do if they were in power. They have deep-seated hostility toward the West, Communism, and Israel. Any ruler who deals with or befriends any of them would be betraying Islam. Excessive wealth, extravagance, severe poverty, exploitation, and usury have no place in a truly Muslim society. They disapprove of nearly all the regimes in the Arab and Muslim Worlds. They attribute many of the decadent aspects of behavior in Egypt either to Western influence or to the squandering of oil money, and they firmly believe that should "true Islam" be implemented, Egypt and the Muslim World would be independent, free, prosperous, just, and righteous societies.[32]

The Muslim militants are mostly like Ilham, the veiled medical student. They come from the middle and lower-middle classes, they are of rural or small-town backgrounds, and they are high achievers and quite intelligent. But they find themselves living in a complicated cosmopolitan world to which they cannot relate and with which they cannot cope. Their talents and energies are neither properly rewarded nor fully recognized by the system. They and their families feel squeezed economically by high inflation. They are startled by the tremendous wealth around them, but anguished as they cannot have a fair share while seeing it being so conspicuously wasted. Their class has always been the reservoir of patriotism: their parents and grandparents fought for independence. But they see their homeland again being trampled upon by what they consider neocolonialism; i.e., the influx of foreigners, multinational corporations, and corrupt ways of life.

The angry Muslim militants of Egypt have their counterparts in Syria, Tunisia, among the Palestinians, and even in Saudi Arabia. At the core they are nationalists, socialists, and anticolonialists, but they do not use these terms because of their former association. Their quest for authenticity, dignity, equality, and independence is now couched in Islamic terms. An earlier generation of young militants couched the same quest in Arab Nationalist terms; two generations earlier it was mostly couched in Egyptian patriotic terms.

Other Images of Change

The six images sketched above are by no means the only ones marking the Arab landscape. Other images of the new social order include that of the Palestinian being transformed from a wretched refugee into a guerilla fighter. The psychological impact of this image is probably far more important than its military or geopolitical bearings in shaping the new Arab social order. The decade of the seventies sensed the turbulence that the Palestinian freedom fighter could cause—in Israel, the Arab World itself, and on the global stage. The raids in occupied Palestine, the street fighting in Amman,[33] the assassination in the Cairo Sheraton Hotel,[34] the attack in Munich at the Olympic Games,[35] addressing the world from the United Nations,[36] the civil war in Lebanon, fighting the Syrians,[37] raising the Palestinian flag on the Israeli Mission building in Tehran,[38] and numerous other acts of defiance or assertion have not gained the Palestinians an inch of their usurped land. But they have driven the message home, loud and clear—to oil producers and oil consumers, to rich Arabs and poor Arabs, to Israeli and Diaspora Jews—that no peace or stability would last before their situation is redressed. The presence of so many Palestinians in the fragile Gulf States, so close to the main oil arteries of the West, makes their message quite credible. The dilemma of the Gulf States is their heavy dependence on Palestinian manpower and at the same time their fear of what these very Palestinians might do should any of the rulers follow in the footsteps of President Sadat.

Another image is that of the embattled Lebanese trying to survive while the state is withering away—or more accurately while one state is proliferating into several. The implications of the Lebanese civil war, however, go far beyond the anguish and individual human tragedies. The war has blown open the entire issue of ethnic and minority groups in all countries in the area. Of course, the Kurds and the South Sudanese had fought for years earlier. But bloody and protracted as they may have been, the battles were on the cultural borderland of the Arab World, and religion was not basically at issue. With Lebanon, the conflict has been much closer to the heart of the Arab homeland. Religious and communal differences were deliberately contrived and drummed up.

Israel, all major Arab states, and the two superpowers were implicated. The whole ethnic question is definitely going to be raised in all neighboring Arab countries, Syria, Jordan, and Egypt included. Indications in both Syria and Egypt show that ethnic tension is already turning into incidents of overt conflict.[39] The flaring up of the Lebanese civil war is, therefore, symptomatic of one aspect of the new Arab social order: diversifiers and primordial forces are at work against political and cultural unifiers that were in full swing during Nasser's years.

All the above images of the new social order have several interlinking threads. One such major thread is the oil syndrome; i.e., the raw material, the energy issue, the money, the geopolitics, and the manpower movement. If any of these images were not a direct function of the oil syndrome, then the syndrome has been somehow affected by them. The mechanized nomad, the Saudi entrepreneur, the *kafil*, the Egyptian peasant out of the Nile Valley—all are direct resultants of the oil syndrome. The other images of change have been indirectly affected by oil. Reveiling and Islamic militancy are both reactions to a multitude of things, among them high inflation, conspicuous consumption, and behavioral patterns brought about by the oil syndrome. Curiously enough, the latter's impact on Islamic militancy is double-tiered, the second being the fact that most militant groups relied heavily on the dues of members and sympathizers working in oil-rich countries.[40] Also some of the Muslim militants from Egypt were active members of the group that seized the Grand Mosque in Mecca in December 1979.[41] The Palestinian Resistance generally and the Palestine Liberation Organization (PLO) in particular rely heavily for financial support on donations and dues from Palestinians working in oil countries. It was rumored that in the Lebanese civil war, oil money found its way to the various factions in the fighting.

In brief, oil, through the movement of money and manpower across the state borders of the Arab World, has been felt in a thousand and one ways. It is therefore important to examine in some detail the most relevant mechanism of the oil impact on the Arab social order: that of migration.

3
Inter-Arab Labor Migration

The new Arab social order has been shaped by the intersection of oil wealth and the already existing demographic and socioeconomic structures of various countries of the Arab World. Manpower movement among the Arab countries in recent years is a manifestation, a product, and a reinforcer of the new social order. Through an investigation of inter-Arab labor migration (henceforth ALM), many of the inputs, dynamics, and outputs of the new order become apparent. I propose to present an overview of this migratory phenomenon in this chapter. In the two following chapters, I will focus on Egypt and Saudi Arabia as representatives of the two ends of the migration stream.

To put ALM into its full demographic context, I present in Table 3.1 some basic population indicators of the Arab World. Briefly described, the total number of Arabs in the mid-1970s was over 136 million, most of whom were children (below 15 years of age), with high birth rates and high but declining death rates. As such, Arab population has been experiencing high rates of natural growth (about 3 percent annually). Yet both economic participation and literacy rates were fairly low (about 30 percent).

This overall profile, of course, conceals some very significant quantitative and qualitative variations, as Table 3.1 clearly reflects. It is these variations, in fact, that have made an inter-Arab migratory system possible.

Movement of Arab individuals, families, and tribes throughout the area extending from Iraq to Morocco had been a common occurrence for centuries (from the eighth to the beginning of the twentieth). Cultural affinities of language, religion, and life-styles facilitated such movement and subsequent adjustment in a new residence; and the absence of rigid national state borders made it all possible. However, with the exception of brief large-scale migrations, namely in the early Arab-Islamic conquest of the seventh and eighth centuries, human movement remained small though frequent. The pilgrimage to Mecca from all over the Arab

TABLE 3.1
The Arab World: Basic Demographic Indicators Mid-1970s

Countries Ranked by Population Size	Population Size in millions (Nationals only)	Area in sq. km. (000)	Density per km2	Crude Birth Rate %	Crude Death Rate %	Natural Growth Rate %	Literacy Rate of Pop. 15 and over %
Egypt	38.2 (1976)	1,001	38	3.5	1.2	2.3	40
Morocco	18.4 (1977)	445	44	4.6	1.5	3.1	26
Algeria	16.9 (1977)	2,383	7	4.4	1.4	3.0	35
Sudan	14.1 (1973)	2,506	7	5.1	1.9	3.2	15
Iraq	11.1 (1975)	435	26	4.2	1.1	3.1	26
Syria	7.3 (1975)	185	41	4.8	1.5	3.3	53
Tunisia	5.6 (1975)	164	36	3.6	0.9	2.7	55
Yemen	5.3 (1975)	195	27	4.9	2.5	2.4	10
Saudi Arabia	4.6 (1975)	2,150	2	5.0	2.0	3.0	33
Somalia	3.2 (1975)	393	8	n.a.	n.a.	n.a.	10
Jordan	2.6 (1975)	98	27	4.7	1.6	3.1	62
Lebanon	2.6 (1975)	10	260	n.a.	n.a.	n.a.	68

Libya	2.3	(1975)	1,757	2	4.7	1.6	3.1	39
Democratic Yemen	1.7	(1975)	288	6	n.a.	n.a.	n.a.	10
Mauritania	1.3	(1975)	670	2	n.a.	n.a.	n.a.	10
Oman	0.6	(1975)	212	3	n.a.	n.a.	n.a.	20
Kuwait	0.5	(1975)	16	31	5.1	0.6	4.5	55
Bahrain	0.3	(1976)	0.6	437	n.a.	n.a.	n.a.	47
U.A.E.	0.2	(1975)	84	3	5.0	1.9	3.1	14
Qatar	0.1	(1975)	22	5	5.0	2.0	3.0	33
TOTAL	136.9		13,015	10				30

Sources: Compiled from various sources: the World Bank's World Development Report 1978 (Table 18, p.11); United Nations Economic Commission for West Asia (UNECWA) Demographic and Related Socio-Economic Data Sheets, Beirut, No.2; The Arab World in the Year 2000 (Beirut, Inst. of Arab Projects and Development, 1975), p.22; UNESCO's Regional Office for Education in Arab Countries, Education and Development in Arab Countries, Cairo, 1976, p.2.

Muslim World has kept at least a minimum of human movement in the area at all times.

The advent of Western colonialism, the Balkanization of the Arab homeland, and the rigid border demarcation and subsequent creation of country-states slowed inter-Arab movement during the first part of the twentieth century. However, the discovery and exploitation of oil in countries of the Arabian Peninsula in mid-century made it possible for ALM to pick up again in the 1950s and 1960s. It was in the 1970s, though, that the scale of ALM assumed a dimension unprecedented since the Arab conquest of the seventh century. Noteworthy are the reverse directions of the historical and the present human movements. The early Arab migration of the seventh century and the Hilaliyya movement of the eleventh century were both from the Arabian peninsula outwards. The present waves are from the outside inward to the Peninsula.

The 1973 Arab-Israeli war, the Arab oil embargo, and the quadrupling of oil prices resulted in an astronomical increase in state revenues of the Arab oil producers. As shown in Table 3.2, these revenues rose from $2.3 billion in 1965 to $12.7 billion in 1973, $53.6 billion in 1974, and $77.5 billion in 1977. At present (1980) these revenues are estimated at $100 billion. Thus if we take 1970 as a benchmark, major Arab producers would have raised their oil revenues from less than $5 billion to $100 billion in one decade, a twentyfold increase (2000 percent).

With this kind of money, the oil-rich or "capital-rich"[1] countries launched very ambitious socioeconomic development plans. Their aims have been (1) to complete the building of basic infrastructures (roads, airports, water desalination plants, power stations, etc.); (2) to expand and consolidate social service institutions (schools, hospitals, housing, community centers, and the appropriate bureaucracies for their maintenance and operation); (3) to diversify the economic base in anticipation of the post-oil era; and (4) to step up and modernize their defense capabilities.

The vast oil revenues put several Arab countries in a category by themselves as the capital-rich—namely Saudi Arabia, Kuwait, Qatar, the United Arab Emirates (UAE), Bahrain, Oman, and Libya. Iraq and Algeria, though they also have substantial oil resources and corresponding revenues, do have large populations, more diverse economic bases, and a high absorptive capacity. The rest of the Arab countries are, by comparison, quite poor in terms of capital, although most of them are substantially populated (e.g., Egypt, Yemen, Tunisia) and have diverse economic bases (e.g., Egypt, Syria, and Lebanon).

With the exception of Iraq and Algeria, all capital-oil-rich Arab coun-

TABLE 3.2
Evolution of Oil Revenues for Major Arab Producers 1965-1979, in $ Millions

Major Producers \ Years	1965	1970	1971	1972	1973	1974	1975	1976	1977	1979
Saudi Arabia	655	1214	1885	2745	4340	22574	25676	37809	36900	
Kuwait	761	899	1407	1634	1980	8645	7706	8063	6800	
Iraq	375	521	840	575	1843	5700	8500	8800	8800	
United Arab Emirates	33	233	431	551	900	5536	6000	7000	8000	
Qatar	69	122	200	255	464	1802	1700	2090	2100	
Libya	371	1351	1674	1563	2223	5999	5101	7500	8600	
Algeria	102	272	321	613	988	3299	3262	3699	3984	
TOTAL	2276	4612	6758	7936	12738	53555	56975	74663	775184	

Sources: Up to 1974 compiled by M.A. Fadil in Oil and Arab Unity (Arabic) (Beirut: Center for Arab Unity Studies, 1979), p.10. Later years from Petroleum Economist, OPEC Oil Report, 2nd edition, 1979.

tries are underpopulated. With a small demographic base, their pool of labor supply would be naturally limited; and in fact it had been all along, even before the 1973 oil boom. These countries had been net labor importers since the 1950s. But now, with an even greater labor demand at all levels to carry out their new ambitious plans, the importation of labor has immensely intensified.

The Size of Inter-Arab Labor Migration

No one knows exactly the size of inter-Arab labor movement. Both sending and receiving countries have not been in the habit of keeping reliable or retrievable records. But from diverse sources, including some gallant scholarly efforts by a score of pioneers,[2] I was able to piece together an approximate picture.

Tables 3.3 and 3.4 show the estimated size of inter-Arab labor migration before and after the 1973 October oil war. The figures indicate that it jumped from less than 680,000 to about 1.3 million—nearly double in four years. The only decisive factor accounting for this phenomenal rise is, naturally, oil revenues. It is readily apparent that Saudi Arabia, for example, increased its share of imported labor from 345,000 to 700,000 in the short interim, over 100 percent increase. Libya nearly tripled its importation of Arab labor in two years from 107,000 in 1973 to 310,000 in 1975.

The leading Arab labor importers and exporters have, nevertheless, remained the same. Saudi Arabia, Libya, and Kuwait topped the list of labor importers before and after 1973. By the same token, Egypt, Yemen, and Jordan/Palestine topped the list of labor exporters. The only noticeable change among the exporters is the trading off of first and second place between Egypt and Yemen before and after 1973. Egypt's share of labor export nearly quadrupled from less than 100,000 to 398,000, and that of Yemen rose from 234,000 to 290,000, a 24 percent increase.

By the late 1970s, the size of ALM had, no doubt, increased even more. But again, exact figures are hard to come by. Table 3.5 gives three estimates, two by international agencies and one by Arab sources. The ILO and Durham University study puts the figure around 1.3 million in 1975. The International Monetary Fund (IMF) two years later gave the figure of 1.4 million on the basis of official data from labor-exporting states, and the figure of 1.6 million on the basis of labor-importing states' data. M. A. Fadil of the Arab Planning Institute (Kuwait) discussed the underreporting bias in these figures. They usually do not take into account illegal migrants, nor the fact that some countries do not require en-

TABLE 3.3
Inter-Arab Labor Migration Before the 1973 Oil Mutation*

Labor Importing Countries \ Labor Exporting Countries	Year	Yemen	Egypt	Syria	Jordan-Palestine**	Lebanon	Oman	Other Arab Countries	TOTAL
Saudi Arabia	1970	225000	u.a.	40000	50000	30000	u.a.	u.a.	345000
Kuwait	1970	7000	18000	13000	41000	8000	10000	24000	121000
Libya	1973	u.a.	61000	6000	8000	8000	--	24000	107000
Lebanon	1970	u.a.	5000	34000	8000	--	u.a.	u.a.	47000
U.A.E.	1968	u.a.	11000	7000	14000	u.a.	7000	4000	43000
Qatar	1970	u.a.	u.a.	u.a.	u.a.	u.a.	u.a.	u.a.	24000
Bahrain	1971	2000	u.a.	u.a.	4000	u.a.	6000	4000	16000
Oman	1973	u.a.	u.a.	u.a.	u.a.	u.a.	u.a.	u.a.	2000
TOTAL	Before Oct. 1973	234000	95000	100000	125000	46000	23000	56000	679000

Source: A.Farrag, "Migration Between Arab Countries" in <u>Manpower and Employment in Arab Countries</u>, Geneva, International Labor Organization, 1976.

* The reference in this and other tables is to gainfully employed migrants and not their dependents.
** Palestine and Jordan are used interchangeably by many official Arab agencies.

u.a. = unavailable.

TABLE 3.4
Inter-Arab Labor Migration in 1975 (After the Oil Price Boom of 1973-74)

Labor Importing Countries	Egypt	%	Yemen	%	Jordan-Palestine	%	Democratic Yemen	%	Syria	%	Lebanon	%
Saudi Arabia	95,000	(23.9)	280,000	(96.6)	175,000	(66.1)	55,000	(78)	15,000	(21)	20,000	(40)
Libya	229,500	(57.8)	----		14,150	(5.3)	----		13,000	(19)	5,700	(12)
Kuwait	37,588	(9.4)	2,757	(1.0)	47,653	(18.0)	8,658	(12)	16,547	(23)	7,200	(15)
United Arab Emirates	12,500	(3.1)	4,500	(1.6)	14,500	(5.5)	4,500	(6)	4,500	(6)	3,000	(6)
Jordan (East Bank)	5,300	(1.3)	----		----		----		20,000	(28)	500	(1)
Iraq	7,000	(1.8)	----		5,000	(1.9)	----		----		1,100	(2)
Qatar	2,850	(0.7)	1,250	(0.4)	6,000	(23)	1,250	(2)	750	(1)	129	(0.2)
Oman	4,600	(1.2)	100	(0.0)	1,600	(0.6)	100	(0.1)	400	(0.6)	----	
Bahrain	1,237	(0.3)	1,212	(0.4)	614	(0.2)	1,222	(2)	68	(0.1)		
Yemen	2,000	(0.5)	----		200	(0.1)	----		150	(0.2)		
TOTAL	397,543	(100.0)	290,128	(100.0)	264,717	(100.0)	70,630	(100.0)	70,415	(100.0)	49,600	(100.0)
%	(30.7)		(22.4)		(20.4)		(5.5)		(5.4)		(3.8)	

Table 3.4 (Cont.)

Labor Importing Countries	Sudan	%	Tunisia	%	Oman	%	Iraq	%	Somalia	%	Algeria Morocco	%	TOTAL
Saudi Arabia	35,000	(76)	----		17,500	(46)	2,000	(10)	5,000	(76)	----		699,900
Libya	7,000	(15)	38,500	(99.6)	----		----		----		2,500	(98)	310,350
Kuwait	873	(2)	79	(0.1)	3,660	(10)	18,000	(78)	247	(4)	47	(2)	43,280
United Arab Emirates	1,500	(3)	----		14,000	(36)	500	(2)	1,000	(15)	----		62,000
Jordan (East Bank)	----		----		----		----		----		----		32,800
Iraq	200	(0.4)	----		----		----		----		----		15,200
Qatar	700	(1)	----		1,870	(5)	----		----		----		14,870
Oman	500	(1)	100	(0.3)	----		----		300	(5)	----		8,800
Bahrain	400	(1)	----		1,383	(4)	126	(4)	----		----		6,200
Yemen	----		----		----		----		----		----		2,350
TOTAL	45,873	(100.0)	38,649	(100.0)	38,413	(100.0)	20,625	(100.0)	6,547	(100.0)	2,547	(100.0)	1,295,750
%	(3.5)		(3.0)		(3.0)		(1.6)		(0.5)		(0.2)		(100.0)

Sources: J.S. Birks & C.A.Sinclair, International Migration and Development in the Arab Region, Geneva: ILO, 1989, pp.134-135.

TABLE 3.5
Comparisons of Various Estimates of Arab Labor Migration
(1975-1977)

Estimates by Countries	A ILO-Durham Univ. (Birks & Sinclair) (1975)	B International Monetary Fund (1977)	C Arab Sources (M.A. Fadil) (1977)
A. Major Arab Labor Exporters			
Egypt	398,000	350,000	600,000
Arab Yemen	290,000	500,000	600,000
Democratic Yemen	70,000	300,000	300,000
Jordan/Palestine	265,000	150,000	225,000
Sudan	46,000	50,000	174,000
Syria	70,000	u.a.	70,000 (1975)
Lebanon	50,000	u.a.	50,000 "
Tunisia	39,000	u.a.	39,000 "
Others	68,000	u.a.	68,000 "
TOTAL	1,296,000	1,350,000	2,126,000
B. Major Arab Labor Importers		(our estimates)	
Saudi Arabia	700,000	900,000	1,170,000
Libya	310,000	325,000	420,000
Kuwait	143,000	276,000	350,000
U.A.E.	62,000	96,000	115,000
Qatar	15,000	19,000	26,000
Oman	9,000	12,000	16,000
Bahrain	6,000	7,000	9,000
Iraq	15,000	u.a.	100,000
TOTAL	1,260,000	1,635,000	2,206,000

Sources: A. : Birks, J.S. & C.A. Sinclair, International Migration and Development in the Arab Region (Geneva:ILO,1980), pp.134-135.
   B. : International Monetary Fund Survey (IMF), Washington D.C. 4 Sept., 1978, pp.260-262.
   C. : Fadil, M.A.,Oil and Arab Unity (Arabic), (Beirut: Center for Arab Unity Studies, 1979), p.30: estimates by the author are based on a wide range of official sources.

u.a. = unavailable.

try visas or registration of citizens from other Arab countries. For example, until very recently Saudi Arabia did not require either one from Yemenis. Iraq is another country that treats Arab immigrants as citizens of its own, and therefore they often do not appear in most official statistics or international agencies' estimates of ALM. Fadil, relying on various Arab sources from exporting countries, comes up with the 2.1 million figure. I supplemented Fadil's estimate with figures from official sources of labor-importing countries and came up with the figure of 2.2 million for 1977.[3]

In 1980, the size of inter-Arab migration was probably in the neighborhood of 3 million. This steady increase is due to more of the same factors operating since 1973: greater rise of oil revenues, more ambitious developmental plans, greater demands on labor than the indigenous pool can supply in capital-rich countries, and greater supply of labor in capital-poor countries than could be indigenously absorbed or enticed to stay.

The labor shortage in most capital-rich countries is not due only to their underpopulation and small demographic base. Additional socioeconomic factors have limited the annual flow of manpower into the active labor market. Most important among these are the social mores barring women from participation in nonhousehold employment, especially in Saudi Arabia.[4] Also, the fact that the demographic pyramids of these countries are quite inflated with a broad base of underage children reduces the proportion of males disposable as an active labor force.[5] Finally, the presence of a sizable nomadic population[6] in all capital-rich countries means at least a 10 percent potential loss of the indigenous deployable labor force in modern sectors. As a result, the crude participation rate in these countries is quite low by both international and regional standards. As Table 3.6 shows, these ratios for the capital-rich oil countries range from 18.4 percent in Qatar to 24.9 percent in Oman, with an overall average for the whole group of 21.7 percent. In most labor-exporting Arab countries, the comparable ratio ranges from 20.4 percent (Jordan) to 33.5 percent (Egypt), with the average for the group as a whole close to 30 percent.[7]

In mid-1970, therefore, we find migrant labor contributing nearly half (48.7 percent) of all the actively employed in capital-rich Arab countries, as shown in Table 3.7. In some of these countries, the share of migrant labor is as high as 85 percent of the work force (e.g., in the United Arab Emirates). This heavy reliance on migrant Arab labor is one of the salient features of the new social order in the Arab World. Its full consequences will be explored later.

TABLE 3.6
Capital-Rich and Capital-Poor Arab States: National Populations and Work Forces Ranked by Size 1975

State	Population (thousands)	Workforce (thousands)	Crude participation rate %
A. Capital-Rich			
Saudi Arabia	4,592.5	1,026.5	22.4
Libya	2,223.7	449.2	20.2
Oman	550.1	137.0	24.9
Kuwait	471.1	91.8	19.4
Bahrain	214.0	45.8	21.4
U.A.E.	200.0	45.0	22.5
Qatar	67.9	12.5	18.4
Sub-Total of Capital-Rich	8,320.2	1,807.8	21.7
B. Capital-Poor			
Egypt	37,364.9	12,522.2	33.5
Sudan	15,031.3	3,700.0	24.6
Syria	7,335.0	1,838.9	25.1
Yemen	5,037.0	1,425.8	28.3
Jordan	2,616.7	532.8	20.4
Democratic Yemen	1,660.0	430.5	25.9
Sub-Total of Capital-Poor	69,044.9	20,450.2	29.6
TOTAL	77,365.1	22,258.0	28.6

Sources: Compiled by Birks, J.S. & C.A. Sinclair, International Migration and Development in the Arab Region (Geneva: ILO, 1980), pp.131-132.

Inter-Arab Labor Migration

THE
UNIVERSITY OF WINNIPEG
PORTAGE & BALMORAL
WINNIPEG, MAN.   R3B 2E9
CANADA

39

TABLE 3.7
Capital-Rich States: Employment by Nationality 1975

State	Nationals		Non-Nationals		Total
	No.	%	No.	%	Employment
Saudi Arabia	1,026,500	57.0	773,400	43.0	1,799,900
Libya	499,200	57.5	332,400	42.5	781,600
Kuwait	91.800	30.6	208,000	69.4	299,800
U.A.E.	45,000	15.2	251,500	84.8	296,500
Oman	137,000	66.0	70,700	34.0	207,700
Bahrain	45,800	60.4	30,000	39.6	75,800
Qatar	12,500	18.9	53,700	81.1	66,200
TOTAL	1,807,800	51.3	1,719,700	48.7	3,527,600

Source: Birks & Sinclair, *ibid*, p.132.

Composition of Arab Labor Migrants

Available data on occupational and educational background of Arab labor migrants indicate that the process is quite selective. As Table 3.8 shows, migrants in Kuwait, Saudi Arabia, Libya, and Oman seem to dominate the construction and building sectors as well as services (education, health, banking, insurance, civil service, etc.), and these tend to be the largest sectors of the economy. In three of the four oil-rich countries shown in Table 3.8, migrant labor makes up more than 60 percent of the construction work force—65 percent in Libya, 67 percent in Oman, and 95 percent in Kuwait. But even in manufacturing and processing, the percentage of migrant labor is quite substantial in Kuwait (86 percent) and Saudi Arabia (62 percent). One sector we have no data on is that of defense. In three of the four selected capital-rich countries, there is no data on the percentage of non-nationals in their armed forces and defense establishments generally. It is no secret that most capital-rich Gulf States recruit non-nationals.

The occupational characteristics of Arab migrant labor seem to have evolved in the last ten years to include all levels of manpower. In the 1950s and early 1960s most Egyptians working in oil countries were professionals (e.g., teachers, doctors, engineers). With the expansion of

TABLE 3.8
Sectoral Distribution of Local and Imported Labor Force in Selected
Oil-Rich Countries (1973-1975)

Economic sector \ Country	S. Arabia (1973)		Libya (1973)		Kuwait (1975)		Oman (1975)	
	local	migrant	local	migrant	local	migrant	local	migrant
Agriculture	37.1	62.9	89.5	10.5	53.0	47.0	n.a.	n.a.
Manufacturing & Processing	38.2	61.8	65.5	34.5	13.6	86.4	64.1	35.9
Construction	52.4	47.6	35.4	64.6	5.5	94.5	33.4	66.6
Gas, Water, & Electricity	78.3	21.7	84.3	15.7	28.0	72.0	80.5	19.5
Commerce	47.2	52.8	90.3	9.7	16.0	84.0	54.0	46.0
Transport & Communication	53.9	46.1	95.6	4.4	29.1	70.9	81.4	18.6
Civil Service & Defense	n.a.	n.a.	96.1	3.9	n.a.	n.a.	n.a.	n.a.
Services (education, health, banking, etc.)	43.7	56.3	81.3	18.7	38.5	61.5	36.0	64.0
TOTAL	57.0	43.0	78.0	22.0	29.1	70.9	66.0	34.0

Sources: Saudi Arabia's Labor Survey for the Private Sector, 1973; Libyan Arab
Jamahiriya's Preliminary Population Census Results of 1973; Kuwait's Population
Census of 1975; Oman's Labor Survey of Private Sector Establishments Employing
Ten or More Persons (Dec. 1974 —August 1975); M.A. Fadil, Oil and Arab Unity
(Beirut: Center for Arab Studies, 1979).

economic activities following the oil price jump of the 1970s, the need for all levels of occupations is reflected in recent data.

Kuwait, which keeps the best statistical records among capital-rich countries, mirrors the pervasive reliance on expatriate labor as shown in Table 3.9. Thus, while the percentage of migrant labor in the two top occupational categories remains high (89.6 and 46 percent, compared with 10.4 and 53.9 percent of the Kuwaitis, respectively), the share of migrant labor in the lower categories is also high. Of all skilled and semiskilled manual workers, for example, migrants make up nearly 86 percent and Kuwaitis only 14 percent. Even in the lower level of manpower (i.e., unskilled manual occupations), non-Kuwaitis account for nearly two thirds of the total (65 percent). Incidentally, the Arab migrant groups that are overrepresented in this low-level manpower are North Yemenis (68 percent), South Yemenis (53 percent), Iraqis (39 percent), and Egyptians (35 percent). Among non-Arab immigrant labor in Kuwait, Indians and Iranians are also heavily represented in unskilled manual occupations (see Table 3.9). The Palestinians, in contrast, are underrepresented in this category (13 percent), and overrepresented in the top professional category (11 percent). Egyptians follow in this top category (7 percent). In other words, Egyptian migrants are heavily represented in both the very top and the very low levels of manpower in Kuwait.

The situation in Kuwait seems to be typical of other capital-rich countries. In a study by M. A. Faris of the Arab Labor Organization, it was revealed that Arab migrant labor occupied 75 percent of all top professional and administrative jobs in Saudi Arabia, 56 percent in Libya, and 85 percent in Oman in the mid-1970s.[8] Commenting on this situation, M. A. Fadil notes that "the migration stream in the new oil era has become more diversified. The new era made it possible for greater numbers of production and ordinary service workers to migrate to the oil countries. These categories were never used to large-scale migration before."[9]

The case of Egyptians is, again, quite typical of other capital-poor countries. In 1965, of all Egyptians working in Kuwait, over 52 percent were professionals and highly specialized. By 1975, however, their share of this high-level manpower dropped to 29.5 percent. In contrast, Egyptian migrant labor in low-level manpower jumped from 21.8 to 38.3 percent during the same period.[10] Of course, the absolute number of Egyptians in both levels continued to rise, but the increase in middle and low levels of manpower was significantly much greater. This is a point worth remembering, for we begin to note some strategic labor shortages even in capital-poor countries like Egypt in the late 1970s—an issue that will be discussed later.

TABLE 3.9
Kuwait: Occupational Distribution of Kuwaitis and Selected Migrant Communities by Skill Level 1975 (percentages)

Occupa-tional Category		Migrant Communties from:											% of the total	
	Kuwait	Pales-tine	Egypt	Jordan	Lebanon	India	Syria	Iraq	Pakistan	Yemen	Democ. Yemen	Iran	Kuwait	Kuwait non-Kuwait
A1	1.2	10.8	7.2	6.5	4.0	3.6	1.7	1.9	2.1	0.3	0.2	0.1	10.4	89.6
A2	5.8	3.3	3.3	2.8	3.8	1.0	1.6	1.2	1.0	1.3	0.5	0.2	53.9	46.1
B	12.0	35.9	21.1	17.6	17.5	9.0	8.8	4.1	5.5	1.3	0.7	2.7	28.6	71.4
C1	24.4	22.7	7.9	26.1	26.5	21.7	21.1	12.7	11.7	16.2	40.9	13.9	35.6	64.4
C2	12.1	14.2	25.6	25.8	27.8	12.9	39.7	40.8	59.5	12.6	4.7	48.3	14.3	85.7
D	44.5	13.1	24.9	2.12	20.4	51.8	27.1	39.3	20.2	68.2	53.0	34.8	35.0	65.0
TOTAL	100	100	100	100	100	100	100	100	100	100	100	100	29.1	70.9
Total No. of Workforce	86621	8200	27300	38900	7200	2400	16500	17800	11000	2700	8600	17500	---	---

Source: Kuwait Census of 1975, Kuwait: Central Dept. of Statistics, Min. of Planning, 1976, p.105.
A1: professional jobs usually requiring science or math.-based univ. degree; A2: professional & sub-professional jobs usually requiring univ. arts degree; B: technicians & others usually requiring 1-3yrs. post-secondary education/training; C1: skilled & semiskilled office & clerical occupations; C2:skilled and semiskilled manual occupations; D: unskilled occupations.

Labor Migrant Replacement and Circulation

Two important characteristics of inter-Arab migration are worth noting here. First is the migration replacement in the Arab countries that are both labor exporters and labor importers.[11] Referring to Table 3.3 it is observed that Jordan, Iraq, Oman, and Yemen fall into this category. In the case of Jordan and Yemen, the balance is still heavily tipped toward labor export, as shown in Table 3.10. But in the case of Iraq and Oman, both of which are oil producers in their own right, the difference is not as large. The main source of labor migrant replacement for the four countries appearing in Table 3.3 is Egypt, Syria, and Lebanon. Of the non-Jordanian labor force of nearly 33,000 in that country in 1975, 20,000 were Syrians, 7,500 were Lebanese, and 5,300 were Egyptians. In Iraq, Oman, and Yemen combined, out of their 26,000 imported Arab laborers, 14,000 were Egyptians (54 percent), 7,000 were Jordanian-Palestinians (27 percent) and 4,000 were Lebanese. It is believed that this kind of replacement labor increased even more by the late 1970s. Thus, as a labor-exporter country begins to experience shortage in its own domestic labor market as a result of the inability to control outmigration, it resorts to importing replacement labor to fill the gap. This applies especially in Jordan, where it is believed that Syrians and Egyptians are simply replacing medium- and low-level manpower Jordanian-Palestinians who outmigrate to oil-rich countries. The replacement labor obviously receives wages markedly higher than those prevailing in its country of origin (e.g., Egypt and Syria) but not as high as those prevailing in the oil-rich countries.

TABLE 3.10
Labor Exporter-Importer Arab Countries 1975

Country	Size of Labor Export	Size of Labor Import	Net
Jordan	264,717	32,800	232,917
Iraq	20,625	15,200	5,425
Oman	38,413	8,800	29,613
Yemen	290,128	2,350	289,778

Source: Table 3.3 q.v.

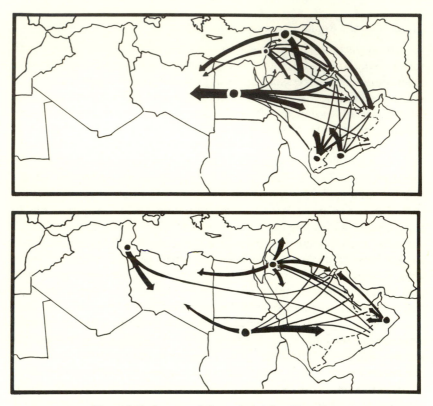

Figure 3.1   Streams of Inter-Arab Labor Migration

The situation with Oman and Yemen is different in the sense that the three-way labor movement is not mechanical replacement. Most likely, the Arab labor imported into Yemen and Oman is of a higher level occupationally, while that exported is of middle and lower levels.

The second phenomenon is migrant Arab labor circulation. Most treatments of the subject analyze ALM statistically and cross-sectionally. The concepts of "stock" and "annual flow" do not take into account the fact that most migrant labor is temporary.[12] In 1970, the average work sojourn for an Egyptian in Kuwait, for example, was about 3.6 years and that of a Yemeni was 4.7 years, while that of a Palestinian was about 6.3 years. As these migrants return home, however, other fellow countrymen replace them in the capital-rich countries. In other words, there is a constant circulation of Arab migrant labor, which means that the process touches many more than the "stock" and "flow" statistics suggest. Thus 1.7 million Egyptians become labor migrants every ten years, not counting their dependents.[13] By the same token, about 2.2 million other Arab labor migrants are affected by the process every decade. According to this view of migrant circulation, a total of nearly 4 million Arabs move across state borders for employment purposes every ten years. If each is a member of an average family of five persons, then a total of 20 million Arabs are directly affected by Arab labor migration every decade, not counting future incremental growth of labor migrants and their dependents.

Arab Labor Migrants and Arab Migrant Communities

So far I have dealt with Arab migrant labor, those actively and gainfully employed outside their countries of origin. Along with some but not all of these migrants go their dependents (wives and children, for example). It is a fact that most migrants do not take their dependents with them, and there is a variety of reasons. Many perceive their stay as short and temporary enough not to warrant bringing their dependents along. Others who may have liked to do so are often deterred by the prohibitive cost of housing and other services in capital-rich countries. Even when they can afford such costs, it would defeat the purposes of migrating in the first place, i.e., to accumulate savings. Finally, some migrants find the environment and quality of life unsuitable for their dependents.

Nevertheless, several categories of Arab labor migrants do bring their families to the country of employment. These include professionals whose housing, family travel, and children's education costs are all paid for by the employer (often the government). Most striking, however, are the Jordanian-Palestinian migrants. These often form a natural population pyramid in the host countries.[14] Again, on the basis of the Kuwaiti data, the population pyramids for several migratory groups are presented in Figure 3.2. It shows the percentage of women and dependent children among the Jordanian-Palestinians to be substantial compared to all others, who tend to be predominantly males. In 1975 the average length of stay for the Palestinian-Jordanians was 7.8 years (compared to 6.3 in 1970), by far the longest of any migratory groups.[15] In fact, as many as 45 percent of members of the Palestinian-Jordanian community in Kuwait were born there, as shown in Figure 3.3. I believe that what the Kuwaiti data reveal is typical of other capital-rich countries: the Palestinian-Jordanians tend to become more of an established community in the host countries. This, of course, is not hard to explain. What we call Jordanian-Palestinians are essentially and mostly Palestinians with Jordanian passports. Their uprootedness and the continued

Figure 3.2

Kuwait: age/sex profiles of selected expatriate communities, 1975.

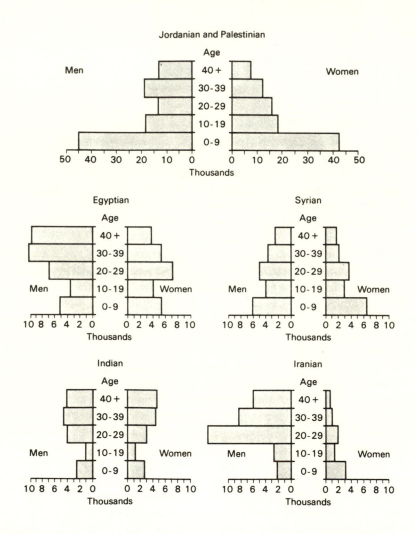

Source: <u>Kuwait Census 1975</u> (Kuwait Ministry of Planning 1976).
Reproduced in Birks & Sinclair, <u>International Migration and
Development in the Arab Region</u> (Geneva:ILO,1980), p.51.

Figure 3.3

Kuwait: age of Jordanians and Palestinians born and living in Kuwait, 1975

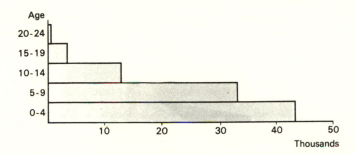

Figure 3.4

Kuwait: distribution of the Jordanian and Palestinian community by length of stay, 1975

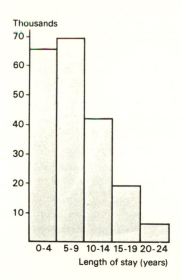

Source: Kuwait Census 1975 (Kuwait Ministry of Planning 1976). Reproduced in Birks & Sinclair, International Migration and Development in the Arab Region (Geneva:ILO, 1980), p.52.

usurpation of their country make it more likely for them to settle temporarily with their dependents wherever they happen to find employment. This, however, has made them the most influential migrant community in oil-rich countries, a fact that has far-reaching political implications. Not only do they constitute between 10 and 20 percent of the labor force in most of the Gulf States, but they are also located in the middle and upper portions of the economic structure. Given the fact that they are the most politicized of all Arabs, with strong affiliation to the PLO, these migrant communities represent subtle deterrence and real constraint on elite behavior and official policies of the oil-rich states.

Non-Arab Migrant Labor

Although ALM constitutes the bulk of the work force in capital-rich countries, there is an increasing presence of non-Arab labor in these countries. Pulled and pushed by the same structural factors in their countries and in the oil-rich countries as are Arab migrants, non-Arab migrants from Asian countries have been trickling in for two decades. However, the trickle turned into a significant stream in the 1970s. Non-Arab migrants come mainly from India, Pakistan, Iran, and Afghanistan. More recently, Koreans and Filippinos have made their appearance on the Arabian landscape as well.

Table 3.11 shows the number of non-Arab migrants in the Gulf States in both absolute and relative terms. The Asians (Indians, Pakistanis, and Orientals) increased from about 84,000 in 1970 to about 248,000 by mid-decade, nearly a 300 percent increase in five years. Although the Asians constituted only 26 percent of the migrant work force in 1970, they grew to make up nearly 46 percent of it by 1975. At that point non-Arab exceeded Arab labor migrants in the Gulf States. Though still growing in absolute numbers (from 166,000 in 1970 to 226,000 in 1975), Arab migrants have slipped in relative terms from 51 percent to 42 percent in the same period. Given the fact that the indigenous populations of the Gulf States are quite modest (about one million in 1975), the growing presence of non-Arab communities could radically change the ethnic makeup of these states. Some voices have been raised in alarm at the process of de-Arabization of the Gulf.[16] But the temptation of cheap labor is too strong to stop the flow of non-Arab migrants.

Prospect of Future Labor Migration

The migratory system set in motion in the 1970s—the labor movement from overpopulated capital-poor countries to underpopulated capital-

TABLE 3.11
Bahrain, Kuwait, Qatar & U.A.E. Work Force
by Ethnic Origin 1970 & 1975

Ethnic origin	1970		1975	
	No.	%	No.	%
Arab (non-nats.)	165,900	51.0	226,400	41.7
Asian	83,900	25.8	247,700	45.7
Iranian, Europ. & other	75,300	23.2	68,400	12.6
Subtotal	325,100	100.0	542,500	100.0
Nationals	147,600	31.2*	195,100	26.5*
Total	472.700	100.0	737,600	100.0

Source: Birks & Sinclair, International Migration...op.cit.
* = percentage of total

rich Arab countries—will continue through the 1980s. In a recent study by the World Bank,[17] manpower requirements for the oil-rich Arab countries are estimated through the mid-1980s (see Table 3.12). Under a high growth scenario, the labor demand is projected to rise from its 1975 level of 9.7 million to about 15.3 million in 1985, a net increase of 5.6 million and a relative growth of 58 percent. Under a low growth scenario, the net increase in manpower requirements in these countries will still be 4.3 million. The sectoral composition of total manpower requirements as shown in Table 3.13 indicates a greater relative labor demand in manufacturing (94 to 109 percent), utilities (119 to 131 percent), construction (112 to 140 percent), trade and finance (65 to 76 percent), and services (55 to 67 percent). The lowest growth demand on labor is projected for the agricultural sector—only about 7 percent under the high growth scenario. In terms of relative share of demand, however, the services sectors will appropriate around 30 percent of the net increase, followed by construction, trade and finance, and manufacturing.

Another projected trend in labor requirements through the mid-1980s is a relatively greater demand on high level manpower. As Table 3.14 shows, even under a low growth scenario, professional-technical occupa-

TABLE 3.12
Major Labor Importing Countries: Total Labor Requirements 1975 and 1985,
by Country (High and Low Growth Rates)

Countries	1975		1985 High Economic Growth Rates			1985 Low Economic Growth Rates		
	Manpower Requirement	Percent Shares	Manpower Requirement	Percent Shares	Percent Increase	Manpower Requirement	Percent Shares	Percent Increase
Algeria	3083000	31.7	4511000	29.4	46.3	3954000	28.1	28.3
Bahrain	79000	0.8	151000	1.0	89.9	129000	0.9	63.3
Iraq	3008000	30.9	4566000	29.8	40.2	4302000	30.7	32.3
Kuwait	297000	3.1	414000	2.7	39.4	393000	2.8	32.3
Libya	735000	7.6	1414000	9.2	92.4	1260000	9.0	71.4
Oman	192000	2.0	257000	1.7	33.9	257000	1.8	33.9
Qatar	74000	0.7	136000	0.9	83.8	133000	0.9	79.7
Saudi Arabia	1968000	20.2	3245000	21.2	64.9	3055000	21.7	55.2
United Arab Emirates	292000	3.0	632000	4.1	116.4	570000	4.1	95.2
TOTAL	9728000	100.0	15326000	100.0	57.5	14053000	100.0	44.5

Source: The World Bank's Research Project on International Labor Migration and Manpower in the Middle East and North Africa (Washington D.C., September 1980, mimeographed), p.36.

TABLE 3.13
Major Labor Importing Countries: Labor Requirements by Sector, and Shares of Total Increase in Requirements 1975 and 1985 (High and Low Growth Rates)

Sectors	1975		1985 High Economic Growth Rates					1985 Low Economic Growth Rates				
	Manpower Requirement	Percent Shares	Manpower Requirement	Percent Shares	Increase 1975-1985 (Number)	Increase 1975-1985 (Percent)	Percent Shares of Increase	Manpower Requirement	Percent Shares	Increase 1975-1985 (Number)	Increase 1975-1985 (Percent)	Percent Shares of Increase
Agriculture	3699000	38.0	3952000	25.8	253000	6.8	4.5	3550000	25.3	-149000	-4.0	-3.4
Mining & Quarrying	145000	1.5	226000	1.5	81000	55.8	1.4	226000	1.6	81000	55.8	1.9
Manufacturing	635000	6.5	1327000	8.7	692000	108.9	12.4	1231000	8.8	596000	93.8	13.8
Utilities	260000	2.7	598000	3.9	338000	130.0	6.0	568000	4.0	308000	118.5	7.1
Construction	1141000	11.7	2734000	17.8	1593000	139.6	28.5	2419000	17.2	1278000	112.0	9.5
Trade & Finance	875000	9.0	1536000	10.0	661000	75.5	11.8	1443000	10.3	568000	64.9	3.1
Transport & Communication	499000	5.1	829000	5.4	330000	66.1	5.9	785000	5.6	286000	57.3	6.4
Services	2474000	25.5	4124000	26.9	1650000	66.7	29.5	3831000	27.2	1357000	54.9	31.4
TOTAL	9728000	100.0	15326000	100.0	5598000	57.5	100.0	14053000	100.0	4325000	44.5	100.0
Percent of Regional Increase							40.2					50.0

Source: Same as Table 3.12.

TABLE 3.14
Major Labor Importing Countries: Labor Requirements, by Occupational Level, and Shares of Total Regional Increase in Requirements 1975 and 1985 (High and Low Growth Rates)

Occupational Level	1975		1985		High Economic Growth Rates			
	Manpower Requirement	Percent Shares	Manpower Requirement	Percent Shares	Increase 1975-1985 (Number)	Increase 1975-1985 (Percent)	Percent Shares of Increase	Percent of Regional Increase
Professional & Technical Occupations (A1)	113000	1.2	321000	2.1	208000	184.1	3.7	1.5
Other Professional Occupations (A2)	246000	2.5	547000	3.4	301000	122.4	5.4	2.2
Subprofessional & Technical Occupations (B1)	186000	1.9	502000	3.3	314000	169.9	5.7	2.3
Other Subprofessional Occupations (B2)	364000	3.7	818000	5.3	454000	126.7	8.1	3.3
Skilled Office & Manual Occupations (C1)	797000	8.2	1504000	9.8	707000	88.7	12.6	5.1
Semiskilled Office & Manual Occupations (C2)	1853000	19.0	3450000	22.5	1597000	86.2	28.5	11.6
Unskilled Occupations (D)	6169000	63.5	8183000	53.4	2014000	32.6	36.0	14.7
TOTAL	9728000	100.0	15325000	100.0	5597000	57.2	100.0	40.8

Table 3.14 (Cont.)

Occupational Level	Manpower Requirement	Percent Shares	1985 Low Economic Growth Rate			
			Increase 1975-1985 (Number)	Increase 1975-1985 (Percent)	Percent Shares of Increase	Percent Regional Increase
Professional & Technical Occupations (A1)	305000	2.2	192000	149.9	4.6	2.2
Other Professional Occupations (A2)	512000	3.6	266000	108.1	6.2	3.1
Subprofessional & Technical Occupations (B1)	455000	3.2	269000	144.6	6.2	3.1
Other Subprofessional Occupations (B2)	762000	5.4	398000	109.3	9.2	4.6
Skilled Office & Manual Occupations (C1)	1395000	9.9	598000	75.0	13.8	6.9
Semiskilled Office & Manual Occupations (C2)	3183000	22.7	1330000	71.8	30.8	15.1
Unskilled Occupations (D)	7441000	53.0	1272000	20.6	29.4	14.6
TOTAL	14053000	100.0	4325000	44.5	100.0	49.7

Source: As for Table 3.12.

tions are projected to increase by around 170 percent followed by technical (108 percent) and subprofessional occupations (145 percent). Manual occupations will have a moderate growth in the 1975–1985 period, ranging from 71 percent for semiskilled to 21 percent for the unskilled. In absolute volume, however, these two categories will still account for most of the net growth of manpower requirements during the ten years ending in 1985.

The question most relevant to the new Arab social order is how much of these manpower requirements would be supplied from indigenous sources and how much would have to come from outside, especially from neighboring Arab countries. The same World Bank study, on the basis of an elaborate model, estimated that the demographic base and educational system outputs of the capital-rich Arab countries would only supply over 50 percent of the net increase in labor required for the lowest occupational level, i.e., semiskilled and manual occupations.[18] This is clearly shown in Table 3.15.

It is, however, middle- and high-level manpower that the capital-rich countries will still be in dire need of through the mid-1980s. Between 50 and 82 percent of manpower requirements in four of the top five occupational levels will have to be filled by expatriates. The volume of expatriates is projected to increase in each of the Arab capital-rich countries. The net growth of manpower requirements of expatriates at all levels is projected at about 1.5 to 1.9 million by 1985 (see Table 3.16). That, of course, is in addition to the 1.7 to 2.0 million who were already working there in 1975. All in all, the size of migrant labor in the seven oil-rich Arab countries would amount to nearly 3.5 million out of the 6.2 million total manpower requirements in 1985 (see Table 3.17).

The above projected evolution of migrant labor indicates clearly that it is going to grow more professional, technical, and highly educated. This profile of expatriate manpower will, no doubt, have serious consequences for the capital-poor labor-exporting countries. More than ever, the demand for manpower is likely to drain the labor-exporting countries of the better qualified workers. In 1975, high proportions of vacancies in professional, technical, and clerical occupations in labor importing countries were constrained by a requirement of Arabic and English language competence. Consequently, it is reasonable to assume that high- and middle-level manpower in Arab labor-exporting countries will be increasingly sought after by public and private employers in the labor-importing countries. The wider recruiting areas of South and Southeast Asia, which have supplied increasingly large shares of additional expatriate manpower since the mid-1970s, may not be appropriate sources of labor in the future as the structure of expatriate manpower re-

TABLE 3.15
Comparison of Projected Net Growth of Manpower Requirements 1976-85 for the Seven Major Labor-Importing Countries

Occupation	Net Growth in Manpower Requirements		National Labor Force Entrants 1976-1985		Supply of Percent of Requirements
	No.	%	No.	%	
Professional & Technical Occupations (A1)	136,700	5.2	24,700	1.9	18.1
Other Professional Occupations (A2)	197,000	7.6	53,700	4.0	27.3
Subprofessional & Technical Occupations (B1)	151,800	5.8	40,300	3.0	26.5
Other Subprofessional Occupations (B2)	234,800	9.0	116,500	8.7	49.6
Skilled Office & Manual Occupations (C1)	446,400	17.1	158,100	11.8	35.4
Semiskilled Office & Manual Occupations (C2)	676,300	25.9	480,400	35.9	71.0
Unskilled Occupations (D)	768,800	29.4	464,000	34.7	60.4
TOTAL	2,611,800	100.0	1,337,700	100.0	51.2

Source: Same as Table 3.12.

TABLE 3.16
Bahrain, Kuwait, Oman, Qatar, Saudi Arabia, and United Arab Emirates: Employment of Nationals and Non-Nationals by Occupation 1975 and 1985 (High and Low Growth Rates)

Occupation	1975			1985 High Economic Growth Rates				
	Total Employment	Percentage per Occupation	Percent Shares	Total Employment	Percentage per Occupation	Percent Shares	Increase 1975-1985 (Number)	Increase 1975-1985 (Percent)
Professional & Technical Occupations (A1)								
Nationals	10496	19.4	0.5	321000	16.0	1.2	21604	205.8
Non-Nationals	43494	80.6	2.7	1587000	83.2	4.5	115206	264.9
Other Professional Occupations (A2)								
Nationals	47407	33.3	2.3	86500	25.4	3.2	38893	81.7
Non-Nationals	95412	66.7	6.0	751600	74.6	7.1	158188	165.8
Subprofessional & Technical Occupations (B1)								
Nationals	13804	70.3	0.7	47600	21.5	1.8	33794	244.8
Non-Nationals	54320	79.7	3.4	173600	78.5	4.9	119280	219.6
Other Subprofessional Occ. (B2)								
Nationals	66320	49.9	3.3	161100	43.7	5.9	94772	142.9
Non-Nationals	66576	50.1	4.1	207700	56.3	5.9	141124	212.0
Skilled Office & Manual Occ. (C1)								
Nationals	161181	37.2	7.9	262100	29.8	9.7	100919	62.6
Non-Nationals	271879	62.8	17.0	418600	70.2	17.4	346721	127.5
Semiskilled Office & Manual Occupations (C2)								
Nationals	347190	52.6	17.0	691400	51.7	25.6	344210	99.1
Non-Nationals	313281	47.4	19.6	645500	48.3	18.2	332219	106.0
Unskilled Occupations (D)								
Nationals	1389986	64.8	68.3	1419700	48.8	52.6	29716	2.1
Non-Nationals	755878	35.2	47.2	1490500	51.2	62.0	734622	97.2
Total								
Nationals	2036594	56.0	100.0	2700500	43.2	100.0	663906	32.6
Non-Nationals	1600840	44.0	100.0	3548200	56.0	100.0	1947360	121.6

Table 3.16 (Cont.)

Occupation	1985 Low Economic Growth Rates				
	Total Employment	Percentage per Occupation	Percent Shares	Increase 1975-1985 (Number)	Increase 1975-1985 (Percent)
Professional & Technical Occupations (A1)					
Nationals	32100	17.8	1.2	21605	205.8
Non-Nationals	148100	82.2	4.8	104606	240.5
Other Professional Occupations (A2)					
Nationals	86600	27.0	3.2	38993	81.9
Non-Nationals	234500	73.0	7.5	139088	145.8
Subprofessional & Technical Occupations (B1)					
Nationals	47600	22.5	1.8	33794	244.8
Non-Nationals	163600	77.5	5.3	109280	201.2
Other Subprofessional Occ. (B2)					
Nationals	161100	45.7	6.0	94722	142.9
Non-Nationals	191100	54.3	6.1	124524	187.0
Skilled Office & Manual Occ. (C1)					
Nationals	262100	31.4	9.8	100919	62.6
Non-Nationals	573100	68.6	18.4	201221	110.8
Semiskilled Office & Manual Occupations (C2)					
Nationals	672500	53.6	25.1	325310	93.7
Non-Nationals	583200	46.4	18.7	269919	86.2
Unskilled Occupations (D)					
Nationals	1420500	53.8	57.9	30514	2.2
Non-Nationals	1270400	46.2	39.2	464522	61.5
Total					
Nationals	2682500	46.3	100.0	645906	31.7
Non-Nationals	3114000	53.7	100.0	1513160	94.5

Source: Same as Table 3.12.

TABLE 3.17
Major Labor Importing Countries: Work Force by Nationality 1975 and 1985
(High and Low Growth Rates)

Countries	1975				1985 High Economic Growth Rates				1985 Low Economic Growth Rates			
	National Work Force	Non-National Work Force	Total	Percent Non-National	National Work Force	Non-National Work Force	Total	Percent Non-National	National Work Force	Non-National Work Force	Total	Percent Non-National
Bahrain	50000	29000	79000	36.7	70000	81000	151000	53.6	70000	60000	130000	46.2
Kuwait	87000	211000	298000	70.8	140000	273000	413000	66.1	140000	252000	392000	64.3
Libya	454000	280000	734000	38.1	695000	719000	1414000	50.8	676000	584000	1260000	46.3
Oman	89000	103000	192000	53.6	150000	107000	257000	41.6	150000	104000	256000	41.4
Qatar	12000	61000	73000	83.6	19000	117000	136000	86.0	19000	115000	134000	85.8
Saudi Arabia	1300000	668000	1968000	33.9	1565000	1680000	3245000	51.8	1565000	1490000	3055000	46.8
U.A.E.	45000	248000	293000	84.6	62000	571000	633000	90.2	57000	508000	570000	49.1
(Total)	(2037000)	(1600000)	(3637000)	44.0	(2701000)	(3548000)	(6249000)	54.8	(2682000)	(3115000)	(5797000)	51.7
Algeria	3073000	10000	3083000	0.3	4248000	263000	4511000	5.8	3832000	122000	3954000	3.1
Iraq	3008000	0	3008000	0	4110000	456000	4566000	10.0	4032000	270000	4302000	4.3
(Total)	(6081000)	(10000)	(6091000)	0.2	(8358000)	(719000)	(9077000)	7.9	(7864000)	(392000)	(8256000)	4.7
GRAND TOTAL	8118000	1610000	9728000	16.6	11059000	4267000	15326000	27.8	10540000	3507000	14053000	25.0

SOURCE: Same as Table 3.12.

quirements shifts from unskilled and semiskilled production and service occupations to more highly skilled and professional occupations.

Nothing illustrates the dynamics of the inter-Arab labor migratory system implied in the above conclusion better than Egypt and Saudi Arabia. In the next two chapters we will focus on causes and consequences of the labor migration in each. Before closing this chapter, however, we must also indicate the future prospect of the ethnic composition of the populations in the seven major oil-rich countries. As Tables 3.18 and 3.19 show, the expatriate migrants to these countries tend increasingly to bring along or later send for their dependents to join them in the country of employment. Although in the 1960s only Palestinians tended to do that, we find that as of the mid-1970s other migrant laborers began to follow suit. In the 1980s this trend is expected to intensify. Thus the projected 3.5 million expatriate workers in oil-rich Arab countries will be accompanied by twice as many of their dependents by 1985—between 6.7 and 7.4 million of them. In other words, migrants are in the process of transforming from aggregates of predominantly adult single males to "natural" communities with a normal age-sex distribution. Their crude activity rate is going down from its previous high of nearly 50 percent in 1975 to a projected low of around 32 percent in 1985. The total non-native population of the seven labor-importing Arab countries will increase from 3.1 million in 1975 to around 10 million in 1985. At least three broad implications of such development will bear significantly on the new Arab social order. First, the natives of most of these countries will become numerical minorities in their own lands. Second, migrant communities will tend to form permanent ethnic enclaves in the seven major labor-importing countries. Third, a high level of cosmopolitanism will be juxtaposed on the substantial remnants of these countries' traditional social structures. Some of these and other implications are elaborated in Chapter 5, which deals with Saudi Arabia.

Conclusion

Oil and the revenues it has generated have triggered an unprecedented inter-Arab migratory system. Its direction has been from heavily populated and capital-poor countries to underpopulated capital-rich countries of the Arab World. Its volume has grown from less than half a million in the sixties, to 0.7 million in the early seventies, to about 2.0 million at the end of the seventies. By 1985, inter-Arab labor migration is projected to reach about 2.5 million. The dependents accompanying this labor are projected to be twice as many, bringing the total inter-Arab migrants to about 6.5 million. In addition, non-Arab migrants, espe-

TABLE 3.18
Bahrain, Kuwait, Libya, Oman, Qatar, Saudi Arabia and U.A.E.: Non-Nationals' Population and Work Force in 1975 and 1985 (High and Low Growth Rates)

Nationality	1975			1985 High Growth Rates			1985 Low Growth Rates		
	Population	Work Force	Crude Activity Rate	Population	Work Force	Crude Activity Rate	Population	Work Force	Crude Activity Rate
Algeria	600	300	50.0	400	200	50.0	400	200	50.0
Egypt	620300	336800	54.3	2328800	716300	30.8	2024200	609300	30.1
India	205700	141900	69.0	997300	321500	37.2	838700	274500	32.7
Iran	147500	69900	49.1	425200	117100	27.5	375300	101000	26.9
Iraq	47000	18700	39.8	57800	12400	21.5	55700	11600	70.8
Jordan	503000	139000	27.6	1308900	246300	18.8	1290300	242000	18.8
Lebanon	57600	28500	54.7	286800	17400	25.2	270900	68500	25.3
Morocco	4700	2000	42.6	53300	12700	23.8	39900	9300	23.3
Oman	56900	30800	54.1	145500	46100	31.7	143400	45100	31.5
Pakistan	353800	205500	58.1	1847100	530500	28.8	1614200	467100	28.9
South East Asia	21500	20500	95.3	372300	346000	92.9	370900	343500	92.6
Sudan	64500	25900	40.2	365800	88800	24.3	345800	80600	23.3
Syria	104600	38100	36.4	412100	96200	23.3	381700	87100	22.8
Tunisia	52400	28000	53.4	225100	64500	28.7	192900	54200	78.1
Yemen (YAR)	607600	378500	54.1	889700	511100	57.4	769400	397700	51.7
Yemen (PDRY)	123100	45800	37.2	374600	84700	22.6	363700	81000	22.3
Rest of World	166900	90400	54.2	859900	281400	32.7	728400	240800	33.1
Total	3127700	1550600	49.6	10945600	3548200	32.4	9805300	3113500	31.8

Source: Same as Table 3.12.

TABLE 3.19
Bahrain, Kuwait, Libya, Oman, Qatar, Saudi Arabia, U.A.E.: Population by Major Ethnic Group in 1975-1985 (High and Low Growth Rates)

Major Ethnic Group	1975 Population	1975 Percent	1985 High Growth Rates Population	Percent	Annual Increase 1975-1985	1985 Low Growth Rates Population	Percent	Annual Increase 1975-1985
Arab Non-Nationals	2237300	71.5	6448800	58.9	11.2	5877800	59.9	10.1
South Asians	559500	17.9	2839400	25.9	17.6	2452900	25.0	15.9
South East Asians	21500	0.7	372300	3.4	33.0	370900	3.8	32.9
Others	309400	9.9	1285100	11.8	15.3	1103700	11.3	13.6
Total	3127700	100.0	10945600	100.0	13.3	9805300	100.0	12.1
Nationals	9758300	75.7	14313300	56.7	3.9	14314400	59.3	3.9
Total	12886000	100.0	25258900	100.0	7.0	24118600	100.0	6.5

Source: Same as Table 3.12.

cially Asians, are projected to increase proportionately and in absolute numbers. By the mid-1980s, non-Arab migrants to rich Arab countries may reach as many as 4 million (over 40 percent of all migrants). Together, Arab and non-Arab migrants (labor and dependents) are projected to be about 11 million by 1985, compared with 14 million natives. The expatriates, therefore, will represent 43 percent of the total population living in the seven capital-rich Arab countries. I believe that this development is having a profound impact on the social landscape of the Arab World.

Causes and Consequences of Labor Exportation: Egypt

Egypt's share in ALM was estimated between 400,000 and 600,000 in 1975.[1] This represents nearly one third of total ALM, which was estimated between 1.3 and 2 million for the same year.[2] Even if we take the minimum estimate of 400,000, it would represent a four-fold increase over what it was in 1965.[3] The two facts that strike any observer of the Arab labor market are (1) the phenomenal growth rate of Egyptian labor supply to capital-rich countries in the first half of the 1970s (a 400 percent increase in five years); and (2) the dominant size of Egypt's share in total Arab labor migration. In most accounts, Egypt is the biggest single supplier among Arab and non-Arab countries involved in the Arab migratory system.[4] Egyptians constitute anywhere from 10 to 60 percent of the labor force of most capital-rich countries. They are found in all levels of manpower, from top political advisors of rulers of the Gulf States, to ditch diggers in the far corners of South Arabia. Libya and Saudi Arabia appropriate most Egyptian labor (about 200,000 each by the late 1970s), followed by Kuwait and the rest of the Gulf States.[5] Cursory observations indicate that Iraq is becoming a major receiver of Egyptian labor, but as yet official statistics are not available.

Causes of Egyptian Labor Migration

The phenomenal growth of labor migration from Egypt occurred in the 1970s. Even though Egypt had traditionally supplied the Arab World and Africa with a high level of manpower since the fifties, the scale was always limited. Thus, as late as 1968 the number of Egyptians granted work permits abroad did not exceed 10,000.[6] Ten years later the number was estimated conservatively at 500,000, a fiftyfold increase. The demand generated by the capital-rich countries is a decisive factor, and it will be discussed again in this volume. But the demand factor alone could not explain this phenomenal growth of Egyptian labor migration.

We postulate three sets of interacting structural forces inside Egypt that made it possible for Egyptian labor to respond to the expanding market in capital-rich countries. These forces are demographic, economic, and sociopolitical. The individual motivation to migrate is basically conditioned by the average Egyptian's perception of these structural forces as they impinge on daily existence and life opportunities. We shall deal with the individual factors in due course.

The Demographic Structure

Egypt's demographic profile is typical of most Third World countries, such as India, Mexico, Turkey, and Thailand. Some of Egypt's demographic indicators were presented in Table 3.1. To recapitulate, Egypt is the most populous Arab country (over 40 million at present), with a natural growth rate of 2.3 percent and an urban growth rate of about 4 percent. In 1976 its population consisted of 56 percent rural and 44 percent urban, but with the historical trend of greater urbanization continuing. This rapidly growing population has a high proportion of young age groups (40 percent below the age of 15), low economic participation rate (36.8 percent), and low literacy rate (44 percent). The largest percentage of the labor force is still engaged in agriculture (48 percent), with the rest engaged in the tertiary and service sectors (38 percent) and industry (14 percent).[7]

This demographic structure is underdeveloped by the standards of the First and Second Worlds. However, by the standards of the Arab World and definitely by those of the oil-rich Arab states, Egypt's population is fairly well developed. It has the highest economic participation rate in the Arab World—almost twice that of the capital-rich countries, which average 21.7 percent (compared with Egypt's 37 percent in the late seventies). With a big base to start with, this population yields a labor force of 13 million. Egypt's literacy rate is one of the highest, at least 10 to 20 percent higher than most capital-rich states. In brief, by Arab standards, Egypt's demographic structure makes it possible to have the largest well-trained deployable labor force in the region.

Egypt has a crude population density of forty persons per square kilometer. In this sense it is not overpopulated. But given the fact that 95 percent of Egypt's territory is uninhabited desert, its real density is about 1,000 per sq. km.—maybe not one of the highest in the world, but definitely one of the highest in the Arab World. With agriculture still the main occupation of most Egyptians, the arable land has increased by only 20 percent in this century (from 5 to 6 million feddans). The population, on the other hand, has quadrupled (from 10 million in 1900 to 42 million in 1980). Thus the per capita measure of agricultural land has fallen off steadily from 0.5 feddans in 1900 to less than 0.15 at present. This is another indication of being "overpopulated."[8]

However, terms such as "overpopulated" or "surplus population" are, and should always be, relative terms. The final measure is probably whether the population is "well-utilized" (as indexed by gainful and productive employment), and whether the population is registering steady improvement in its standard or quality of living (as indexed, say, by income per capita, literacy rates, infant mortality rates, etc.). This takes us to the next set of structural factors—economic—that make it possible for Egyptian labor to flow into the capital-rich Arab countries. The point remains, however, that Egypt's demographic structure made it possible but not inevitable for it to become a labor-exporting country.

The Economic Structure

On the eve of the oil price boom, Egypt had an economy that was typical of most Third World countries. "A low level of gross domestic product per capita; a low level of consumption per capita; a low level of domestic savings; a low level of domestic capital formation; an uneven pattern of income distribution; widespread unemployment; hidden employment and rapid rural-to-urban migration."[9] In the case of Egypt there were added economic shackles: huge defense burdens, high inflation, foreign debts, and a rapidly deteriorating infrastructure.

Egypt's economic expansion and industrialization, which were in full swing from 1955 to 1965, came to a halt in the late 1960s. The major, but not the only factor in halting Egypt's socioeconomic development was the 1967 defeat in the third Arab-Israeli War. The decade of economic expansion was coupled with activist socialist policies. This was the period in which central planning, the public sector, workers' participation in management, land reform, and rent controls were all in vogue.[10] The share of industry in Egypt's GNP was steadily rising, and the transformation of Egypt's labor force to modern sectors looked irreversible.[11] With such socioeconomic forces at work, the thought of massive labor transfer to other countries was unthinkable. At the time, permitting Egyptians to work abroad was motivated mainly by nationalist and political, but not economic, considerations, a point we shall elaborate upon shortly. Numerous restrictions were placed on Egypt's manpower lest some of it should migrate and thus adversely affect Egypt's own development.[12]

In the late 1960s, Egypt's rate of economic growth dropped from its previous 6.5 percent annually to about 2 percent, with some years recording negative growth.[13] The main reason was the fact that most of Egypt's resources, which would otherwise have gone to productive investment, were now diverted to the war efforts. Employment opportunities froze, and an increasing number of would-be entrants into the labor force were drafted into the army. However, this seemed no more than a temporary economic halt, not necessitating a retreat in Egypt's socialist orientation while Nasser was still at the helm.

But with Nasser's death in 1970 and Sadat's emergence as Egypt's strong man after a showdown with his challengers in May 1971, a new orientation was set in motion. The economic slowdown of the late sixties continued in the early seventies, but now coupled with steady retreat from socialism.[14] The public sector was to be "stabilized" or "consolidated"—a polite term for its freezing or liquidation, as it turned out. The private sector was to be allowed freedom of action, a polite term for a wholehearted official endorsement of a capitalist orientation, as became crystal clear by 1974.

What the new economic orientation amounted to was no less than minimum government involvement in socioeconomic development. The task was to be left to private initiatives—domestic, Arab, and foreign. The new orientation translated itself in Law No. 43 of 1974, Law No. 132 of 1977, and numerous other decrees, which altogether came to be called the Open Door Policy.

With little or no state commitment to economic planning, most of the Nasser manpower policies seemed not only irrelevant but an outright impediment to the economic orientation. Thus, guaranteeing employment for high school and university graduates seemed an unnecessary burden. Restriction on manpower movement was gradually lifted. The new architects of Egypt's economy now deemed it more important to compete for the lucrative Arab labor market and capital. Outright encouragement of labor migration became official policy after the quadrupling of oil prices in 1973, following the October War. This coincided with the subsequent release of thousands of young Egyptians from military service in mid-1974. Thus the economic rationale for exporting labor was becoming quite persuasive, and may be summarized as aiming at the following: reduction of population pressure, reduction of hidden and open unemployment, and capturing an appropriate share of the oil revenue boom in the form of wages and remittances. The latter was believed to have a multiplier effect. It would earn for Egypt badly needed foreign currency and thus help correct its balance of payments deficit. The remittances were to enhance the sagging rate of saving and boost the process of capital formation.

Exporting Egyptian labor and attracting investments from outside the border have become integral parts of a new policy evolved to deal with Egypt's economic woes. Here, a self-fulfilling diagnosis-prognosis was at work. Egypt's problems, viewed as overpopulation, surplus labor, low rates of saving and capital formation, indicated that the solution must lie in reducing what Egypt had too much of and increasing what it had too little of. Phrased differently, the economic approach is to export "negatives" (i.e., surplus population, the unemployed, and the underemployed) and import "positives" (e.g., remittances, capital, and new technology). In brief, it is seeking external solutions for internal problems. With the state reducing its direct involvement in developmental efforts, this "diagnosis-prognosis" would have a surface validity: it becomes self-fulfilling.

Sociopolitical Forces

The demographic-economic interplay discussed above was acted upon by a regime that seems committed to the interests of the upper-middle and upper classes. These classes represent a social force that felt its golden opportunity to control Egypt had come with Nasser's defeat in 1967 and his final departure in 1970. They are a mixture of prerevolutionary big landowners and businessmen-capitalists on one hand, and post-revolutionary professionals, top technocrats, and managers of the public sector on the other.[15] If the urge of the first group to reorient society to nonsocialist philosophy is understandable, a word of explanation is in order for that urge among the newer groups. Simply stated, technocrats and top managers who benefited greatly from Egypt's economic and social transformation in the two previous decades had reached the ceiling by the late 1960s. They could go no higher, yet most of them were still in their 40s and 50s. They and the echelon immediately below them felt the need for an outlet. Immediately after the 1967 defeat they timidly toyed with the ideas that later became the cornerstone of Sadat's socioeconomic orientation: exporting labor, open migration, encouraging the private sector, attracting foreign capital. However, Nasser's presence, even in defeat, still symbolized unmistakable socialist orientation and commitment to the lower half of society. But upon his death, the timid voices of the old and the new upper classes became loud and clear. They were aided by their Arab counterparts from the oil-rich countries, especially after the 1973 War.

Thus the early years of the 1970s witnessed the confluence of inputs from Egypt's demographic, economic, and social structures. Aided by regional, and later international factors, this confluence of forces translated into a full-fledged philosophy, orientation, and a set of policies symbolized by President Sadat. This coalition of old and new social forces wed itself to the ruling elite in more than a metaphorical manner. The expansion of President Sadat's kinship group through intermarriage added a literal dimension to the metaphor.[16] By the end of the 1970s, four major thrusts of this orientation were quite clear: the open door policy, limited democratization, alignment with the West (especially the United States), and accommodation with Israel.

Of concern to us here is the open door policy as it bears on Egypt's exportation of labor. Most important of all, the 1971 constitution, in Article 52, established migration, permanent or temporary, as a citizen's right. Immediately after, a series of laws and presidential and ministerial decrees were issued operationalizing this constitutional right even before the formal baptism of the open door policy.[17] Presidential Decree No. 73 of 1971 was designed to encourage temporary and permanent migration. The decree gave Egyptian migrants the right to be reinstated in their formal government positions within one year of their resignation. The aim was to assure potential migrants that in case they faced difficulties abroad, the risk would be minimal, for they could come back to their old jobs. In the same year the government enacted an 18-point plan removing a number of bureaucratic and administrative restrictions, thus making it much easier for Egyptians to migrate. In 1972, a cabinet-level commission was formed, headed by the minister of manpower, to review all relevant migrant issues with the aim of enhancing the process without "harming" internal socioeconomic development. Law No. 97 of 1969 was amended to allow former ministers and top-ranking officials (e.g., former managers of the public sector) to work abroad without the five-year waiting period previously stipulated. In 1975 the People's Assembly ratified a treaty for manpower movement among Arab countries. Two laws by presidential decree, No. 31 and No. 795 of 1976, established the Supreme Commission for Affairs of Egyptians Abroad and the Supreme Council of Manpower and Training, with the explicit stipulation that the aim was to enhance Egyptian labor migration. There were some objections from development-oriented ministries, such as industry and health, to this swift change in manpower migration, especially with regard to doctors and engineers.[18] But obviously these were muffled or overruled. The deluge of laws and decrees with regard to travel, secondment, conscription, currency, exchange rates, self-import, etc., has continued. It is matched only by the number of official bureaucratic bodies created to facilitate the process of "sending people out" and "receiving money in." Ali Dessouki, after listing at least eleven such entities in 1978, concludes that "the multiplicity of committees is a fair indicator of the amount of official attention that has recently been given to the issue of migration."[19]

In brief, the interplay among demographic, economic, and sociopolitical factors set the stage for the massive labor transfer of the 1970s. It is expected to continue through the 1980s.

Individual Factors

With structural forces in full swing in Egypt and the Arab oil states, Egyptians as individuals and as reference groups began to entertain the idea and then crave for migration. Here we must remember how the mounting socioeconomic bottlenecks were closing in on the average Egyptian. With serious developmental efforts arrested since the late 1960s, the hardening of social arteries for upward mobility,[20] high inflation, serious shortages (especially in housing), and low wage levels, the prospect of migrating became very attractive. The idea for the majority was initially to migrate temporarily for two or three years, accumulate sufficient savings to secure an apartment and/or get married, and acquire some durable household appliances.

After quite a while, however, these objectives became quite elastic for an increasing number of migrants and "would-be" migrants, especially among the middle and upper-middle classes. We have the findings of two small-scale surveys by Amr Mohie El-Din[21] and Suzanne Messeiha[22] on Egyptian university professors and schoolteachers on secondment in Arab countries. Both studies confirm this elasticity of "needs," which invariably expands from basic to nonbasic, to luxury items, and ultimately to simply saving and investing.

The other striking fact is that the salary differentials are simply mind-boggling for any individual who can calculate. Mohie El-Din found in his sample that the maximum salary for a professor was LE150 a month in Egypt, and the earnings from salary throughout thirty years of academic life would be LE48,600. At the market exchange rate, the same professor on secondment to Kuwait would earn LE1,750 (700 dinars or $2,450) per month plus free housing; earnings in four years of secondment (the standard length allowed by Egyptian authorities) would be LE84,000. Simply stated, an Egyptian professor would earn in only four years twice as much as would be earned in thirty years of an entire professional career in Egypt.[23] The same comparison applies to associate and assistant (lecture) professors, as well as to schoolteachers.

In Mohie El-Din's sample, it turned out that most university professors on secondment to capital-rich countries did in fact have most of their durable goods from their earnings in Egypt before secondment, as shown in Table 4.1.

In brief, individual factors seem to be a reflection of the structural forces discussed earlier. Individual Egyptians are simply responding to a prevailing mood for having "more" and to a new orientation symbolized by the regime itself for seeking solutions to problems outside the societal boundaries.

TABLE 4.1
Type of Consumer Durables Possessed by a Sample of
Egyptian Professors Before Secondment to Arab Countries

Type of Durable	Number	Percentage
Television set	45	95.7
Recorder	45	95.7
Refrigerator	46	97.9
Washing machine	44	93.6
Gas stove & oven	47	100.0
Heaters (water heaters)	44	93.6
Telephone	33	70.2
Motorcar	32	68.1
not indicated	3	6.0

Source: Amr Mohie El-Din, The Emigration of University
Academic Staff, draft mimeo. report prepared for the Project
on Egyptian Migration of Cairo Univ. & MIT's Technology
Adaptation Program, Cairo: Jan.1980, p.50.

Consequences of Egyptian Labor Migration

As in most large-scale societal processes, the consequences of Egyptian migration are quite complex. The "positive" and "negative" are so entangled that it is hard to assess their relative weights or tradeoffs for the society at large in both the short and the long run. The consequences for individuals seem, on the surface at least, to be mostly positive. Many of them do indeed solve their immediate economic and financial problems. A "utilitarian" approach may argue that what is good for most individuals must be good for their society. But it is now axiomatic in social science that society is a "product," not a simple "sum," of its individuals or their actions. Thus, what may be beneficial for individual Egyptians may not be beneficial for Egypt. Earlier public optimism regarding the outcome of exporting Egyptian labor has given way to a more sober appraisal in the last few years. While there is no indication at present of any official policy reversal in allowing Egyptians to migrate, there is increased awareness of several deleterious effects of such migration on Egypt's economy and society.

The advantages and disadvantages of labor exportation must be viewed in dialectical and relative terms. What may seem as an advantage at one point in time may evolve into a disadvantage at a later point, and vice versa. Thus, remittances from Egyptians working abroad may help at one stage to ease the chronic deficit in Egypt's balance of payments. At another point, however, the volume of such remittances and the patterns in which they are spent could result in inflationary pressures that offset the earlier advantage. By the same token, labor migration may be thought to reduce the overall rate of unemployment in the country, but if such migration is "selective," as we shall see to be the case, then sectoral labor shortfalls can create problems far more serious than any advantage gained by reducing the overall rate of unemployment.

Remittances of Egyptians Abroad and Multiplier Effects

The most concrete outcome of Egyptian labor abroad is its remittances in hard currencies. Table 4.2 indicates the value of these remittances for a selected number of labor-exporting countries, including Egypt, between 1974 and 1978 in the aftermath of the oil price rise. The Egyptians increased their remittances from $268 million in 1974 to $1,761 million in 1978, nearly a 600 percent increase in four years. The phenomenal growth is even more staggering if we take, say, 1970 as a base year. Remittances then did not exceed $10 million. By 1979, according to official Egyptian sources, the level had reached or exceeded the $2 billion mark.[24] Thus, in one decade, Egyptians abroad raised their monetary transfers from $10 million to $2,000 million—two-hundredfold. This amount equals or exceeds the combined returns of Egypt's cotton export, the Suez Canal revenues, tourism, and the value added from the Aswan High Dam.[25] Proponents of the open door policy may well argue that Nasser's Egypt waged battles and spilled blood for the Suez Canal and the Aswan Dam, yet the silent outcome of one measure of the open door policy brings to Egypt much more hard currency.

Theoretically these growing remittances should help Egypt's balance of payments and stimulate the process of capital formation. The remittances represented 11 percent of all of Egypt's exports in 1974, but by 1977 the percentage had risen to 66 percent—a sixfold relative increase. As a percentage of Egypt's imports, it rose from 5 to 27 percent in the same four years.[26] By any measure, this is quite impressive. Of course, as Table 4.2 shows, other countries benefited as much (with the exception of Algeria, whose labor market is essentially Western Europe and not the capital-rich countries). Yemen especially seems to have reaped greater relative increases in remittances from its labor abroad, from $136 million to $900 million between 1974 and 1977. The value of these remittances represented over 1,300 percent of its export in 1974 and over 5,000 percent of its export in 1977.[27] All in all, by the end of the 1970s remittances from Arab workers in capital-rich Arab countries totaled about $5 billion annually—they more than tripled in six years.

TABLE 4.2
Net Transfers by Country of Receipt 1974 to 1978
($US Current Prices)

Country	1974	1975	1976	1977	1978
Algeria	352.4	397.0	428.3	309.4	330.6
Egypt	268.2	365.5	755.1	896.7	1761.2
Jordan	75.4	166.6	411.0	455.3	520.2
Morocco	319.9	489.3	498.8	535.9	699.9
Syria	44.5	52.2	53.1	140.2	93.9
Tunisia	107.0	126.3	121.2	144.8	191.6
Yemen Arab Republic	135.5	279.0	676.5	914.3	899.6
Democratic Yemen	41.1	55.9	115.2	172.6	254.8
TOTAL	1344.0	1931.8	3059.2	3569.2	4751.8

Source: IMF Master Files, Data compiled by G. Swamy and
cited in the World Bank's Report of Research Project on
International Labor Migration and Manpower in the Middle
East and North Africa, mimeographed, (Washington D.C.,
Sept. 1980, p.196).

The Egyptian balance of payments did show marked improvement by
the end of the 1970s. The trade deficit, which was LE1,785 million in
1978, decreased to LE1,466 in 1979, an improvement of 34.7 percent.[28]
By the end of 1980, Egypt's balance of payments recorded a surplus of
$120 million for the first time in two decades.[29] Although such improve-
ment is due to several factors (including Egypt's increased earnings from
oil, the Suez Canal revenues, and tourism), officials singled out remittances of Egyptians working abroad as a crucial factor.[30]

Bank deposits (one indicator of savings) were estimated at $3.4 billion
in 1978 and rose to $4.7 billion in 1979, a growth rate of 33 percent in one
year. This is a far cry from the early 1970s when Egypt's savings rates fell
to their lowest in several decades.[31]

Some economists still argue, however, that the levels of remittances
and savings would have been much higher had there been effective channels for attracting and using the immense financial resources of Egyptians
working abroad.[32]

Recent figures of investments under both Law No. 43 of 1974 and Law No. 32 of 1977 (the open door policy) indicate that most investment has been made by Egyptians. At the end of 1977, of all such investments in the previous five years, foreigners contributed 17 percent, Arabs 25 percent, with the share of Egyptians amounting to 57 percent.[33] It is hard to pin down the sources of these Egyptian investments, but it is assumed that a substantial part of them come from Egyptian workers abroad. It is known, for example, that at least a number of sizable ventures (banks, real estate development, and industrial firms) were initiated by Egyptians in the Gulf.[34]

The foregoing discussion relates to transfers by Egyptians working abroad through official channels. But any observer familiar with the Egyptian scene realizes that additional substantial amounts are transferred through a currency black market. The black market earns the remittant about 17 percent more than the government "Encouragement Exchange Rate" of LE0.68 to the US dollar (the black market rate in 1979 and 1980 averaged LE0.80 to the dollar). Egyptian authorities are quite aware of this thriving market, and there has been no attempt to curb it. As a matter of fact, in most banks in Cairo there is an informal currency exchanger by the door. Not only do bank clients deal with him, but so do some foreign banks' employees who receive all or part of their salaries in US dollars. No one knows exactly how much of the remittances are traded through the currency black market. Estimates vary from 20 to 100 percent equivalent of the amounts transferred through official channels.[35]

Equally important are remittances in kind. The reference here is to durable goods (e.g., cars, refrigerators, television sets) that Egyptians working abroad bring with them when returning to their country. Again, we do not have reliable figures on the real monetary value of such remittances in kind, but they were estimated to be several hundred million dollars in 1979.[36]

Sectoral Labor Shortages and Their Multiplier Effects

The initial euphoria surrounding mass labor migration from Egypt gave way recently to a more sober assessment of its implication for the development of Egypt itself. As it turned out, it was not surplus labor or surplus population that was tapped by migration to capital-rich countries. Rather, it was the high-level manpower, the trained, and the most skilled medium-level manpower of Egypt's labor force. To be sure, some of the unskilled managed to filter through the borders of the oil-rich countries. But by and large the bulk of Egypt's migrants have been Egypt's best labor. In essence, therefore, most of Egypt's unemployed at home were unemployable abroad. They have remained in Egypt. Migration has not reduced the rate of unemployment, which, as shown in Table 4.3, stood at 11.5 percent in 1976. It has been hovering around 11 percent since the late 1960s, i.e., since the halting of Egypt's development plans. In other words, migration did not do what it was supposed to do for Egypt: reduce unemployment and population pressure. In effect, it has deprived Egypt of its most valuable brains and hands.

The effect of this loss is now acknowledged by most observers, but it is hard to assess its real economic and social cost. One argument may contend that the best brains are not properly used in Egypt under the present regime anyway. The Cairo University-MIT research team, which has so far investigated two important migrant groups, argue differently. Egypt's construction workers are one of the most sought-after groups all over the region. This is understandable in view of all the infrastructure prerequisites for any subsequent development. Choucri, Eckaus, and Mohie El-Din noted that employment in Egypt's construction sector is symptomatic of Egypt's economy in the past two decades.[37] It grew rapidly

TABLE 4.3
Estimate of Employment in Egypt by Sector 1976

Sector	Number	Percentage
Agriculture *	6,490,000	50.7
Government **	1,740,000	13.6
Public Sector **	1,210,000	9.4
Private Sector **	950,000	7.4
Armed Forces ***	342,000	2.7
Workers Abroad ****	600,000	4.7
Unemployed *	1,479,000	11.5
TOTAL	12,811,500	100.0

* estimate by Birks & Sinclair of employment in agriculture;
** Min. of Planning Five Year Plan 1978-82 Vol.I Table 4,p.31;
*** International Inst. for Strategic Studies The Military Balance 1977-78 Table 3, p.85; **** Min. of Planning, op.cit. II, p.184.

Source: J.S.Birks and C.A.Sinclair, "Egypt, Frustrated Labor Exporter," in Middle East Journal Vol.31 (Summer 1979), pp.288-303 & p.290.

between 1960 and 1966 (31 percent at an average annual 4.5 percent increase), then it slowed down between 1966 and 1974 (with a modest increase of 14 percent in eight years). That period was characterized by declining levels of investment. Then came the 1973 boom and mounting demand on Egypt's construction labor. The instant response created a domestic shortage leading to an increase of money and real wages for construction workers, as shown in Tables 4.4 and 4.5. Table 4.5, es-

TABLE 4.4
Average Wages Per Worker 1959/60–1978 in Egypt
(in Egyptian Pounds)

Year	Construction	Agriculture	Services	Mining & Industry
1960	161.6	30.2	164.5	147.6
1961	164.4	27.5	162.5	147.7
1962	159.3	32.5	161.7	153.3
1963	150.1	34.8	185.5	172.2
1964	156.2	37.9	190.2	174.8
1965	155.6	44.6	208.4	181.3
1966	170.4	50.8	209.3	183.4
1967	180.4	53.3	213.5	183.3
1968	182.8	51.7	208.7	181.9
1969	182.8	53.1	223.4	184.3
1970	184.6	53.9	238.6	187.6
1971	184.2	55.0	241.0	190.0
1972	190.4	55.4	251.0	255.2
1973	233.3	60.5	266.0	287.1
1974	233.2	70.8	295.0	297.0
1975	376.2	106.5	314.8	292.4
1976	378.7	107.0	327.1	305.9
1977*	328.3	107.6	340.0	320.0
1978*	354.7	108.0	353.4	334.7
Increase: 119%		258%	115%	127%
Average Annual Increase: 4.4%		7.1%	4.2%	4.5%
Increase from 1974–78: 52.1%		52.5%	19.8%	12.7%

Source: <u>Ministry of Planning Follow-up Report, 1977.</u>

* Projections

TABLE 4.5
Average Daily Wage for Different Occupations of Construction Labor in Egypt
(LE per day)

Occupation	Average Daily Wage Rate					% Change
	1970	1973	1975	1977 (1)	1977 (2)	1970–1977
Stonecutter	0.6	0.9	1.5	2	1.76	193
Builder (bricklayer)	1.5	2.5	3.5	4.5	5.7	280
Assistant builder	0.6	1.5	2.0	3.0	3.5	483
Whitewasher	0.75	0.9	2.0	3.0	3.5	366
Assistant whitewasher	0.5	0.6	1.0	2.0	1.76	250
Painter (for building)	0.8	1.0	2.0	2.5	3.23	300
Assistant painter	0.5	0.7	1.25	1.5	1.58	216
Carpenter for concrete forms	0.9	1.25	2.0	3.0	3.49	287
Assistant concrete carpenter	0.6	0.8	1.5	2.0	2.5	316
Metalworker for reinforced concrete	0.6	0.9	2.0	3.0	3.55	491
Assistant metalworker for reinforced concrete	0.5	0.7	1.5	2.5	2.06	312
Reinforced concrete worker	0.45	0.6	1.5	2.5	1.35	200
Blacksmith	0.7	1.0	2.0	3.5	3.0	328
Machine Joiner	0.8	1.0	2.5	4.0	---	400
Door & window Carpenter (Joiner)	0.8	1.25	2.0	3.5	3.49	338

Assistant door & window Joiner	0.5	0.8	1.25	2.0	2.5	400
Concrete specialist	0.6	0.9	2.0	3.0	1.45	142
Assistant concrete specialist	0.5	0.8	1.75	2.75	0.85	70
Tile Fitter	0.9	1.5	3.0	5.70	5.7	533
Assistant tile fitter	0.60	1.25	2.0	3.60	3.5	483
Tile Maker	0.75	1.25	2.5	4.0	---	433
Stone Breaker	0.8	1.25	2.5	3.5	1.58	98
Glazed Tile Worker	1.5	3.0	5.0	7.0	5.7	280
Marble Worker	1.0	1.7	2.5	4.0	3.5	250
Woodcutter	1.75	1.25	3.0	3.5	1.58	-10
Sanitary ware Plumber	0.8	1.5	4.0	5.0	3.5	338
Asst. sanitary ware plumber	0.5	0.9	2.0	2.5	1.5	200
Installations Electrician	0.75	1.0	2.0	3.0	3.23	331
Asst. installations elec.	0.5	0.75	1.5	2.0	1.45	190
Architectural Worker	0.5	0.6	1.25	2.0	1.06	165
Construction Foreman	0.5	0.8	1.25	2.0	3.23	546
Glassfitter	1.0	1.8	3.5	5.0	---	400
Concrete Plate Porter	0.6	0.9	1.25	2.5	1.35	316
Marble Cutter	1.0	2.25	3.5	4.5	3.55	350
Cement Paster	0.8	1.0	1.25	1.8	1.76	125

Source: These values were obtained from the files of "Anwar El-Hamaki, Engineers and Contractors," Private Contractors; the data for No.2 for 1977 were obtained from the file of the "Arabic Company Contractors" Ltd., compiled by N.Choucri et.al. and cited in Migration and Employment in the Construction Sector: Critical Factors in Egyptian Development, Cairo: Cairo Univ.–MIT Technology Adaptation Program 1978, pp.49-52.

pecially, shows that some construction labor categories (e.g., assistant builders) registered over 480 percent wage increases between 1970 and 1977. Most other categories have at least doubled their wages. Much of that rise, it should be noticed, occurred from 1973 on.

Table 4.4 gives average wages from 1969 to 1978 for construction workers as well as those in three other sectors. All of them registered impressive increases. But it should be noted that wages in agriculture have increased the most over the eighteen-year period (280 percent). Part of this exceptional rate of increase is due to the very low wage base in 1960. But most of it, especially since 1974, is due to sectoral replacement in construction. In other words, with domestic shortage due to migration, some agricultural labor was drawn and enticed into construction by higher wages. That, in turn, created some shortages in agricultural labor, a condition that usually raises wages.

It should be pointed out that these wage increases have not been matched by increase in labor productivity, and possibly the latter declined because of undertrained replacements. In other words, the wage rise is due mainly to shortage created by migration. This means a higher corresponding construction labor cost for the consumer. This is one way of creating inflationary pressures within the economy. The rising wages are, no doubt, beneficial to the workers involved (about 300,000 in construction in 1977) and to other groups whose incomes rose at the same or higher rates. But this has not been the case for 3.2 million government and public sector employees who are on fixed incomes, nor for their dependents (another 6 million). The income per capita in Egypt as a whole, estimated at between $200 and $240 in the mid-1970s, did not rise at the same rate (52 percent in four years). The closest indication of the rate of increase for government employees is seen in the *services* column in Table 4.4, because most civil servants are included there. The service sector wages rose by only 19.8 percent in the same four-year period, less than half the rate of those in construction and agriculture.

Of course, the sectional shortages and their inflationary consequences could have been avoided, or at least minimized, had there been a rational labor training and labor exporting policy. As it exists now, Egypt's labor market does not have the flexibility that makes quick adjustments and intersectoral replacements possible. Birks and Sinclair describe Egypt's labor market as highly segmented with relatively little occupational mobility between segments.[38] This situation is represented in Fig. 4.1. On the basis of available data they conclude that

> the Egyptian labor market is characterized by extraordinary immobility between even relatively similar occupations. There are in the first place obvious barriers to occupational mobility—for instance between classes 1, 2,

Figure 4.1

Egypt: diagrammatic representation of the labour market showing the propensity
to migrate internationally and the degree of internal mobility, 1975

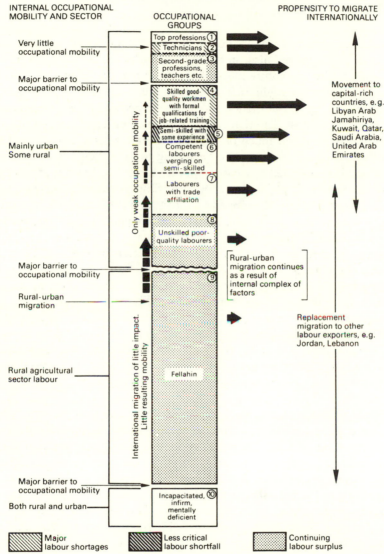

Note: This diagram must not be taken to represent absolute numbers or accurate proportions; it is merely schematic.

Source: Adapted from J.S.Birks & C.A.Sinclair, *International
Migration and Development in the Arab Region* (Geneva: ILO,
1980), p.95.

and 3 (the professional and technically qualified workers) and class 4 which lies beneath them (the skilled and qualified craftsmen). . . . Apart from this market boundary to occupational mobility, there would seem to be rather little vertical transfer of occupations between other more similar classes of labor.[39]

This occupational rigidity not only has made it difficult to offset shortages inside Egypt but also, in the view of Birks and Sinclair, has limited Egypt's ability to capture more of the Arab market. Obviously the two authors seem to argue that Egyptian labor migration is something valuable for Egypt but there is too little of it because of this occupational immobility.[40] Most Egyptian critics, on the other hand, contend at present that there is too much of Egypt's best labor force abroad and that strategic sectoral shortages are beginning to take their toll.[41] Construction workers are cited as a case in point. Table 4.5 shows that some categories within that sector that are simply skilled workers (e.g., bricklayers) had by 1977 topped architects and civil engineers in terms of daily wages. This is an exceptional phenomenon because engineers especially were the highest paid category even among high-level manpower during the heyday of Nasser's industrialization in the late 1950s and 1960s. As a matter of fact, so valuable and scarce were engineers then that a law by presidential decree was issued to "draft" them upon graduation from college to serve in various public and state functions. This was, incidentally, the year that Egypt's Ministry of Labor was established,[42] and the first industrialization plan was enacted soon after. The point here is that by the late 1970s engineers, still undoubtedly needed, were being outearned by certain skilled manual workers who suddenly were in short supply because of migration to neighboring countries.

If the shortage of construction workers has caused inflationary havoc in the building industry, hurting especially those on fixed incomes (the majority of Egyptians), shortages in other sectors have caused an alarming decline in quality of service. One such case is university professors. The pioneering work of Amr Mohie El-Din on the subject is quite enlightening.[43] He first shows that the total registered academic staff in Egypt's three largest universities (Cairo, Ein Shams, and Alexandria) grew from 3,177 in 1970 to 4,081 in 1975, an increase of 904 or 28.4 percent in five years. However, by 1976 the number "brain drained" to the West was 1,058, more than the net increase in the previous five years and more than 25 percent of the total staff of the three institutions that year. As for those seconded to Arab countries (temporary migrants), their number grew steadily from 388 in 1970/71 to 605 in 1974/75, a 63 percent increase in five years. Thus, while the growth rate of the total academic staff was 6.3 percent per annum between 1970 and 1975, the emigration rate to Arab countries increased at over 12 percent, and the brain drain rate to the West was 5 percent per annum during the same period. (Tables 4.6, 4.7, and 4.8.)

Table 4.9 shows the average rate of secondment of academics by field of specialization between 1970 and 1975. In some fields as many as 30 percent of the total faculty were out of their institutions and teaching somewhere else in the region.

The impact of this phenomenon on the quality of Egypt's higher education is hardly positive. The ratio of students to faculty in most American universities is 20 to 1; in Egypt, in 1970, it was five times as high in social sciences and the humanities—100 students to every faculty member—if all the teaching faculty were present. With nearly 25 percent of them on secondment to Arab countries, the ratio in 1970/71 was 123 to 1. The following year (Table 4.10) the ratio jumped from 111 to 1 before emigration of the staff, to 144 to 1 after emigration. Table 4.11 shows in de-

TABLE 4.6
Distribution of Academic Staff in Egypt's Three Major
Universities According to Branch of Specialization

Branch of Specialization	1970–1971		1974–1975	
	No.	%	No.	%
Literature & Human Studies	288	9.07	370	9.07
Legal Studies	126	3.97	132	3.24
Commercial Studies	83	2.61	95	2.33
Basic Sciences	401	12.62	533	13.67
Medical Sciences	970	20.53	1,253	30.70
Pharmaceutical Sciences	111	3.49	156	3.82
Veterinary Sciences	79	2.49	104	2.55
Engineering Sciences	470	14.79	577	16.15
Agricultural Sciences	407	12.81	522	12.79
Educational Sciences	197	6.20	269	6.59
Economics and Statistics	45	1.42	69	1.69
TOTAL	3,177	100.00	4,081	100.00

Source: Amr Mohie El-Din, *The Emigration of University Academic Staff*, Cairo, Cairo Univ.–MIT Technology Adaptation Program, 1980.

TABLE 4.7
Individuals on Scholarships and Study Leaves Abroad Who
Refused to Come Back as of March 1976

Place of Study	No. of Scholarships	No. of Study Leaves	Total
U.S.A	224	234	558
Canada	6	51	57
England	64	98	162
W.Germany	45	46	91
Switzerland	29	9	33
France	20	34	54
Austria	3	2	5
Spain	1	3	4
Sweden	1	4	5
Italy	1	6	7
U.S.S.A.	4	1	5
Hungary	2	12	14
G.D.R.	4	10	14
Finland	1	–	1
Norway	–	4	4
Holland	5	7	12
Denmark	–	1	1
Greece	–	2	2
Belgium	–	5	5
Yugoslavia	–	2	2
Poland	–	8	8
Bulgaria	–	2	2
India	–	3	3
Japan	–	3	3
Lebanon	–	1	1
TOTAL	510	548	1,058

Source: Cairo University, Study on the Organization of Secondment of University Staff Outside Egypt. Prepared by a Committee
formed by a decision from the Higher Council of Universities in
1970. Cairo, 1976, and cited in the same source as in Table 4.6.

tail the same trend for Cairo University. If the ratio in physical sciences
has not worsened as quickly as it has in the humanities and social
science, it is only a matter of time. Most rich Arab countries, in their
rush to open new universities, found it easier to start with social sciences
and humanities (including law and business), which do not require set-
ting up laboratories and complicated equipment. By the end of the 1970s,
however, they were beginning to open engineering and medical schools.

TABLE 4.8
Members of the Academic Staff of Egypt's Three Universities
Who Were on Temporary Emigration (Secondment) and Did Not
Come Back 1970-1975

Year	1. Temporary Emigration	2. Those Who Did Not Return	2/1. % Who Did Not Return
1970-1971	338	11	2.81
1971-1972	454	18	3.96
1972-1973	515	17	3.30
1973-1974	548	16	2.92
1974-1975	605	11	1.82

Source: 1. Annual Reports of the Directors of the Three Universities of Cairo, Alexandria, and Ein Shams for the years
1971-1973-1975. 2. The Calendar Year Book of the Three Universities 1971-1973-1975. 3. A Study on the Organization of
University Staff Members Secondments. A Report by a Committee
Formed by a Decision of the Higher Council of Universities in
1976. Cairo University, 1976. Cited in the same source as in
Table 4.6.

TABLE 4.9
Average Number of Staff and of Emigration from Cairo University
(1967/68 - 1974/75)

Field of Specialization	Academic Staff		Emigration		Emigration/ Academic Staff %
	Avg.	%	Avg.	%	
Literature & Human Studies	164	11.48	33	17.60	20.12
Legal Studies	51	3.57	13	6.99	25.49
Commercial Studies	28	1.96	8	4.30	28.57
Economics & Statistics	48	3.36	14	7.53	29.37
Basic Sciences	168	11.75	25	13.44	16.88
Medical Sciences	457	31.97	24	12.91	5.25
Veterinary Science	60	4.20	3	1.61	5.00
Engineering Science	85	5.95	11	5.91	12.94
Agricultural Science	189	13.23	31	16.67	6.88
TOTAL	1,429	100.00	186	100.00	13.02

Source: As for Table 4.6.

TABLE 4.10
The Ratio of Students to Each Staff Member Before & After Migration
for Egypt's Three Major Universities

| Year | Human Sciences | | | Physical Sciences | | |
	Before Emigration	After Emigration	% Change	Before Emigration	After Emigration	% Change
1970/71	100 to 1	123 to 1	23	25 to 1	28 to 1	12
1971/72	111 to 1	144 to 1	32	25 to 1	28 to 1	12

Source: As for Table 4.6.

TABLE 4.11
The Ratio of Students to Each Staff Member Before and After Migration
for Cairo University

| Year | Human Sciences | | | Physical Sciences | | |
	Before Emigration	After Emigration	% Change	Before Emigration	After Emigration	% Change
1967/68	76 to 1	89 to 1	17	24 to 1	28 to 1	17
1968/69	76 to 1	103 to 1	36	24 to 1	28 to 1	17
1969/70	77 to 1	111 to 1	44	23 to 1	28 to 1	22
1970/71	79 to 1	100 to 1	27	23 to 1	28 to 1	22
1971/72	90 to 1	118 to 1	31	23 to 1	26 to 1	13
1972/73	107 to 1	146 to 1	36	22 to 1	25 to 1	14
1973/74	122 to 1	172 to 1	41	22 to 1	26 to 1	18
1974/75	123 to 1	180 to 1	46	22 to 1	26 to 1	18

Source: As for Table 4.6.

No doubt there will be a similar run on Egyptian professors in these fields as well.

The point made here is that even in sectors in which Egypt had shortages to begin with, an "oil rush" has taken place. This has caused the quality of service, low to begin with, to deteriorate further. The case of university professors is illustrative of the immense social cost to Egypt, despite whatever material gain there is for the migrants themselves. And here, as in the case of doctors and engineers, even Birks and Sinclair's misgivings on the rigidity of Egypt's labor force hardly apply. No easy or quick replacement from one sector to any of the above can be effected in Egypt (or in any society for that matter). It takes nearly twenty years to train a professor. As much lead time would be required to effect any substantial replacement. This is unlike a construction worker who may take no more than one or two years to train. A. Kandil pointed out that more than 95 percent of Egyptians working abroad have four to eight years of work experience.[44] Thus they are already well trained and are not seeking employment for the first time.

Downgrading of Egypt's Labor Force

Since most Egyptian labor moving to capital-rich countries is seeking not simply employment but mainly higher wages, a number of essentially negative effects have been observed. For one thing, it is noted that most of the labor has been transferred from sectors with highly productive activities in Egypt. This is unlike Turkish, North African, and Southern European workers who migrated in the fifties and sixties to Western and Northern Europe.[45] In the latter, workers were essentially moving from low-productive activities to high-productive ones in the host countries. Therefore, the migratory process entailed for them labor upgrading—they acquired new skills and experience.[46]

In the case of Egypt, the situation may be almost the opposite. The wages in the capital-rich countries being so high, they bear little direct correlation to productivity or performance when compared to the standards back home. This has led, among other things, to many Egyptians accepting jobs far below their skill levels so long as the pay is so much higher than anything they can get in Egypt. This is quite detrimental to the skilled workers, to Egypt, and to the entire Arab World in the long run. Some of these workers simply lose their skills over time. At best, they stop learning and improving.[47] Even in cases where the job description formally matches the qualification level of the migrant, it turns out that so little is often required in the way of performance that productivity indeed deteriorates. This applies, for example, in the case of university professors. While the capital-rich countries may recruit the best academics from Egypt, Palestine, or Lebanon, very little is required of them besides teaching six to nine hours a week—much less than they do back home, but for ten times as much pay. Some Egyptian professors, while quite prolific in Egypt, published very little during their four years of secondment in Kuwait or Saudi Arabia.[48] Seniority rather than performance is the criterion for the salary scale.

As M. A. Fadil puts it, the tenure of Egyptian laborers abroad "seems to involve an element of 'rent' which has nothing to do whatsoever with productive efficiency compared to their respective fields back home. Thus one of the most negative effects of the oil era is a widening gap between productivity of labor and cost of labor in the Arab World at large."[49]

The Spread of Conspicuous Consumption

The rapid increase of money wealth for Egyptians working abroad has naturally led to new consumption patterns. This has been made all the easier in the host countries by the endless demonstration of the latest products from the industrial machine of the First World. For those Egyptians who have never owned standard durable goods (refrigerators, washing machines, cooking stoves, televisions, etc.) these are the first items to be acquired, either from the capital-rich countries for shipment to Egypt, or from the numerous duty-free shops in Egypt itself (which sell only in hard currency). Egyptians who acquired these standard durables while still in Egypt went for cars, color television sets, air conditioners, etc. For those who had all of these before departing, the consumption pattern usually reaches a higher order: either a second one of everything, or more sophisticated items such as videotapes, stereo systems, expensive rugs, expensive imported clothes, etc. The observations are confirmed by the results of two surveys of schoolteachers and university professors.

Messeiha found in her sample of schoolteachers on secondment to Saudi Arabia[50] that: (1) on the average they spend 46 percent of their earnings in Saudi Arabia, save 28 percent, remit 15 percent, and spend 11 percent on goods brought back to Egypt annually; and (2) on final return to Egypt their savings on the average are allocated as follows: 28 percent for home appliances, 13 percent for clothes, 12 percent for gifts to relatives and friends, 11 percent for other goods, and 30 percent in bank accounts and 16 percent in direct investment. No one in the sample reported paying Egyptian taxes (an explicit question asked by the researcher).

In other words, of all the accumulated savings of four years, the average schoolteacher ends up spending 64 percent on consumer items, with about 36 percent allocated to savings and investments. Messeiha calculated the average amount spent on all consumer goods by the average member of her sample and came up with the figure of LE6,877. The mean monthly salary of a teacher with a university degree and five years of experience in Egypt is about LE40, or LE480 a year. Thus, what the average teacher spends on consumer goods at the end of four years of secondment is equivalent to about fifteen years of total salary earnings in Egypt. The appliances part of that expenditure (LE3,667) is equivalent to about eight years of salary, and the expense for nondurable items (LE3,210) is equivalent to the total salary in seven years.

Mohie El-Din found the saving and consumption pattern among his sample of university professors (a much higher income group than schoolteachers) to be as follows: (1) an average (mean) of 44 percent of the salary earned abroad is saved; (2) the rest, 56 percent, is spent in the host country and on consumer goods (about evenly divided); (3) the consumer goods acquired are mainly imported cloth and finished garments, a second motorcar, color television, home utensils, carpets, washing machines, refrigerators, and other electronic equipment. As for the allocation of savings, more than half (55 percent of the sample) would buy a new home or a condominium, and an equal number would put their funds in time deposits (savings); one third (33 percent) would invest in a moneymaking enterprise.[51]

It is clear that Egyptians working abroad do achieve a much higher standard of living. The consumption patterns they enjoy create a demonstration effect. Those at home who may not have quite the same level of income or savings from working abroad begin to crave similar consumption tendencies, most of which are quite conspicuous and go beyond basics or even average luxuries. Those who cannot afford to consume at the same level but who belong to the same reference group (e.g., other university professors) would soon develop an irresistible urge to be seconded to an oil-rich country.

For the returnee there are adjustment problems vis-à-vis premigration work, earnings, and expenditure pattern. People can adjust quickly to a higher standard of living, but not vice versa. It is often difficult for returnees to live on a "modest" Egyptian salary after having been used to lavish spending for four years. So they begin to dip into their savings until that money is nearly exhausted. At such a point, if not before, they will be caught up in the struggle for a new secondment. Work and productivity become quite marginal or secondary to a returnee's existence in either case, a point we take up next.

The high individual expenditure pattern among citizens of the oil-rich countries spreads down to migrant laborers in these countries, and through the usual "demonstration effect" it spreads, in turn, to the capital-poor countries. The only difference, of course, is that the latter cannot afford it. Material expectations have by far outdistanced any possible earning level of most of the Egyptian population. Finding employment in a capital-rich country has therefore become the dream of many Egyptians, spanning the entire class and age structures of the society. The quick money and the dazzling consumer goods it can buy have become part of the "Egyptian national imagination" in recent years.

The role of the state in all this is far from neutral. For one thing, the leadership at the highest level feeds these high material expectations. The model projected by President Sadat to the Egyptian people is not limited to his own behavior and consumption patterns; it is encouraged by his verbal assertion that the goal of every Egyptian should be to have a car and a "villa."[52] Very few would object to such a dream in principle, but the ability to fulfill this material aspiration does not exist inside Egypt for the vast majority of Egyptians. The only way to make the dream come true is to work in an oil country. In essence, then, the state, in the person of the president, is selling a dream that can only be fulfilled if most people leave their country on a temporary labor migration. The state has also pampered those who work abroad. It has done away with the law that required them to transfer a minimum of 10 percent of their earnings to Egypt at the official exchange rate. More than that, it exempted them from paying any taxes on their earnings abroad.[53] In other words, there is no attempt on the part of the state to check the conspicuous consumption by resorting to some of the conventional fiscal policies at its command.

Furthermore, the state reinforces conspicuous consumption by its own deliberate policies. By allowing "own-import"[54] and general import of all kinds of luxury items, the markets of Cairo and Port Said are now full of a dazzling array of goods that only a few Egyptians can afford on their earnings inside Egypt. Not counting what Egyptians abroad bring with them, Egypt's imports of consumer goods have steadily grown from LE36 million in 1970 to LE133 million in 1975, to LE1,224 in 1979, and are projected to reach LE1,331 million in 1980. In short, Egypt's imports of consumer goods in one decade have increased by 3,600 percent (compared with only a 2,000 percent increase in capital goods).[55] Neither population growth nor the rate of inflation in one decade would justify this steep rise in the importation of consumer goods. The main factor that explains it is the real increase in levels of consumption, especially of luxury goods.

Thus we are witnessing an emerging breed of Egyptians who are earning a lot, consuming conspicuously, and are quite hostile to any notion of paying taxes or transferring money at the official exchange rate. Their behavior is reinforced by the state, and the demonstration effect is taking hold among an increasing number of Egyptians. This, in turn, stimulates an all-willing state to import more consumer goods to satisfy the consumers' insatiable appetite. The trade deficit, as a result, has grown from less than LE200 million in 1970 to over LE2,000 million in 1977. Consumer goods accounted for 19 percent of Egypt's total imports in 1970; in 1975 it was over 45 percent. The state has financed the annual deficits by increasingly relying on foreign aid or borrowing.[56] In brief, the state's behavior and that of the new Egyptian breed are alike in many ways.

Decline of Work Ethics

One of the most devastating effects of the oil wealth and its chain reaction has been the near collapse of work ethics in the Arab World. Easily earned money and easily spent money undermine the value of productive work. This, of course, may apply anywhere, and the Arabs are no exception.

We have already alluded to the fact that the huge wage differentials between poor and rich Arab states have led to a gradual downgrading of work skills of Egyptian migrants. This operates, as we saw, when a worker accepts a job far below his skill level so long as there is significantly higher pay than anything he could earn back home. Aside from this, there is a subtle and yet damaging change of attitudes toward work, regardless of the skill level required. The belief that "hard work" and "achievement" are the essential means of professional and financial success is no longer supported by empirical facts in Egypt or the rest of the Arab World. The accumulated perceptions of "others," especially of those who have made it financially, are beginning to strike root in the psyche of an increasing number of Egyptians. The code words now for success are *"huzz"* (luck), *"Essouᶜidiyya"* (Saudi Arabia), *"Ekkwait"* (Kuwait), *"intidab"* (secondment), *"fursah"* (opportunity), and *"ᶜakd"* (a contract). Rarely does an average Egyptian ask how much work is involved, what skill is required, or what the working conditions are—not that he or she does not entirely care; but these are now secondary matters, removed to the periphery of consciousness. Rarely does one hear returnees describing their work in any professional detail, or conveying the impression that they enjoyed what they were doing or derived any intrinsic gratification from occupational achievement. The rare occasions when "work" is mentioned at all by a vacationer or a returnee is in the context of competition for renewal of a contract or to obtain work for a friend, or of a conflict with other "national groups" (like Palestinians, Syrians, or Pakistanis) to get to the ear of the native boss or to get rid of one another in the "host country." In brief, just "being there" means success, with a minimum of work. Money means consumption of things, which "significant others" (one's reference groups) cannot obtain on their incomes back home.

Another devastating effect on work attitudes pertains to those who are still in Egypt. Most are waiting for their "turn" *(al-dour)* to be seconded if they are government employees, or waiting for a "contract" from a relative, a friend, an agent, or a *kafil*. And because "getting there" is not contingent on anything exceptional in the way of work performance in Egypt, the work itself suffers in the process. People are either anticipating a secondment, waiting for a contract, preparing to leave, or otherwise lamenting their "luck" and feeling demoralized. In all these mental states, job performance in Egypt itself becomes as marginal as it is for the lucky ones who are "over there."

In other words, healthy attitudes toward work have been undermined both in the capital-rich and the capital-poor countries.[57] In neither case is "hard work" proportionately rewarded or poor work proportionately penalized. What matters now in most cases in the Arab World is really where one is geographically situated, i.e., on which side of the wealth divide.

Thus a new attitudinal syndrome is developing toward "success," "work," and "consumption." All such attitudinal objects are being redefined in the Arab societal context. The usual instrumental links among them are being supplemented or altogether replaced by new ones that bear very little on productivity or creativity. Among these links in the new syndrome are "luck," "opportunity," "secondment," "contract," and "being there." This layer of attitudinal qualities is added to the ones already described as conspicuous consumption.

Devaluation of Authenticity

Related to the new oil syndrome is a steady decline of pride in authentic objects and values. Thus, consuming Egyptian-made products is no longer a source of national pride, nor does it represent a statement of conscience. The majority consume local products because they cannot afford to consume foreign goods. They do not have the money because they have not been "there."

Even if one has "money" for the transaction of certain items, such money has to be of a special kind: non-Egyptian "hard currency." This degrading attitude toward authentic objects, including the country's products and its own national currency, may have begun with those working abroad. But by the late 1970s the attitude had become so widespread that it was adopted by the government. In 1979, Egypt's minister of national economy issued Decree No. 600, which stipulated that customs and tariffs on imported goods must be paid in hard currency. And for several years government agencies and private companies have given priority to applicants and customers for the purchase of housing, real estate, and durable goods (even when made in Egypt) if they pay in hard currency. Even the release of tenders by some state organizations for Egyptian contractors and suppliers has become conditional on paying the required fee in U.S. dollars.[58]

This phenomenon is both a cause and an effect at the same time. It is a symptom created by a glut of money in the hands of a substantial minority that made it in the capital-rich countries. Given the scarcity of goods and services in a still ailing Egyptian economy, having such money acquires an added exaggerated dimension that depresses the value of local currency even more. The symptom however, has become a moving cause in its own right: people now compete for foreign jobs to be able to afford foreign goods and even some of the local scarce goods (e.g., housing and cars).

This phenomenon, initially triggered by Egyptian labor migrants, has been further reinforced by other components of the open door policy. The opening of branches of foreign banks and companies (both by Arabs and Westerners) has fueled the trend of devaluing Egyptian items. Since the mid-seventies, another way of striking it rich has been to associate with foreign institutions in Egypt. Working for national institutions is no longer "rewarding." People working in the latter seem to be doing it only because they have not yet managed or are unable to go to an oil-rich country or join a foreign institution in Egypt. A recent graduate of the American University in Cairo (AUC) working for a Cairo-based foreign institution usually gets a starting salary of at least ten times that of his counterpart from a national university working for a national institution in Egypt. Little wonder that AUC, a private institution, which in the late 1950s and 1960s admitted those who were unable to enter national universities because of low grades, is now a dream for many young Egyptians.

The Feminization of the Egyptian Family

One curious effect of labor migration is the *feminization* of Egyptian households. It is estimated that as many as half of the married male Egyptian migrants to the Arab countries leave their wives and children behind. The result is that the wife often takes upon herself the total management of the household, including the exclusive upbringing of the children in their most formative years. A whole generation of Egyptian youngsters is now growing up in one-parent families, with the other parent no more than a periodic visitor. It is hard to label this effect as positive or negative, and it is not possible to gauge its long-range repercussions. Feminists may hail the phenomenon as giving women greater sexual power and self-assertion.[59] Others may think of it as no more than explicating what usually takes place even with the fathers around, i.e., that women have undertaken most of the socialization process all along.

Another related phenomenon is the increasing number of female labor migrants to the capital-rich countries. The number of female Egyptians hired in 1979 in Saudi Arabia alone was 7,817, not including wives accompanying their spouses. They represented about 6 percent of all Egyptians hired to work in Saudi Arabia that year (totaling 136,855).[60] These tend to be mostly professional, subprofessional, and white collar workers. Some are domestic workers (e.g., maids and nannies). Nothing in this process is problematic if the woman is accompanied by a spouse who is equally employed. But in several cases these women are either unmarried or married but without their spouses accompanying them. The latter situation may be dictated by the same factors that can lead a husband to migrate alone (saving, the schooling of children, etc.). Often it is because the husband cannot obtain a job in the host country and cannot, or does not want to, leave his job at home. Whatever the case, this phenomenon is rather novel on the Egyptian social scene. The splitting of females from their families of origin or families of orientation may be hailed as another step in the emancipation of women: they are on their own and earning money in another country. But it may also be perceived as yet another factor in the destabilization of the Egyptian family by oil money.

Probably the hardest situation for a married couple is when the wife has a job and the husband does not in a country like Saudi Arabia, which requires that employed married females be accompanied by a *"mahram,"* a husband or an older male relative. This happens especially when the wife has an employable skill with a salary far exceeding the couple's combined income in Egypt. No systematic research has been done on this phenomenon with regard to Egyptians, but cases with which I am familiar are quite distressful. The "role reversal" for an Egyptian husband is still very hard to take. The boredom of staying at home and the feeling of worthlessness is emasculating for many of them.

The Political Venting Function

For the political stability of the regime, out-migration may represent a positive effect. Because the migratory process is quite selective, it is often the young or the ambitious who are more likely to go. Had these restless elements remained in large numbers inside Egypt in the absence of channels to absorb their energy, they would most likely be a source of trouble for the regime. There is empirical evidence that channels of upward social mobility for young adults of lower and lower-middle classes have become increasingly clogged in Egypt in the 1970s.[61] In fact, quite a few such youngsters join militant Islamic groups, which seek to overthrow the regime.[62] In the aftermath of the 1977 violent confrontation between RHF and the Egyptian government, it was revealed that substantial funding comes to the group from its members working in oil-rich Arab countries. More important, many of the group's members fled Egypt to Saudi Arabia to escape arrest in the summer of 1977.[63] As it turned out, some of the same elements participated, two years later, alongside Muslim Saudi dissidents in the seizure of the Grand Mosque at Mecca (an incident treated in the next chapter).

Iraq, Libya, and Algeria have served as political refuges and workplaces for many Egyptian dissidents of Nasserist and leftist persuasions. These elements are not confined to the young. They include former cabinet members, army generals, famous writers, and journalists.[64]

The presence of Egyptian political dissidents in neighboring oil countries is a mixed blessing for President Sadat's regime. In one sense, their absence from the Egyptian scene weakens the internal opposition. The regime would no doubt welcome such a development if these dissidents concentrated on "making money" instead of "making revolution." Some of them have in fact turned away from politics and rechanneled their energies into business and professional activities outside Egypt. Quite a few, however, have been vocal in criticizing the Sadat regime and have found easy access to the mass media of the host countries. Anti-Sadat broadcastings by Egyptian dissidents are beamed to Egyptian listeners from Baghdad and Tripoli. Several well-known Egyptian figures have formed opposition "national fronts" with the aim of overthrowing the Sadat regime, especially since the signing of the Peace Treaty with Israel.

Conclusion

It should be obvious by now that the consequences of Egyptian labor migration to capital-rich Arab countries are quite mixed. The "positive" and the "negative" are quite intertwined for both individuals and society. On balance, the "negatives" at this point may seem to far exceed the "positives" for Egypt as a labor exporter, as a developing country, and as a one-time pacesetter for the entire Arab Nation. But in any dialectical social process, "negatives" of today may turn into "positives" of tomorrow. And, of course, there is no "One Egypt" in abstract. In reality there are several, and what may seem "positive" for one may very well be "negative" for another. It is this very fact that sets the stage parameters for social conflict with all its creative and destructive functions, as discussed in the final section for Egypt and the rest of the Arab World. In concluding this chapter I would also note that several of the consequences discussed above apply to other Arab labor-exporting countries: Tunisia, Sudan, Jordan-Palestine, and Yemen.

Causes and Consequences
of Labor Importation:
Saudi Arabia

Saudi Arabia is the largest Arab oil producer with around nine million barrels a day; in 1979 it accounted for nearly half of the total Arab oil production. Saudi oil revenue increased from $0.6 billion in 1965 to $1.2 billion in 1970 and $4.3 billion in 1973. But in 1974 it jumped to $22.5 billion as a result of price quadrupling in the aftermath of the October-Ramadan War. In 1977 Saudi oil revenue hit the $37 billion mark and nearly doubled again to about $70.0 billion in 1979 in the aftermath of the Iranian Revolution. Middle Eastern crises, so far, seem to result in quantum jumps in oil revenues (see Table 3.2).

Being the leader in production and revenues, Saudi Arabia has naturally embarked on the most ambitious public expenditure programs in the Arab World. Its 1975–1980 Five-Year Plan called for an expenditure of $145 billion. Its 1980–1985 Plan nearly doubles this amount ($268 billion). This in turn has set in motion an accelerated labor importation process. Of the 700,000 inter-Arab migrants in 1970, Saudi Arabia received one half (see Table 3.3), while the other seven labor importers shared one half. The same trend continued after 1973, and in 1977 Saudi Arabia's share was about 1.2 million out of 2.2 million Arab migrants (see Table 3.4).

To appreciate the relative magnitude of labor importation in oil-rich countries, we must recall that in some of them expatriates now outnumber the native population (e.g., the U.A.E., Qatar, and Kuwait). This has not quite happened yet in Saudi Arabia. Even with the most conservative estimates native Saudis still outnumber migrants 2 to 1. But in terms of contribution to labor force in Saudi Arabia, migrants accounted for 43 percent of the total in the mid-1970s. In some sectors their share of employment was even higher, as may be seen from Table 5.1. Expatriates comprised more than 50 percent in five economic sectors:

TABLE 5.1
Saudi Arabia: Employment by Economic Sector and Nationality 1975

| Sector | Saudi Arabian | | Non-National | | | Saudi Arabians' share of all employment % |
	No.	%	No.	%	Total	
Agriculture and fishing	530,700	51.7	54,900	7.1	585,600	90.6
Mining and petroleum	15,400	1.5	11,600	1.5	27,000	57.0
Manufacturing	21,550	2.1	94,350	12.2	115,900	18.6
Electricity, gas, & water	7,200	0.7	13,150	1.7	20,350	35.4
Construction	35,900	3.5	203,400	26.3	239,300	15.0
Wholesale & retail trade	30,600	5.9	131,500	17.0	192,100	31.5
Transport, storage, and communication	72,900	7.1	30,950	4.0	103,850	70.2
Finance and insurance	5,150	0.5	6,950	0.9	12,100	42.6
Community & personal services	277,100	27.0	226,600	29.3	503,700	55.0
TOTAL	1,026,500	100.0	773,400	100.0	1,799,900	57.0

Sources: Saudi Arabia, Population Census 1974, Volumes I-XIV, Dammam: Ministry of Finance and National Planning, Central Department of Statistics — and cited in J.Birks and C. Sinclair, International Migration and Development in the Arab Region, Geneva:ILO, 1980, pp.159-160.

manufacturing, electricity, construction, trade, and finance. The largest nonagricultural sector by far is that of construction, employing about 240,000 in 1975; 85 percent of the employees in that sector were expatriates.

Table 5.1 also reveals salient aspects of the Saudi sociodemographic-economic structure. For example, more than half of the native Saudi manpower (52 percent) is engaged in agriculture and related activities. This is curious in a country in which 99 percent of its territory is barren, uncultivable desert. Outsiders' stereotype of the Saudis is anything but a peasant society. Most likely the high proportion of manpower in the agricultural sector is due to the inclusion of pastoral population in the official figures. The agricultural sector, broadly defined as such, is one in which native Saudis predominate: 91 percent vs 9 percent for expatriates. Despite this preponderance of agricultural employment, this sector's contribution to the Saudi GNP is no more than 5 percent. In other words, 52 percent of the native work force is engaged in activities covering less than 1 percent of the country's territory and contributing less than 5 percent of its GNP. In strictly economic terms this represents a high degree of "marginality." To put it more bluntly, most of the Saudi work force is "irrelevant" to the Saudi national economy.

Another important feature revealed by Table 5.1 is equally startling but in an opposite way. The oil and mining sector, which generates more than 90 percent of the Saudi Government's revenues, employs only 27,000 (compared to the agriculture sector's 586,000). In relative terms, oil employs 1.5 percent of Saudi manpower (compared with 52 percent in agriculture). In other words, a minuscule part of the work force accounts for much of the generated wealth of the country. Such lopsided incongruency is one of several that will be pointed out in this volume. This particular disequilibrium, however, is easily explainable. For one thing, oil production is highly capital-intensive. Although in the exploratory phase more people are employed, once production starts a relatively small number of managers, technicians, and workers are required. In the postwar era, the oil industry has become progressively more automated with an ever increasing capital-to-labor ratio. Some observers of the industry attribute this tendency to political as much as economic reasons. Fred Halliday states that the "companies have deliberately reduced the labor component of oil production, partly in response to technical developments and partly to make output less vulnerable to political pressure. In several countries oil output has multiplied while the absolute number of those employed has declined."[1]

Probably more important in explaining the low labor input in the oil sector in Saudi Arabia and in the Arab World in general is that the most labor-intensive phase of the oil industry is somewhere else. Most of the refining of raw oil and the related petrochemical industries are not located in the producing Arab countries, they are in the consuming Western countries. It is estimated that tens of thousands more workers in Western Europe and Japan are employed in refining, processing, and related chemical industries based on oil brought from the Arab World. Were these activities and the facilities required for them situated in the Arab World, the number of Arabs employed in the oil sector would easily double or triple.[2]

Table 5.1 shows that in 1975 native Saudis made up only 57 percent of the employment in the oil sector in that country—merely 15,400 workers. The sociological significance of this fact is no less startling. In a country whose entire economic existence at present depends on oil, less than 16,000 out of a population of about 5 million are engaged in that industry. All accounts indicate that even this minute number of natives is heavily concentrated in the lower rungs (unskilled labor) rather than in the managerial and technical levels of the oil industry. Many of the higher-level jobs are performed by expatriates, who make up as much as 43 percent. In other words, the social organization of the oil industry in Saudi Arabia has kept the natives, by and large, outside its intricate operating "secrets" or "knowhow". If this was logically understandable in the 1930s, when oil was first drilled, it is quite odd and socially alienating that this remains the case fifty years later.

Most of the Arab migrants to Saudi Arabia come from Yemen, Egypt, Jordan-Palestine, and Sudan. The estimated number of Yemenis in Saudi Arabia varies widely from one source to another. Some contend that over one million Yemenis are often counted by the authorities when the total figure of Saudi population is given (7.5 million in the 1974 census), although never acknowledged as such. This inclusion of Yemenis is due to the fact that until recently they were not required to obtain visas or work permits to enter the kingdom. At any rate, the figure officially acknowledged for Yemenis in 1975 was 280,400.[3] Even with this decided underestimation, migrant laborers from Arab Yemen ranked first in terms of number and accounted for more than 36 percent of all migrant labor that year. If we add those from Democratic Yemen (55,000), the total for both Yemens would be 43.4 percent (see Table 5.2). The Jordanian-Palestinians ranked as the second largest migrant group in Saudi Arabia in 1975. They numbered 175,000 and accounted for nearly 23 percent of all expatriate labor. Given the fact that they are strategically locted in the middle and higher levels of manpower and are highly politicized, this substantial presence of Palestinians in Saudi Arabia is no less significant than it is in Kuwait (where they are the largest migrant

TABLE 5.2
Saudi Arabia: Migrant Workers by Country or Area of Origin,
Ranked by Size 1975

Country or Area of Origin	No.	%
Yemen	280,400	36.3
Jordan and Palestine	175,000	22.7
Egypt	95,000	12.3
Democratic Yemen	55,000	7.1
Sudan	35,000	4.5
Lebanon	20,000	2.6
Oman	17,500	2.3
Syrian Arab Republic	15,000	1.9
Somalia	5,000	0.6
Iraq	2,000	0.3
Total Arab	699,900	90.6
Pakistan	15,000	1.9
India	15,000	1.9
Other Asian	8,000	1.0
Total Asian	38,000	4.8
Europe and America	15,000	1.9
Africa	10,000	1.3
Iran	10,000	0.1
Turkey	500	0.1
Total	773,400	100.0

Sources: Saudi Arabia, Population Census 1974, Volumes I-XIV,
Dammam: Ministry of Finance and National Planning, Central
Department of Statistics -- and cited in J. Birks and
C. Sinclair, International Migration and Development in the
Arab Region, Geneva: ILO, 1980, pp.159-160.

community) and other Gulf states. Egyptians came in third with nearly
100,000 or 12.0 percent of all migrant labor in Saudi Arabia. Although
no figure is available for the late 1970s, the number and percentage of
Egyptians in Saudi Arabia seems to have increased markedly. At present,
they probably approach the same size as Yemenis, or decidedly rank a
close second. The absolute and proportionate increase of Egyptian labor
in Saudi Arabia was accelerated as relations between Egypt and Libya
steadily worsened from 1975 on.

All in all, Saudi Arabia showed in the mid-1970s a preponderance of Arab migrant labor force (91 percent). As Table 5.2 shows, the Asians accounted for less than 5 percent. All other nationalities combined, including Westerners, accounted for less than 5 percent. Future projections, however, indicate a decline in the percentage of Arabs in Saudi imported labor in favor of Pakistanis and other Asians by the mid-1980s (see Table 5.3).

As discussed in Chapter 3, Saudi Arabia may be able to develop its work force to meet low-level manual labor needs by 1985, but it will have greater needs than at present for middle and high levels of manpower. The size of the expatriate population in Saudi Arabia is projected to increase from 1.4 million in 1975 to 4.8 million in 1985. As Table 5.3 shows, such expatriate population will jump from less than 20 percent in the mid-1970s to around 35 percent of the country's total population in the mid-1980s. At such time Egyptians are projected to be the largest foreign community in Saudi Arabia (874,000), followed by Yemenis (844,000), Pakistanis (621,000), and Jordanian-Palestinians (473,000). The sociopolitical implications of this increased reliance on expatriate population are dealt with later in this chapter.

Causes of Labor Importation

I have already alluded to the causes propelling oil-rich countries to import labor. Small demographic base, low economic participation rate in the labor force, and low skill levels among native population are all factors constraining the supply of indigenous labor. On the demand side of the equation, its increase in the last decade was as phenomenal as the growth of oil revenues. The latter set in motion very ambitious developmental plans. If all the above applied to all capital-rich Arab countries, the case of Saudi Arabia was even more accentuated.

The Saudi population is relatively small compared to its territorial size of 830,000 square miles. Despite Saudi official claims, most students of the subject estimated its population at 5 to 5.5 million in 1975.[4] This figure included some resident aliens (e.g., Yemenis), which means a native Saudi population of no more than 4.5 million. This is about 2 to 3 million less than most official Saudi estimates of 7.5 million.[5]

Even with 4.5 million in 1975, Saudi Arabia would have been less reliant on imported labor if the participation rate had been, say, as high as 35 percent. At such a rate, which is not uncommon in several Third World countries, Saudi Arabia could have supplied a work force of 1.6 million. This would have been only 200,000 short of its actual work force

TABLE 5.3
Saudi Arabia: Non-National Populations in 1975 and 1985 (High and Low Growth Rates)

	1975		High Growth Rate 1985		Annual Increase 1975-1985	Low Growth Rate 1985		Annual Increase 1975-1985
	Number	Percent	Number	Percent	Percent	Number	Percent	Percent
Egypt	154700	11.1	873500	18.0	18.9	798400	17.9	17.8
India	15200	1.1	222700	4.6	30.8	187700	4.2	28.6
Iran	25000	1.8	83500	1.7	12.8	68900	1.5	10.7
Jordan	186600	13.3	473000	9.8	9.7	481700	10.8	9.9
Lebanon	9600	0.7	67100	1.4	21.5	67600	1.5	21.6
Morocco	1400	0.1	5300	0.1	14.2	5300	0.1	14.2
Oman	19000	1.3	71000	1.5	14.1	70600	1.6	14.0
Pakistan	111800	8.0	620900	12.8	18.7	563500	12.6	17.6
South East Asia	18300	1.3	213400	4.4	27.8	239200	5.3	29.3
Sudan	41500	3.0	272200	5.6	20.7	261500	5.9	20.2
Syria	55100	3.9	241800	5.0	15.9	225200	5.1	15.1
Tunisia	2200	0.1	10100	0.2	16.5	10000	0.2	16.3
Yemen (YAR)	586700	42.0	844200	17.4	3.7	726900	16.3	2.2
Yemen (PDRY)	86500	6.2	296000	6.1	13.1	290000	6.5	12.9
Rest of World	84700	6.1	554300	11.4	20.7	468800	10.5	18.7
Total Non-Nationals	1398300	100.0	4849700	100.0	13.2	4465300	100.0	12.3
Total Nationals	5935900	80.9	5757100	64.4	4.0	8757100	66.2	4.0
Total Population	7334200	100.0	13606800	100.0	6.4	13222400	100.0	6.1

in 1975, instead of the shortage of nearly 800,000, which was filled by expatriates that year.

Underlying the low participation rate in Saudi Arabia are several factors alluded to already, and I recapitulate them here briefly. The preponderance of young age groups in the population is one such factor. With one of the highest birth rates in the Arab World (5.0 percent), and a rapidly declining death rate (2.0 percent), the result is a fairly young population, and a low participation rate (22 percent). Additional factors contribute to the underutilization of the Saudi work force, which is small to begin with. Over half of the native work force is employed in the traditional rather than the modern sector. This includes subsistence farming and herding. Thus in the modern sectors, which are the targets of the Saudi ambitious developmental planning, the participation rate of native Saudis is even much smaller, as could be deduced from Table 5.1.

Many native Saudis, especially with well-known tribal origin, are reluctant to take up certain manual jobs that were at one time performed by slaves. Until the early 1960s "slavery" was still legal in Saudi Arabia.[6] Although that system was abolished when the state bought all the slaves in the kingdom and set them free, the legacy has lingered on. Thus construction work, sanitation jobs, hotel services and the like are occupational areas that many native Saudis shy away from even if they are poor and the financial pay for these jobs is good. With greater material wealth the demand on such services naturally increases. But even when the training and skill level required for them could be met easily by indigenous Saudi personnel, they do not opt for them, thus increasing the need for importing expatriates to perform them.

A closer examination of Table 5.1 reveals yet another factor that contributes heavily to labor importation. The second largest sector in which native Saudis are engaged (after agriculture) is what is labelled in the official census as "community and personal services." In the mid-1970s it had more than 277,000, or 27 percent, of the indigenous work force. Most of these are government employees, who in practice do very little yet draw a decent salary. The immense wealth of the state makes this practice possible as a way of indirect subsidized welfare to natives who have little or no skills and who are not inclined to take up training to do more productive work. In other words, the present social organization in Saudi Arabia does not have enough built-in incentives to motivate the indigenous labor force to adjust itself to the real employment requirements of the modern sector.

Some observers[7] have noted a related phenomenon that leads to the continuation of this underutilization of native Saudis. It is referred to as "nonwage income" opportunities. This includes family support, royal patronage, land grants, and of course being a *"kafil"* (a sponsor).[8] Some of these deliberate policies or charitable practices have "an enervating effect on individuals to whom the Government is looking most urgently to participate in modern economy."[9]

The rapid expansion of Saudi military and security forces in the last decade is yet another factor that limits the supply of indigenous Saudi manpower to modern sectors. Here there is a convergence between the political imperative as perceived by the ruling elite and the tribal value system of many of the natives themselves. Naturally, the ruling elite prefer to assign such sensitive tasks to native Saudis who, especially if they are of Bedouin background, opt for military occupations because of the high pay and because of the "honor" associated with being a "fighter." Together, the Saudi Armed Forces, the National Guard, the internal police and security forces, and their support of civilian bureaucracy number in the neighborhood of 200,000.

The rapid expansion of education is one more factor that limits the supply of indigenous labor. The ratio of school enrollment in the primary level has jumped from 12 percent of the respective age group in 1960, to 34 percent in 1970 and 47 percent in the mid-1970s. In the secondary level of education the enrollment ratio has also risen, from 2 percent in 1960, to 9 percent in 1970 and 19 percent in the mid-1970s.[10] This may be of long range benefit to Saudi Arabia, but for the present it is restricting the flow of new Saudi entrants into the labor force.

Finally, the Saudi puritanical mores have made the incorporation of women into the modern labor force quite negligible. Saudi women, if allowed at all, are restricted to a few occupations (e.g., teaching in girls' schools or social work in feminine spheres).

All in all, then, the factors that make Saudi Arabia a heavy importer of expatriate labor derive from its demographic structure (smallness and youthfulness of the population), sociocultural impediments, social organization of work, and the accelerating demand on labor for expansion of the modern sector.

Consequences of Labor Importation

The consequences of labor importation are as mixed and complicated for Saudi Arabia as those of labor exportation are for Egypt. The question of which of these consequences are positive and which are negative is value-loaded. For example, would the breakdown of certain indigenous values and practices (e.g., slavery and women's seclusion), as a result of massive contact with outsiders, be viewed as positive or negative? The case for abolishing slavery may be universally endorsed even

within the most conservative quarters of Saudi society, but the same
would not apply to attitudes toward women. The argument for their
continued seclusion and veiling is still quite strong—so much so that
many non-Saudi females coming to work in the country find it both expedient and necessary to veil. By the same token, it is hard to evaluate
the impact of the vast number of expatriate laborers on the political
vulnerability or stability of the regime.

It should be noted at the outset, however, that the specific consequences of labor importation cannot be separated from their overall context. They are in one sense interactive with the other chain-effects of oil.
To appreciate this point, we may recall a similar scale of labor importation from Turkey, Yugoslavia, and North Africa to Western Europe in
the postwar period. But it hardly had an impact similar to that in oil-rich
Arab countries, despite similarity in volume.[11] One reason for this differential impact is due to the prime mover and the vastly dissimilar
socioeconomic structures of host countries in both instances of labor importation. Despite its large scale, migrant labor represented a relatively
small percentage of both population and manpower of each Western
European society. The latter had a highly developed industrial and institutional structure that the migrants were to fit into, not create. In
Western Europe, migrant labor from southern countries was to perform
only unskilled or at best semiskilled work, while the indigenous manpower was engaged in skilled, technical, and managerial jobs. Finally,
migrant laborers in Western Europe found themselves in a vastly different alien culture. For that reason they could not penetrate it, much less
get acculturated or incorporated in the mainstream of Western societies.
Very few, if any, of these conditions apply to Saudi labor importation
from "sister" but capital-poor Arab countries. Here the language and the
cultural affinities are much greater. The labor migrants span the occupational spectrum from professionals and top managers to unskilled manpower. They come from societies that in many cases are more advanced
educationally and industrially, with much more differentiated social
structure and more crystallized social formations. The migrant labor to
Saudi Arabia, furthermore, is virtually shaping the host country's new
institutions and forging its modern infrastructure almost from scratch.

It is because of these qualitative differences between the labor migration experiences that the respective consequences are vastly different.
The sociocultural impacts of labor importation were quite minimal on
Western European societies. In Saudi Arabia and other capital-rich Arab
countries the impact is quite significant. The absolute and relative size of
migrant labor, its pervasive role in the economy, and the fragility of

social structures of host countries account for this vastly more significant impact. Awareness of such an impact is equally shared by social scientists and ruling elite in the oil countries. No matter how socially committed they may be, scholars' interests are still mainly intellectual. For the ruling elite, however, it is a far more serious question. In some instances it puts them on the horns of a dilemma—they are damned if they do and damned if they do not. If these apprehensions were mere conjecture a few years ago, after the Iranian Revolution they acquired a deadly reality as far as the ruling elite are concerned. This is particularly true in the case of Saudi Arabia, with its vast territory (over 2.1 million square kilometers), its small native population (around 5 million) dispersed in pocket-like oases, its quasitribal social organization, its undiversified economy, and its long borders along frontiers of nine other countries and two sensitive bodies of water.

The Building of Modern Infrastructure

Before we deal with the elite's cause for concern, let us quickly review some of the decidedly positive consequences of oil and labor importation.

As late as 1955, Saudi Arabia had only three secondary schools in the entire kingdom, with a total enrollment of fewer than 3,000 students. There were no girls' schools at all, and no universities. Today, there are 1.3 million students enrolled in several thousand schools, and 60,000 college students in five universities and several institutes for higher learning. In 1960 the first girls' school was opened against the will of Saudi Arabia's arch-conservative religious establishment. Two decades later, there exist 300 such schools, and girls are admitted to all-women colleges, albeit separated from male students and male faculty.[12]

In the last decade alone (1970–1980), 2,000 villages were electrified, 15,000 kilometers of paved roads were built, 700,000 telephones were installed, and 300,000 housing units were constructed. Health facilities (hospitals and dispensaries) quadrupled and the number of doctors grew from less than 1,000 to 4,600. Two huge industrial complexes are under way in Yanbu and Jubail; one of them is the world's largest.[13] The list of these and other indicators of socioeconomic growth is phenomenal by any world standard.

The accomplishment of this impressive growth could not have taken place without three necessary conditions: the oil revenues, expatriate labor, and the leadership's decision to plunge in with the full weight of the state into a deliberate growth process.

The role of expatriate labor in building the country's infrastructure virtually from the ground up needs no further emphasis. More important, however, is its role in maintaining and operating this socioeconomic infrastructure and the institutions erected upon it. We have already seen that even in the oil industry, which triggered all these developments, the expatriates are heavily represented in the skilled and managerial aspects of it. We do not wish to belabor the point. But to give a few more examples, not only did imported labor build the 3,000 or more schools now in operation, but also nearly 70 percent of all teachers are expatriates from Arab countries, especially Egypt and Palestine. More than 80 percent of all Saudi Arabia's university academic staff are from neighboring Arab countries (mostly Egyptian). Only 8 percent of the 4,600 doctors manning the country's health facilities are Saudi; the other 92 percent are mostly Arabs (with a few Pakistanis and Westerners).[14]

Building schools for over one million Saudis, and hospitals, roads, and power stations to serve the country has to be judged among the positive consequences of labor importation. Without it, it simply could not have happened.

Indirectly, the presence of about one million migrants in Saudi Arabia also has its role in energizing the business sector of the economy. Their purchasing power has expanded the domestic market tremendously and accelerated the circulation of money. Their sheer presence and interaction with the indigenous population has added a cosmopolitan dimension to many Saudi communities, a phenomenon hitherto confined to the three cities of Jeddah, Medina, and Mecca in the Hijaz, where Muslim pilgrimage is conducted. The subtle influence of such contact is bound to expand the frame of reference of hundreds of thousands of Saudis, children and adults alike.

The Undermining of Traditional Culture

Any such large-scale cultural and human contact in a relatively short period of time is bound to create all kinds of stress and strain on the local culture and population. Saudi Arabia is one of only two Arab countries without a direct colonial experience (the other is Yemen). As a result, most of its society had remained until midcentury virtually locked up in the hinterland of the Arabian Peninsula (the exception being the western and to a lesser extent the eastern peripheries of Arabia). This insular geographic existence had been compounded by a puritan fundamentalist belief system and practice brought about by the Wahhabi movement in the late eighteenth century.[15] The fact that King Abd Al-Aziz, the modern unifier of the country, had to battle with his religious establishment in the 1930s and 1940s to introduce the automobile, the radio, and the telephone, testifies to that degree of insularity and the deep suspicion toward the modern world. It took another thirty years to persuade the same establishment to open the first girls' school (1960), and only with the provision that it would be under the supervision of the religious ulama.[16]

It must therefore be appreciated how actually and potentially stressful it must be as the outside world is suddenly being thrust on such a simple, fundamentalist, quasitribal social structure. The outside world came in two major forms: expatriates, and everything money can buy. Each form entails its own limitless adjustments on the part of the indigenous population. We saw in an earlier section three ideal typical ways and images of coping with the sudden flow of money, technology, and people from outside the Peninsula.

Problems have arisen as a result of the accelerated pace of material growth and the sustained human influx into Saudi Arabia as in other oil-rich countries. Some of these problems pertain mainly to the indigenous population; others to the migrants; and still a third kind of problem affects both.

Despite all claims, and obviously wishes, of the Saudi leadership (both secular and religious) of modernizing on "Islamic bases," there is a steady erosion of "traditional" culture. New and diverse life-styles introduced by Westerners and Asians, as well as northern Arabs, may be disdained, avoided, or admired, but they are being constantly watched by young Saudis. The growing number of schooled Saudis (1.3 million in 1980, nearly one fourth of the entire native population) means exposure to modern science and to living human models (teachers) from various backgrounds. The impact of such experience may not be instant, but the "sleeper effect" is no doubt constantly at work. Such effects are further reinforced by increasing travel abroad for study (in 1980 there were 15,000 Saudi students in the U.S. alone). The growing population of modern educated Saudis means an emerging "world view" at marked variance with that of their elders and that of their uneducated counterparts. The volume and diversity of cultural contacts between Saudis and the outside world may be inferred from Tables 5.4 and 5.5. The number of foreigners visiting Saudi Arabia in 1979 was about 2.5 million from some seventy-two countries. This number equals about half of the total native Saudi population. It is equivalent to 120 million foreigners visiting the U.S. in one year, or 20 million visiting Egypt (the actual number for Egypt that year was about 1 million foreign visitors).[17] In other words, on the average, one of every two Saudis came into contact with at least one foreigner that year. Equally impressive is the number of Saudis traveling abroad. As Table 5.5 shows, as many as 900,000 traveled outside Saudi Arabia in 1979. That is nearly one fifth of the total native Saudi population. It would be equivalent to about 50 million Americans

TABLE 5.4
Number of Foreigners Entering and Leaving Saudi Arabia
in 1979 (1399 H.)

Nationality Groups	Entering		Leaving	
	No.	%	No.	%
Arabs (20 countries)	1,555,171	(62.6)	1,543,404	(63.7)
Asians (16 countries)	556,353	(22.4)	452,910	(18.7)
Africans (18 countries)	21,441	(0.8)	24,097	(1.0)
Europeans (18 countries)	232,094	(9.3)	278,731	(11.5)
The Americas and Australia (11 countries)	119,690	(4.8)	124,405	(5.1)
Total	2,484,749	(100.0)	2,423,547	(100.0)

Source: Compiled from Saudi Arabia's Ministry of the Interior Statistical Year Book, 1979, Riyadh:1980, pp.222-231.

or 8 million Egyptians traveling abroad in one year. Culturally even more significant is the fact that of all Saudis traveling abroad about 15 percent were females. To appreciate the social implications of this we must remember that a Saudi woman still cannot move about outside her own home without being veiled, nor can she drive a car; these taboos are not observed while she is abroad. In many ways, such contacts with the outside world for a people who remained culturally insulated until very recently amount to another "silent revolution."

Although Saudi officials keep a tight lid on figures pertaining to crime, divorce, alcoholism, and other indicators of social problems, observers with a long-standing interest in Saudi Arabia report a rapid increase in all such phenomena.[18] From scattered published official sources we may infer this rapid increase. Between 1971 and 1975 (two years before and two years after the 1973 oil boom), the administrative manpower of Saudi prisons more than doubled. It grew from a total of 2,255 policemen and civilians to 5,541, a 146 percent increase in five years,[19] indicating possible doubling of the number of prison inmates. Substantiation of this inference became explicit by the late 1970s. As Table 5.6 shows, in the span of a single year the number of crimes officially reported increased by 169 percent (not taking into account either political crimes or crimes possibly committed but not reported). A close ex-

TABLE 5.5
Number of Saudis Traveling Abroad in 1979 (1399 H.)

Leaving to or Entering from	Leaving			Entering		
	Males	Females	Total	Males	Females	Total
Arab Countries	683,224	112,371	795,595	721,842	117,057	838,899
Europe and the Americas	43,626	17,179	60,805	38,749	14,805	53,554
Asian and African Countries	19,635	5,323	24,958	16,875	4,479	21,354
Total	746,485	134,873	881,358	777,466	136,341	913,807

Source: Computed from Saudi Arabia's Ministry of the Interior Statistical Year Book, 1979, Riyadh; 1980, p.264.

TABLE 5.6
Number and Types of Crime in the Kingdom of Saudi Arabia
in 1978 and 1979 (1398-1399 H.)

Year \ Type of Crime	Murder	Economic & Financial	Moral (sexual)	Fraud	Other crimes	Total
1398 (1978)	70	1186	546	28	23	1853
1399 (1979)	136	3006	1368	117	353	4980
% increase	94.3	153.5	150.5	317.9	1434.8	168.8

Sources: Computed from Saudi Arabia's Ministry of Interior
Statistical Year Book, 1979, Riyadh:1980, pp.270-300.

amination of Table 5.6 indicates that the traditional crime of murder,
which is mostly related to honor and vendetta, increased by 94 percent
but showed the slowest rate of growth. In contrast, economic and financial crimes grew by 154 percent; and those involving fraud more than
tripled (318 percent). These offenses are no doubt related to the tremendous influx of money and the relentless scrambling over it.

What is labelled in Table 5.6 as "other crimes" includes alcohol and
drug offenses, which increased phenomenally, by more than 1,400 percent in one year. Along with moral crimes (i.e., sexual), these "other
crimes" reflect the stress and strain of the Saudi individuals and society.
We do not have a time series showing the contribution of expatriates to
the criminal scene in Saudi Arabia, but Table 5.7 gives a one-year
breakdown of convicted offenders by nationality and type of crime in
1978. Most of the convicted were Saudis, but foreigners accounted for 40
percent of the total. Their greatest concentration was in financial crimes
and crimes of fraud (49 percent and 42 percent, respectively). All in all,
these fragmented data suggest the growing incidence of social
breakdowns in Saudi Arabia.

A related phenomenon is the growing duality or discrepancy between
publicly sanctioned mores and privately practiced behavior. The upper
echelon has for years espoused public strictness with regard to Islamic taboos (e.g., drinking, movies, gambling, sexual freedom). But members
of this same stratum are known to freely indulge in such behavior in the
privacy of their palaces or while traveling abroad.[20] In recent years, the
same moral duality has spread rapidly among the growing new middle

TABLE 5.7
Convicted Offenders by Type of Crime and Nationality in
Saudi Arabia in 1978 (1398 H.)

Nationality \ Type of Crime	Murder	Financial	Moral	Fraud	Other crimes	Total
Saudis	86.7	50.8	70.4	57.6	63.4	59.9
Non-Saudis	13.3	49.2	29.5	42.4	36.6	40.1
Total	100.0	100.0	100.0	100.0	100.0	100.0

Source: Computed from the same source as Table 5.6, pp.270-300.

class. Thus while public theaters are still prohibited by law, private cinema clubs and home-owned videotapes are quite common in all major urban areas where all kinds of motion pictures are shown, including X-rated movies and hardcore pornography. The phenomenon is so prevalent and yet so publicly hushed that it has the appearance of a collective "social conspiracy."

Varieties of Social Discontent

The rapid but imbalanced changes are creating a growing disaffection among the older generation as well as among younger puritanical Saudis.[21] The young Muslim militants who seized the Grand Mosque at Mecca on November 20, 1979, declared as one of their objectives the "cleansing" of Saudi society of all such immoralities but specifically the "moral hypocrisy" of the ruling elite.[22]

Another source of disaffection among certain sectors of Saudi society results from the uneven distribution of growth and its concomitant differential rewards. While the ruling elite has tried to spread wealth to all corners of the kingdom, the laissez-faire, laissez-passer economic ideology has also remained the prevalent practice. As a result, certain groups have benefited in disproportion to others.[23] Big Saudi contractors, for example, who number no more than a few hundred individuals, exercise a tight hold over the lion's share of the construction sector. Even when they subcontract foreign companies to perform the actual work, they still end up with a net profit margin ranging between 10 and 20 percent. The volume of construction contracts in 1978 was nearly $10 billion (SR31,959 million).[24] This would mean at least one billion dollars in net profits in one year. The same may be said of commissions in the sale of oil, purchase of arms, or procuring of other services for the government.[25] Land seizure and laying claim to it outside major cities was freely practiced by a few hundred shrewd Saudis in the late 1960s and early 1970s. Land value skyrocketed following the oil price revolution in 1973. The construction boom and mounting demand for housing, accentuated by hundreds of thousands of immigrating workers, fueled the inflation of land prices. The price of a square meter in the desert fringe of Riyadh was less than one Saudi Riyal in the late 1960s. In the late 1970s, the same land was selling from anywhere between SR100 and 500 a square meter. Several hundred people have become millionaires as a result of land speculation alone, not to mention other similar speculative activities. There are, of course, several times as many Saudis, who, though living well, have missed out on such opportunities. Given the principles of "distributive justice" and "relative deprivation," these people are quite disgruntled. They "feel" poor.

Becoming instant millionaires in Saudi Arabia is still the fortune of a minority, but there are enough such individuals for others to see. An emulation "rat race" has engulfed most Saudis in urban communities. This is not the familiar American "rags to riches" mythology, which still emphasizes individual hard work. In the Saudi context it is rather from "rich to richer" with little or no work and with the shortest route possible.[26] I have already described the new Saudi entrepreneur and the "kafil" (see Chapter 2); what may be added in this regard is that many Saudis in government service have a business on the side. It is not uncommon to devote more attention to the side business than to one's official "full-time" job with the state. Reporting in the morning, then leaving for several hours to attend to the private business is not a rare practice. The phenomenon reached such a dimension in the sensitive Ministry of the Interior (in charge of internal security) that a crackdown and stiff penalties were decreed by the minister in June 1977. But even that did not seem sufficient deterrence. The minister resorted to what seemed a more effective measure at the time: he doubled the policemen's salaries.[27] In less sensitive departments, the government simply ignores the practice because most of those who would be enforcers of job attendance and work performance also have their own businesses on the side. Teachers, professors, and high level technocrats are no exception.

What all this amounts to is a steady erosion of work ethics. Being a "Saudi" seems increasingly to make the native feel entitled to getting richer with a minimum of effort.[28] The practice of hiring expatriates to do the work has become a generalized attitude from the state down to the "kafil," even when natives themselves can do the job. It is not an unfamiliar scene to encounter a typical middle class urban Saudi family with Indian or Ethiopian maids and nannies for their children, Yemeni or

Pakistani workers constructing its new villa, Lebanese or Palestinians running the side business, and an Egyptian subordinate doing the government office work of the head of the family.

The uneven growth in Saudi Arabia has created yet another source of discontent. Discrepancies among various provinces in the relative share of government projects and services have revived some old regional and tribal rivalries and animosities.[29] The poorest and most deprived are the southwestern, southeastern, and northern areas. Tribal and population groupings in these regions envy their counterparts in central (Najd), eastern (Dhahran-Dammam), and western (Jeddah-Mecca-Medina) provinces. But even inhabitants of both the eastern and western provinces envy their central counterparts, not only for their greater share of the kingdom's wealth, but also for their near monopoly of political power. Although these mutual regional sentiments are not at all new, they have been revived and magnified in the last ten years as a result of the sudden influx of money, goods, and foreign labor.

Finally, the heterogeneous mix of people, life-styles, and exposure to new ideas and modern education have made younger elements of the rising middle class more questioning of the entire socioeconomic-political system. The ruling elite have proven flexible enough in recent years to accommodate most of the economic ambitions of these elements. Even politically, some of the brightest among them have been appointed to ministerial and subcabinet positions. In the past decade nonroyal names have begun to glitter on both the national and international scene: Sheikh Zaki al-Yamani, Minister of Oil, Dr. Hisham al-Nazir, Minister of Planning, Dr. Ghazi al-Gosaibi, Minister of Industry. These and others are quite articulate and competent, and have served the regime well. But they remain a minute number in a growing class of modern-educated technocrats. Most of the major and sensitive positions are still exclusively monopolized by members of the Royal Family and of the house of Al-Sheikh. The circulation of top elite positions remains extremely limited.[30] As the experience of other societies shows, becoming materially well-to-do is never a total substitute for political participation. It is no accident that most of the attempted coups d'etat in Saudi Arabia were led by elements from the new middle class.[31] This is one of the pressing issues that the ruling house of Al-Saud has to contend with, especially after what happened across the Gulf in neighboring Iran.

Problems of Imported Labor

The problems peculiar to imported labor in the kingdom are no less varied or complex. Almost every migrant is quite eager and indeed feels lucky to get to an oil-rich Arab country. The wage differentials more than justify such feelings, at least in the beginning while the reference point of comparison is back home. Over time, however, the reference point gradually shifts in the direction of his Saudi counterpart. The migrant's attitude changes from one of content to one of ambivalence toward the host country as he increasingly senses differential treatment and occasionally blatant discrimination.[32] Invariably the migrant receives much less pay for the same work, has no freedom of movement, and is almost entirely at the mercy of the employer. As the novelty and excitement of the migratory experience wears off, the sources of discontent become magnified. Although most migrants come from Arab countries with no political freedom to speak of, some of them begin to anguish at the added denial of many civil liberties and lack of social freedom. This condition is compounded by the lack of recreational opportunities, especially for single migrants and those without their families. Some unscrupulous private sector employers force the migrants to work in appalling conditions and live in minimal residences without any protection from other migrants or from abuse by citizens of the host country. Such conditions naturally breed restlessness and malcontent among migrants.[33] While Asians are perceived as a docile work force, Arabs feel they should be entitled to some "rights" of a sort. As one commentator points out, "they [Arabs] are attuned to political and social currents, which though very discreet today, they can eventually turn to their advantage."[34]

The migrant work force has not been organized to defend its minimum rights. Any such attempt is mercilessly quelled by the Saudi authorities. As one observer notes, "naturally a regime that does not recognize trade union rights for its own people is very intolerant of anything that smacks of collective agitation among its foreign helots."[35] In 1977 there was some mild public protest by Turkish workers in the northern town of Tabuk. Saudi Air Force C-135 transport planes were summoned to ship all of them out immediately without any investigation of the legitimacy of their grievance.[36]

There are reasons besides the Saudi government's harsh attitude for the difficulty of organizing migrant laborers. For one thing, they come from many diverse national and ethnic backgrounds. They are separated from the indigenous work force both by vast pay differentials and in most cases by physical insulation on work sites. Many of them have no savings or strike pay to fall back on. They realize that they are dispensable since the oil states can deport them and replace them quickly by others who are eager to come in.[37]

Despite lack of organization and stern governmental policies, the objective conditions drive some migrants to flare up occasionally. Even groups that are believed to be as industrious and disciplined as the South Koreans are reported to have caused trouble on one or two occasions; as usual, they have been sent home immediately without fuss.[38] In the last two years rumors began to spread around the Gulf States about the Koreans. They are mostly in their twenties, work a forty-hour week for only $800 per month, usually stay for no more than a year's tour of duty, and live in military-like camps. They are now suspected by some quarters to be South Korean Army reserves, readily deployable by Western powers to take over the oil fields in an emergency.[39] Farfetched as it may sound, expressing such suspicions in print reflects the sensitivity of the whole question of imported labor in the area.

The increased incidence of expatriates' frustration still expresses itself mainly in individual acts of "deviance." More of them are arrested and penalized every year for smuggling, illegal entry, drugs and alcohol use or peddling, sexual immorality, fraud, embezzlement, and petty and grand theft (see Table 5.7). Some of the latter categories of crimes were rarely encountered in Saudi Arabia in the past. Recently, for example, the Saudi media reported a SR6 million (about $2 million) payroll theft, by a couple of West Germans, from the military hospital at Riyadh.[40]

Convergence of Dissidence: The Seizure of the Grand Mosque at Mecca

Of greater alarm to Saudi authorities than individual criminal acts is migrants' involvement in political protest activities in alliance with dissident Saudi citizens. The November 20, 1979, attack and seizure of the Grand Mosque at Mecca is a dramatic case in point. The incident involved over 400 heavily armed dissidents using well-rehearsed military tactics.[41] Equipped with walkie-talkies, machine guns, and bazookas, they stormed the Mosque and moved into strategic positions during the confusion of a well-attended dawn prayer ceremony on the first day of the Muslim New Year ending the 14th Hijra century. The group, calling itself *Al-Ikhwan* (the Brothers),[42] was reported to have planned the arrest of King Khaled and other members of the Saudi ruling elite who were scheduled to attend the ceremony as a step in a well-phased takeover of power. The King did not attend because of a sudden illness, and the plot was foiled after several days of fighting, which left about 300 killed (mostly government counterattacking National Guardsmen), more injured, and some 160 of the dissidents arrested. The subsequent interrogation and trials revealed some significant facts quite relevant to our present analysis.

First, the dissidents reflected a complex microcosm of the present Saudi scene: 80 percent of them were Saudis, but the other 20 percent (about eighty dissidents) included Yemenis, Egyptians, Iraqis, Moroccans, Pakistanis, and others from the Arab Gulf States. Although including some low-level educated persons, the majority were middle- and high-educated. The group had some doctors and engineers as members.

Second, among the Saudis themselves there were some from the eastern and southwestern provinces. But more significant was the fact that some of the dissidents, including the leader Juhiman al-Otaybi, were from central Najd tribes, long believed to be loyal to the ruling house of Al-Saud.

Third, among the Saudi dissidents there were some former and present members of the National Guard. It was rumored that this fact explains the tenacity and fighting skills of the dissidents. The weapons used were said to have been stolen from the National Guard's armories around the country by these members. The National Guard has long been thought of as a very loyal fighting force especially designed to protect the regime against possible coups d'etat by other branches of the Saudi Armed Forces. For some former or present members of the National Guard to defect is an indicator of serious internal social discontent.

Finally, the attack style, the youthful makeup, and the ideological proclamations of the dissidents are quite similar to their counterparts in Egypt in 1974 and Tunisia in 1979.[43] Without evidence of organic links among the groups involved in the three incidents or suggesting any "conspiracy theory," such similarity provides food for thought. Some unconfirmed reports claimed that the Egyptian participants in the Mecca attack were former members of Egypt's militant group Jama'at al-Takfir w'al-Hijra (Repentance and Holy Flight), which violently confronted the Egyptian government in July 1977, and then managed to escape to Saudi Arabia.[44] Regardless of such possible links, it is more likely that similarities of structural forces give rise to similar protest movements. Demonstration effect, since the former incidents were well-publicized all over the Arab World, gives rise to adoption of similar tactics.

The participation of migrants in any such movement with their Saudi counterparts means that some migrants, by no means a majority yet, are no longer reluctant to channel their discontent politically. The banner of Islam serves as a unifier among dissidents despite their diverse national or ethnic backgrounds. Enslaving migrants or segmenting them from native Saudis by vastly differential monetary and legal treatment seems to have its limitations. This may particularly be true in the case of middle and highly educated Saudis as well as expatriates.

Oil, development, and related labor importation have generated other problems pertaining to expatriates and natives. Among such problems I would cite inflation, mounting pressure on services, overurbanization, and urban sprawl. In this sense there is a convergence of discontent of expatriates and Saudis.

Inflation is one of the most destabilizing factors of sociopolitical regimes in today's world. It has been running high in Saudi Arabia in the last ten years—about 20 percent annually.[45] Part of this inflationary pressure is imported from the capitalist world system to which the Saudi economy is closely linked. Part of it is a recycled inflation. Saudi Arabia and other OPEC countries raise oil prices, and industrial importing countries (U.S., Western European nations, and Japan) raise the prices of their goods in which oil figures heavily. Thus Saudi Arabia and others have to pay higher prices when they import such goods. The most important cause of inflation, however, is the vast increase in money supply at rates way outdistancing the indigenous productive capacity of Saudi Arabia outside the oil sector. Whatever the relative weight of each factor, inflation hurts natives and expatriates alike. This is particularly the case with groups on fixed incomes, e.g., state employees and people in nonurban traditional sectors. The Saudi government, thanks to abundance of oil revenues, raises salaries periodically, but there is always an inevitable time lag in which these groups suffer. It is this fact, among others, that leads some state employees to engage in other economic activities on the side, as discussed earlier.

Another problem common to both natives and expatriates is the mounting pressure on services. This has come about as a result of the influx of migrants at an accelerated rate in the post-1973 years. The service sectors could not adjust and expand quickly enough to keep pace with the newcomers or with the rising demands of Saudis themselves, who now have plenty of money to spend. To cite one ironic example, in the summer of 1977 there was a shortage of automobile fuel in most urban areas of Saudi Arabia.[46] Breakdowns of power stations are common because of overloading resulting from a greater consumption of electricity (more air conditioners and other electrical appliances). But probably the most serious problem in this regard is the housing shortage. Despite the frantic pace of construction in the 1970s, it could not keep up with the influx of expatriates. With less supply than the actual demand, rentals skyrocketed in the mid-1970s, adding, of course, to the inflationary spiral discussed above.

The influx of expatriates has mainly been to major urban areas of Saudi Arabia. Along with an older trend of internal rural-urban migration, this influx led to more than doubling of the city population of the kingdom in the last decade, from slightly over one million to about two and a half million.[47] Most Saudi cities are built out because of the natives' preference for single dwellings. The result is a rapid urban sprawl in the desert, which makes motorcars indispensable. All new buildings are made of concrete or prefabricated material à la Western style. Little attention is paid to environmental specificities of an arid desert climate, and none of the long-proven architectural principles or motifs that maximize shade and natural cooling and ventilation are observed. Most of the "modern-style" buildings are energy guzzlers for cooling in the summer and heating in the winter. The worst part of the new urban forms in Saudi Arabia, however, is their social segregationist nature. Certain districts are exclusively set aside for Saudis, others for expatriates.[48] Within each domain there is further, though subtle, segregation by class. As a result of housing shortage and exorbitant rentals, slum areas have sprung up around and inside major urban centers, especially Riyadh and Jeddah. These slums are referred to invariably as *ʿashish* (huts), *moudun al-cartoun* (cardboard cities), or *moudun al-safih* (bidonville or tin cities),[49] reflecting the flimsy materials used by their inhabitants in building these wildcat shelters. They are overcrowded, unsanitary, and lack running water and electricity. Their population is made up of unskilled expatriates (including illegal migrants) as well as recent native Saudi migrants from rural areas and former nomadic Bedouins. These slums have the ominous appearance of a lumpen proletariat siege around pockets of oil-based Saudi opulence. Again, if Iran was a prelude of things to come, such slums represent a social time bomb.

Growth vs. Security: A Saudi Dilemma

The dilemma of the Saudi political elite derives from the hard choices confronting them and the price tag attached to each choice. We can identify several paradoxes in which choices may work at cross-purposes. The one treated below is security vs growth for it is directly related to labor importation. The vast oil and financial resources of Saudi Arabia have placed equally heavy obligations on the ruling elite to modernize the country, create new and viable institutions, build an elaborate infrastructure, raise the standard of living, and diversify the economic base in anticipation of the post-oil era. By the same token, these vast resources with their regional and global geopolitical implications thrust the kingdom into a sudden position of importance and vulnerability at the same time. This has made the ruling elite quite sensitive to questions of national security, and they have called for beefing up the country's defense capabilities in terms of manpower in the armed forces and weapon systems.

But national security also means internal stability. That calls for, among other things, reducing dependence on expatriate labor. At present, as we have seen, Saudi Arabia has become so dependent on expatriates that if they were to leave, according to economic experts, "the whole kingdom would grind to a halt."[50] In brief, the equation of growth and security is quite tenuous. Saudi defense spending rose from $171 million in 1968 to over $13 billion in 1978—more than 770 percent.[51] The per capita defense expenditure is $1,704, compared to Algeria's $25, Egypt's $112, Iraq's $224, and Israel's $887.[52] With a population of less than one fifth of Egypt's, the Saudi defense budget in 1978 was three times bigger than that of Egypt. This no doubt reflects the overconcern of the ruling elite with security questions. And if there is any doubt about the internal component of security, one has only to look at the allocations and beefing up of the Saudi National Guard (sometimes called the White Guard), whose exclusive concern is the protection of the regime of the Al-Saud Royal Family.[53] It grew from less than 10,000 in the 1960s to 41,000 in 1978.[54] Designed to quell any internal disturbances or military coups d'etat, the National Guard is a match for the Saudi regular army (45,000), the air force (12,000), and the navy (1,500). While these regular armed forces are dispersed along the Saudi frontiers, the National Guard has its concentrations and installations near most of the important cities.[55] The guard, which until the early 1970s was armed with lighter arms than the country's regular ground forces, has undergone total modernization. Accordingly, it now has armored vehicles, mechanized infantry battalions, artillery batteries, air-defense weapons (antiaircraft guns), TOW missiles, and other antitank capability.[56]

The concern with internal security must have seemed more than justified in view of repeated coups d'etat, the latest and most spectacular of which, as we saw, was the one involving the seizure of the Grand Mosque housing the Kaʿaba Shrine, by Saudi and non-Saudi dissidents. It was the National Guard that was called upon to counterattack and "liberate" the Holy Place.

Thus the goal of rapid socioeconomic development, in some ways, works at cross-purposes with the goal of internal security and the political stability of the regime. The leadership's solution for this difficult equation has been to increase investments on both fronts. As defense and security-related expenditures skyrocketed in the last decade, so did development expenditures. The first Five-Year Plan (1970–1975) earmarked about $12 billion (SR41.3 billion) for development projects at an annual allocation of $2.5 billion. The second Five-year Plan (1975–1980) was pegged at $149 billion, averaging about $30 billion annually. The third Five-Year Plan (1980–1985), announced in June 1980, would invest $285 billion at an average annual rate of $57 billion.[57] In other words, the annual expenditure on development jumped from $2.5 billion in 1970 to $57 billion in 1980, a 2,200 percent increase in one decade. This huge investment on development in a country with a very modest demographic base has dictated the massive importation of labor on all levels. The influx of such large-scale heterogeneous population into a fragile and basically conservative social structure was bound to create all types of stress and strain, as described earlier. Here I would add simply that "security" is one such strain, as evidenced by the participation of expatriates from other Arab and Muslim countries in the seizure of the Grand Mosque.

The Saudis' financial ability to deal with the apparent contradiction of the goals of security and development by escalating expenditure on both does not insure a "desirable" outcome. Iran under the Shah is a glaring case in point. In that situation there was even less cause for alarm because the number of expatriates was so minuscule.

The Saudi leadership awareness of the potential danger of a huge amount of foreign labor has made it resort to a number of protective measures and policies. These range from prohibiting any form of labor organization, to swiftly and ruthlessly dealing with the slightest labor unrest. Wholesale deportation of expatriates on a few hours' notice is common, as described earlier.

One way of containing the flood of expatriates, or at least neutralizing their existence in the country, is through what may be called "enclave labor camps." Both Saudi Arabia and Kuwait have recently encouraged this new style, for which the South Korean contractors are most notorious. The contractor brings his entire work force with him and then takes it away again upon completing the job. The Koreans have very little, if any, contact with the native population.[58] By the end of 1979, the *Arab Economist* estimated the number of Koreans in Saudi Arabia at about 80,000.[59] These Korean-style labor camps, however, are only suitable for construction programs, of which there were plenty in the first two Five-year Plans. The 1980–85 plan, while still containing a substantial component of infrastructure projects, concentrates on services, social welfare, institution building, and human development. For carrying out the plan's targets, there is no major substitute for Arab manpower.[60]

A variant of the same practice of insulating expatriates from the natives is "enclave development projects." This is another compromise chosen by political leaders and technocrats for the difficult equation of security vs development. Here, the concept is to physically separate new industrial areas on which future growth will be based from existing urban centers. It is hoped that this would minimize any close or prolonged contacts between expatriates and indigenous Saudis. It also reduces the economic cost of supporting migrant labor because standard social services (like education and health) are not easily available for them, which in turn discourages their dependents from joining them. Examples of such industrial enclaves are the multibillion-dollar projects at Yanbu and Jubail. Other capital-rich Arab states have done the same[61]—Ruwais in Abu Dhabi, Jebek Ali in Dubai, Shuaiba in Kuwait, and Um Said in Qatar. The optimistic assumption, of course, is that upon completing these projects indigenous manpower would have been trained and be available to operate and maintain them.

The inherent sociological naiveté in all this is astounding, but this is not the place for elaborating on it. Suffice it to say that the Saudi elite, and the entire system along with it, wants to have its cake and eat it too. This is not confined to the dilemma of security vs growth, but applies to many other aspects of contemporary Saudi society.

One such paradox is equating growth with development and confusing one for the other. Although expanding education is commendable, one wonders if, in this sparsely populated country, there is a need to build the world's largest university campus in Riyadh, where two universities are already functioning (and there are three others elsewhere in the kingdom, at Jeddah, Mecca, and Dhahran). One questions such an effort at billions of dollars cost when the government has failed to motivate enough Saudis to enroll in the several vocational training centers, most of which stand empty and hard pressed for recruits.

The same mistaken sense of priorities and scale applies to the issue of economic diversification: the industrial complex now under construction in Yanbu is the world's largest. It will include refineries and petrochemical industries. The concept of processing oil products, instead of exporting it crude, is no doubt very sound and long overdue. But under present manpower realities, the Saudis have to rely heavily on expatriates for running and maintaining the complex for several years to come. It would have made more sense, given the present Saudi population policy, to plan smaller-scale projects and spread them along the Jubail-Yanbu axis. Or alternatively, if the Saudis want to maintain the projected colossal scale it would be reasonable to consider a new population policy that allows settling expatriates and granting them citizenship after a certain number of years of residence. The fear that such a course may alter the demographic-cultural composition of the country is only an academic one, for this is the case *de facto*. By adding a *de jure* component, expatriates will have a stake in the development process and will internalize a deeper commitment to their "new country." Not only would that reduce the security risk, it would also help thicken the demographic base of an otherwise underpopulated country. It would gradually eliminate the present pecuniary and mercenary mentality that prevails among most expatriates. Instead, the Saudi leadership continues to follow a course replete with the seeds of destabilization: quantitative growth mistaken for development and self-fulfilling distrustful population policy.

Conclusion

Many of the paradoxes of the Saudi society may be attributed to its unique developmental experience: a quasicapitalist mode of development juxtaposed on a semitribal traditional society, with the state playing the major economic role; abundant financial resources; a small population; little of anything else; and presided over by a theocratically-based autocratic monarchy. This hodgepodge has proved an amazing tenacity so far, thanks to the *esprit de corps* and inner solidarity of the large clan of Al-Saud and their minor partners, Al-Sheikh. But again, with Iran in the back of our minds, it may be a house of steel built on quicksand. The Khaldunian cycle of Arab dynasties may be entering its final phase. The same paradoxes exist in other opulent oil sheikdoms on the Gulf. They have most of the same structural forces at work. The difference between them and Saudi Arabia is only in the order of magnitude.

Inter-Arab Stratification

Parameters and Issues

The most salient feature of the new Arab social order is its stratification system. It is uncommon among social scientists to treat a group of "sovereign states" as one societal unit and, hence, deal with a stratification system encompassing them all. I beg to digress from the convention and treat the Arab World with its twenty "sovereign states" as one societal unit, at least with regard to stratification. There are multiple reasons for such treatment.

First, the Arab political regimes, on the normative prescriptive level, consider their states as parts of one nation.[1] No Arab regime in any of the twenty sovereign states has dared formally to go against this proclaimed national self-identification. None, in theory, equates its present legal status of a "sovereign state" with that of a "sovereign *nation*-state." Despite many practices to the contrary, the explicit or implicit assumption is that the present state of affairs, i.e., separation into several sovereign countries, is only "temporary."[2] The prescribed goal, in theory again, is for these separate Arab states to *ultimately* unite in one "nation-state." This is not so much asserted today as it was in the 1950s and 1960s, but no leader or government has gone the other way to negate the prescribed norm either. In brief, the norm in believing in one Arab Nation to which all Arabs belong is still nominally observed—though not actually practiced—by most regimes at present.

Second, the belief in being one Arab Nation is shared by most people in all countries, classes, and subgroupings in the population living in the area extending from Iraq to Morocco. In a recent attitudinal survey conducted in ten Arab countries (Kuwait, Qatar, Yemen, Jordan, Palestine, Lebanon, Egypt, Sudan, Tunisia, and Morocco), about 80 percent of a cross section of the adult population identified themselves as Arabs, belonging to one Arab Nation[3] (see Figure 6.1). Of course, there were intercountry variations, but in no country did the percentage of people holding this belief fall below 60 percent (e.g., Lebanon, Morocco, and

124

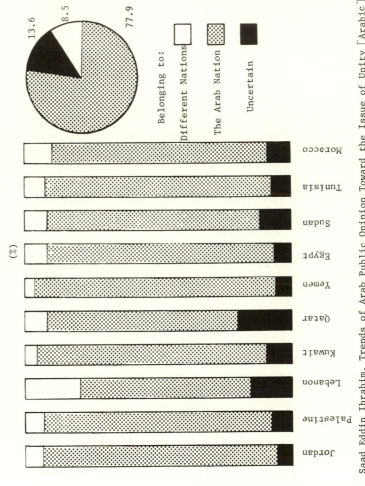

Figure 6.1

Beliefs of National Belonging Among Respondents from Ten Arab Countries in 1978

Source: Saad Eddin Ibrahim, Trends of Arab Public Opinion Toward the Issue of Unity [Arabic] (Beirut: Center for Arab Unity Studies), p.80.

Sudan); it was about 90 percent in others (e.g., Yemen, Kuwait, and Jordan).[4] Underlying this common belief is people's perception of shared language, religion, way of life, and problems. Islam especially was considered crucial in forging the Arab Nation.[5] The majority of those surveyed expressed their aspiration in seeing the Arab countries united politically, although only a minority saw that happening in the short run.[6]

Third, it is because of both governmental and popular belief in being parts of the same nation that several pan-Arab organizations have been created to foster closer cooperation, if not outright integration. The League of Arab States (established in 1945) and some twenty specialized agencies have sprung up over the last three decades in nearly every field of human endeavor.[7] Even countries that have been blessed with oil wealth have found it morally obliging and politically expedient to set up individual and collective funds to extend aid for development in "poor sister states."[8] Many of these efforts fall short of what "ought to be" in the views of ardent Arab nationalists.[9] Nevertheless, they have given this region of the world an appearance of a "unity" of sorts, hardly matched in any other region of the Third World. Such unity has particularly asserted itself in times of regional crisis (e.g., Arab-Israeli wars, the 1956 Suez Crisis, the resignation of Nasser in 1967 and his death in 1970).

Fourth, the increased volume of human movement and interaction across state lines in the last thirty years has added a sociological dimension to both the pan-Arab political norms and institutional arrangements. In the 1950s and the 1960s, the bulk of interstate human movement was for study and tourism. In the 1970s, as discussed in Chapter 3, most of such movement was for work.

The above reasons, and others, justify looking at the Arab World as one cultural area or as one societal unit. In this respect, it stands socioculturally at a midpoint between, say, Western Europe and North America, i.e., more culturally homogeneous than the former but less politically united than the latter. Thus, while no Italian or Frenchman would readily identify himself abroad as simply "European," a Syrian or a Saudi would readily identify himself as simply an Arab. But while a U.S. citizen would hardly identify himself abroad as a "Californian" or "New Yorker," many citizens of the Arab countries would easily identify themselves as "Egyptians," "Yemenis," or "Tunisians." In other words, there are concentric political-cultural-legal identities for most Arabs, all of them equally or near equally salient and readily invokable. The broader political-cultural identity as an "Arab" is readily invoked when the person is outside the Arab World. The particularistic-country-legal identity (Syrian, Egyptian, Saudi, Iraqi, etc.) is mostly invoked within the Arab World itself, or when crossing sovereign state borders.

These concentric identities are quite confusing to non-Arab outsiders, but also problematic in inter-Arab relations. Many a leader, political regime, and political party has acted on the basis of the broadest identity (e.g., Nasser, Qaddafi, and the Baath Party). By the logic of "sovereign state" *(raison d'état)* this would be considered meddling in internal affairs of other "sister states." At times such "meddling" is taken as complaints to the councils of the Arab League or all the way to the United Nations.[10] But for the "meddler" or would-be "meddler," such action is perfectly justified for a concerned or zealot Arab nationalist. Regimes in one country have helped quell political uprisings in another on such grounds.[11] Similarly, they have used sabotage or outright armed intervention against one another, not to mention propaganda wars and boycotts.[12]

The relevance of the above considerations to inter-Arab stratification lurks in the back of the minds of Arab governments and individuals alike. On the governmental level, regimes of Arab countries which bore the brunt of Arab-Israeli wars consider their heavy material and human sacrifice as being made on behalf of the entire Arab Nation. Their argument has taken an explicit and vehement form in the wake of the 1973 October War. They consider the windfall quadrupling of oil revenue a direct result of their "triumphant" war.[13] A "petro-dollar" versus "petro-blood" debate has been raging on both sides of the wealth divide since the mid-1970s.[14] The debate involved journalists, intellectuals and scholarly writers, and heads of states.[15] On the side of petro-wealth, the supportive argument ranges from religious justification (the holy Quran says "God gives whom He wants and denies whom He wants") to economic reasoning (most oil countries are poor in other resources; oil is depletable, and therefore its revenues must be used or invested by these countries to insure their post-oil future).[16] Holders of oil wealth further argue that they are already giving plenty of aid, loans, and grants to their brothers in less fortunate Arab countries—$3 billion to $4 billion a year, more than either superpower is annually dispensing in foreign aid. They would even give or invest more if there were less corruption, more absorbing capacity, or more assurances against the risk of future confiscation and nationalization in poor Arab countries.

On the other side of the wealth divide, the arguments are no less complex or persuasive.[17] Not only are brotherly feelings and responsibilities invoked frequently for a greater share of oil-wealth, but also national, political, and economic reasoning is advanced. Even for the religious argument of oil wealth holders, there is a counterargument (the holy Quran says, "in thy wealth, there is a determined right for he who asks and he who is deprived"). The more sustained arguments, however, are predicated on nationalist, political, and economic grounds. I have already alluded to the nationalist argument concerning the burden incurred by some of the poor Arab states (i.e., Egypt, Syria, and Jordan) on behalf of all Arabs in the conflict with Israel. To that a reminder is frequently added that in the pre-oil era, the "poor" today were the "rich" of yesteryear who then readily helped their "poor sister states" with gratis educational and health missions. Now the tables are turned. The potential political and social instability caused by poverty in the non-oil countries, the argument often implies, would be detrimental to the entire area, including the rich states. Economically, the argument goes, oil-rich sister states are not duly compensating the labor-exporting poor Arab states. The amount of inter-Arab aid ($3 to 4 billion annually) is a miniscule part of what capital-rich Arab states deposit in Western banks (about $40 billion) or lose annually as a result of inflation and currency devaluation in Western countries. As to investment risks in poor Arab countries, the counterargument is that Arab money in the West is no safer—e.g., the freezing of Egyptian assets in the U.S., U.K., and France during the Suez crisis, or those of Iran in the U.S. because of the 1979–80 hostage crisis.[18]

One important aspect of this debate is that no side dismisses the other as irrelevant or as having no right to make its argument. In other words, both sides perceive the issue of Arab wealth distribution as a "legitimate" arena for debate. Significantly, neither side invokes "state sovereignty" as an argument justifying sharing or not sharing oil wealth, although in actuality this is the most decisive factor.[19] Additionally, this kind of debate is reminiscent of any debate that takes place within a single "national society" (e.g., Great Britain in the nineteenth century, or the U.S. more recently). Rarely, if ever, would such a debate take place between societies of neighboring nation-states (e.g., Italians debating Germans over their respective differential wealth). And since the inter-Arab debate rages in media of mass communication, private citizens are not incognizant of the issue. Significant also is the fact that some of the proponents of more equitable distribution of Arab wealth are from oil-rich countries themselves,[20] thus making the debate less polarized in appearance along sovereign state lines.

Individual Arabs are neither unaware nor disinterested in the issues of distribution and inequities on the pan-Arab level. In the recent survey (Figure 6.1), as many as 53 percent of respondents in ten Arab countries believed that poor Arab states hope to gain materially from any drive toward Arab unification.[21] As many as 69 percent said they would stand to gain personally from such unification. A greater percentage, 82 percent, stated that their own children would gain even more (see Figures 6.2 and 6.3). However, the intercountry variations are revealing. When asked whether some countries would benefit and others would lose by any

128

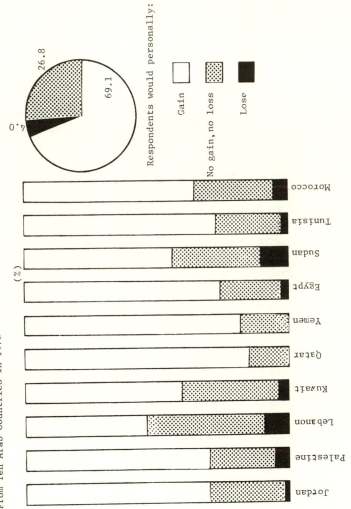

Figure 6.2

Evaluation of Possible Outcomes of Any Arab Unification on the Personal Lot of Respondents From Ten Arab Countries in 1978

Respondents would personally:

Gain

No gain, no loss

Lose

Source: Same as in Figure 6.1, p.202.

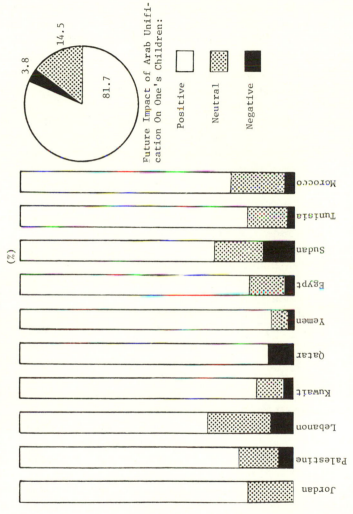

Figure 6.3

Evaluation of Respondents from Ten Arab Countries of Possible Impact of Arab Unification on the Future of Their Children (1978)

Future Impact of Arab Unification On One's Children:

Positive

Neutral

Negative

Source: Same as in Figure 6.1, p.204.

prospective Arab unification, 66 percent of the entire sample indicated a benefit for all and 34 percent saw otherwise. But when the sample is broken down by country (Figure 6.4), as many as 45 percent of the Qataris and 42 percent of the Kuwaitis (respondents from oil-rich countries) saw great harm or some harm to some Arab countries (presumably theirs), and were joined in this respect by a sizable percentage of Lebanese (47 percent) and Sudanese (44 percent) respondents. In contrast, those who saw unification as harming some and benefiting others did not exceed 35 percent in any of the other six Arab countries, e.g., Yemen (32 percent) and Morocco (36 percent). This differential perception of gains and losses from possible integration among Arab states seems to be a function of either the respondent's country's wealth (Kuwait and Qatar) or its ethnic and religious diversity (Sudan and Lebanon). The fact remains, however, that only 5 percent of the Kuwaitis and none of the Qataris perceived Arab political integration as harming them personally (Figure 6.2), as opposed to 11 percent of the Sudanese and 9 percent of the Lebanese. In other words, even though oil-richness has a mildly depressing effect on disposition toward Arab unification, it is by no means the most salient factor in this regard. Ethnic politics seems to be a greater determinant of attitudes toward unification.

More important to this point is the relatively greater attitudinal support for Arab unification on utilitarian grounds among most respondents from non-oil countries (with the exception of Lebanon and Sudan). In other words, individual Arabs feel it is quite legitimate to be entitled to personal gain from any pan-Arab enterprise. This expectation, among other things, explains the resentment many Arab migrants feel at discriminatory practices in oil-rich countries. As Arabs, they feel entitled to certain rights in any Arab country. They may not expect such rights in a non-Arab country. Highly educated Arab migrants are naturally the most articulate and vehement in expressing their bitterness vis-à-vis discriminatory practices in the host countries.[22]

Thus, on the normative, institutional, and individual attitudinal levels, most Arabs and their governments are quite disposed to feeling, and sometimes behaving, as belonging to "one" big society, extending from Iraq to Morocco. But another set of "realities" operates simultaneously to remind them that the "one" sentimental-cultural entity is in fact "several" socioeconomic entities, and the latter are quite sharply stratified in terms of wealth. The accident of birth in one of the several entities overshadows the broader cultural accident of belonging to "one Arab Nation" when it comes to material fortune. The situation is analogous in some respects to an ascribed "caste system." All Indians feel they belong to one Mother India, but Brahma, the Creator, has ordained

Figure 6.4

Assessment of Differential Impact of Possible Arab Unification on Singular
Countries as Expressed by Respondents from Ten Arab Countries in 1978

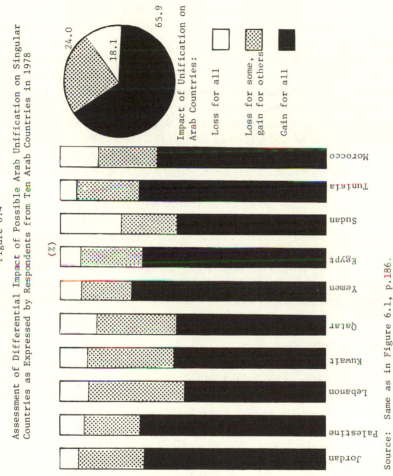

(%)

Impact of Unification on
Arab Countries:

☐ Loss for all

▦ Loss for some,
gain for others

■ Gain for all

Morocco Tunisia Sudan Egypt Yemen Qatar Kuwait Lebanon Palestine Jordan

Source: Same as in Figure 6.1, p.186.

(or condemned) them to a hierarchy of well-ordered castes. The temporary Brahma of the Arabs is oil.

Inter-Arab Stratification By Income

Combined total Arab GNP in 1977 was estimated at $144 billion, as shown in Table 6.1. Given a total population of 142 million, the average GNP per capita for the entire Arab World would be slightly above $1,000 per annum. This is less than one eighth of its counterpart in the U.S. ($8,520), but above the world average ($800), and about twice that of the Third World average ($600).[23] Thus the Arab World as a whole is not poor. But contrary to the recently emerging stereotype, the Arab World is not rich either. It is still closer in income per capita to the Third World than to the First World (the U.S. and Western Europe which together average $6,980 GNP per capita).[24]

Even this overall average of per capita GNP is quite misleading because its distribution among Arab states is quite skewed. The range is so vast, from $110 in Somalia to about $16,000 in Kuwait, that it is mindboggling for people to perceive themselves as belonging to the same "Arab Nation." This amounts to a 1:144 ratio between the lowest and highest per capita GNP. Of course, within each Arab state there are rich and poor, an aspect I shall discuss later. But the interstate variations are so tremendous within the same cultural region that they justify looking at them as constituting a "state-class" system. I have grouped the twenty Arab countries into four strata in Table 6.1; we now look at each stratum in some detail.

The Rich Arab States

At the top of the inter-Arab stratification are five states with a combined population of less than 8 million. Comprised of Kuwait, the United Arab Emirates (U.A.E.), Libya, Qatar, and Saudi Arabia, the five underpopulated countries represent the "rich" of the Arab World, at least in terms of income per capita. As a group, they appropriated nearly $56 billion out of the $142 billion Arab GNP in 1977. In relative terms, the rich accounted for less than 6 percent of the Arab World's population but appropriated 39 percent of its GNP.

The average GNP per capita for the five countries of this stratum was over $7,000 in 1977, which is seven times larger than the average for the Arab World as a whole. Within this group of five, however, there is marked variation as well. At the top of the stratum, Kuwait stood at nearly $16,000 per capita GNP per annum, which is more than twice that of the bottom three (Libya, Qatar, and Saudi Arabia). Thus Kuwait and

TABLE 6.1
Inter-Arab Stratification by Income

Country	GNP ($ Million)	Indigenous Population (000)	Per Capita GNP ($)
Stratum I (The Rich)			
1. Kuwait	7,478	0,472	15,840
2. U.A.E.	2,798	0,200	13,990
3. Libya	17,368	2,600	6,680
4. Qatar	429	0,068	6,310
5. Saudi Arabia	27,784	4,600	6,040
Subtotal	55,857 (38.7%)	7,940 (5.6%)	7,035
Stratum II (The Well-to-do)			
6. Oman	1,474	0,550	2,680
7. Bahrain	482	0,225	2,140
8. Iraq	18,290	11,800	1,550
9. Lebanon	3,480	2,900	1,200
10. Algeria	18,803	16,940	1,110
Subtotal	42,529 (29.5%)	32,415 (22.7%)	1,312
Stratum III (The Struggling Middle)			
11. Syria	7,098	7,800	910
12. Tunisia	5,074	5,900	860
13. Jordan	2,059	2,900	710
14. Morocco	10,120	18,400	550
Subtotal	24,351 (16.9%)	35,000 (24.6%)	696
Stratum IV (The Poor)			
15. Yemen (A)	2,166	5,027	430
16. Yemen (D)	578	1,700	340
17. Egypt	12,998	38,228	320
18. Sudan	4,901	16,900	290
19. Mauritania	405	1,500	270
20. Somalia	407	3,700	110
Subtotal	21,455 (14.9%)	67,165 (47.1%)	319
GRAND TOTAL	144,192 (100.0%)	142,520 (100.0%)	1,010

Source: The World Development Report, Washington, D.C.: The
World Bank, August 1979, pp.126-127.

the U.A.E. may qualify for a subcategorization as the "super rich." Their respective per capita GNP is the highest not only in the Arab lands but also in the world.[25]

Thirty years ago, the five countries of this stratum were among the poorest in the Arab World. Except for Saudi Arabia, none of them was an independent or viable state. The great fortune of all five is exclusively a function of "geological accident": oil. They have little or no other natural resources and are thinly populated, with more than 98 percent of their respective territories barren desert. None of the five has a major river or fresh water lake. Simply put, without the oil revenues, they would be among the world's poorest countries. Many observers, Arabs and non-Arabs, consider the rich group as nonviable states even with oil.[26] Halliday likens them to Botswana, Chad, and Niger. He contends that even with oil, "there are still substantial obstacles and limits to any overall industrialization. The kinds of development seen in Saudi Arabia, Libya (and Oman) are not therefore indicative of general development possibilities as are comparable experiences in Iran or Iraq."[27]

Three of the five rich Arab countries are essentially "city-states": Kuwait, Qatar, and the U.A.E. Over 80 percent of their populations are concentrated in one or two cities. The other two, Saudi Arabia and Libya, are vast desert expanses comprising disparate regions that were only united in one polity during the second quarter of this century.

Countries of the rich stratum are the major labor importers of Arab and other expatriate labor. Among them they account for nearly 90 percent of all imported Arab labor (about 2 million; see Table 3.4). It is this importation of labor from the two lowest strata of Arab countries that gives the inter-Arab stratification system its organic links. Expatriates in three of the five rich countries outnumber the indigenous population, and in the other two, they outnumber the native work force, at least in the modern sectors of the economy. The near total reliance of the rich Arab countries on imported labor and oil revenues for their survival is unique among all four strata. It is also the reason many observers cast serious doubts on their viability as "sovereign states." This harsh assessment, however, may not be totally applicable to Saudi Arabia and Libya. Even the other three could survive in the post-oil era, as do other dynamic city-states like Hong Kong and Singapore.[28]

The Well-to-do Arab States

Below the rich comes the second stratum, which by Arab standards may be described as the "well-to-do" countries. This stratum also comprises five Arab states: Oman, Bahrain, Iraq, Lebanon, and Algeria. Together they have over 32 million in population and account for nearly $43 billion in GNP. In other words, the well-to-do stratum makes up about 30 percent of the total population of the Arab World and appropriates about 30 percent of its combined GNP. The average per capita GNP for the five well-to-do countries combined was $1,312 per annum in 1977, $300 above the Arab average. But within this group we also note some marked variations. Oman and Bahrain, for example, boast twice as high per capita GNP as the bottom two, Lebanon and Algeria.

Unlike the rich, this group has a more diversified economic base. None of them relies exclusively on oil, and they are not major importers of labor. With the exception of Lebanon, members of this stratum are producers and exporters of oil, more so for Iraq and Algeria than for Oman and Bahrain. But all have other natural and human resources. All but Bahrain, for example, have sizable agricultural sectors.

The largest two countries in this group, Algeria and Iraq, have many structural similarities as well as common policy orientations. If it were not for oil they would have been like any standard developing country in the Arab World (e.g., Egypt, Morocco, Syria, and Tunisia) or the Third World (e.g., Turkey, Latin America, and South Asia). In other words, with large populations mainly situated in rural areas, few "oversize" cities, slim industrial sectors, a growing but half-parasitic service sector, mushrooming bureaucracy and scarce capital, they would be hard pressed in their developmental drive. Without oil, Algeria and Iraq would have joined the ranks of Stratum III (The Struggling Middle) at best; and at worst, they would be in Stratum IV (The Poor). Oil revenues have removed one major element of the underdevelopment trap: lack of capital for investment. They also have reduced the need to squeeze the rural sector for the required capital.[29] Both Algeria and Iraq have a quasisocialist orientation with central planning, a leading public sector, and a host of state controls on imports and currency regulation. With Libya (which has a similar policy orientation), they are the only three oil-exporting countries that do not deposit or invest a sizable share of their oil earnings abroad. Iraq (like Libya) does so by limiting its oil production to its actual development allocation needs, and Algeria by investing all that it earns from oil and gas export into internal development. Algeria has on occasion even requested loans from Arab and international agencies to meet its investment targets. The two countries, of all Arab oil producers, have the greatest potential for development and for eminence as major regional powers. They have a sizable population, relatively trained indigenous work force, diversified economic base, a growing industrial sector, and a modern military establishment. Each has its own problems, however. Algeria still has a high rate of unemployment because of its propensity for highly capital-intensive industrial investment, and an economic drain caused by its entanglement with Morocco over the Sahara. Iraq has recurrent internal problems because of its pluralistic makeup (sizable Kurdish and Shia populations).

Lebanon and Bahrain are alike also in several respects. Although oil is a major source of revenue for Bahrain and not for Lebanon, the two countries have a thriving transit trade and banking, communication, and other infrastructural services that cater to the Middle Eastern region as a whole. Significantly, when the Lebanese Civil War broke out in 1975, it was Bahrain, rather than Cairo or Damascus, that picked up the fleeing regional and international businesses. Most outside observers often categorize Bahrain with the other Gulf States because of its geographic location, its tribal ruling elite, and city-state character; but aside from these three characteristics, Bahrain is quite different structurally from the rest of the Gulf States. Modern education, including girls' schools, started in Bahrain as early as the 1920s, at least thirty years ahead of its neighbors. It has a fairly well-trained and sizable indigenous work force. It has known an active trade union movement. It hardly relies on expatriate labor (which did not exceed 20,000 in 1977). Of all the small oil-exporting countries in the Gulf, Bahrain has evolved a relatively more balanced overall development. It has very few of the bottlenecks that overheated growth has created for its rich neighbors.

Oman, the richest among this group of the well-to-do, is the least developed in everything else. Partly because of its semifeudal structure and partly because of a protracted guerrilla struggle that only recently seemed to have ended for the time being,[30] the country did not begin building its infrastructure until well into the 1970s. Oman's reliance on expatriates is modest and often confined to middle- and high-level manpower. In fact, Oman is both an importer and an exporter of labor—the latter usually is unskilled. Among oil exporters in the Gulf area, Oman has the smallest reserves, predicted to run out by the early 1990s.

The Struggling Middle

About one-third down the Arab stratification pyramid, we find a layer of four countries: Syria, Tunisia, Jordan, and Morocco. Their combined population in 1977 was 35 million, and their GNP was slightly over $24 billion. In relative terms, Stratum III accounted for 25 percent of the Arab World's total population and for 17 percent of its GNP.

Again, within this stratum there is marked income per capita variation. Thus, while the average for the group is about $700 per capita GNP, Syria is $200 above and Morocco is $150 below the group average (see Table 6.1). The per capita of Stratum III is slightly above one half that of Stratum II, and about one tenth that of Stratum I (The Rich); but it is more than twice the per capita GNP of Stratum IV.

We have called this group the "struggling middle" because they display most of the characteristics of most standard developing countries. Their middle position in the Arab stratification pyramid is quite precarious. Any one of the four countries in the group can easily slip down into Stratum IV. In fact, until the mid-1960s, this was the case of two of them, Jordan and Morocco, who then had lower GNP per capita than, say, Egypt. Thanks to the rising international price of phosphate (the main export of Morocco), tourism, and remittances of nationals abroad, the two countries moved up the ladder. A protracted conflict or a fluctuation in the price of raw materials can easily set them back, as happened in the case of Egypt.

None of the countries in Stratum III is a major exporter of oil. Agriculture is a major economic activity in all four, and tourism is a main foreign currency earner in at least three of them (Morocco, Tunisia, and Jordan). The same three have a substantial labor force abroad (Moroccans in Europe, Tunisians in Libya and Europe, and Jordanians in oil-rich Arab states), thus earning them additional hard currency.

All four of the Struggling Middle countries have rapidly growing population and urban centers. Their industrial growth, though steady, is quite modest. They all have the potential for faster economic growth if more capital is made available for investment. In other words, countries of this stratum are like those of the stratum above them in terms of growth potential, but without oil. They are also in many ways similar to most of the countries in the stratum below them, except for fewer problems and some temporary comparative economic advantages.

In all four countries there has been political continuity of leadership for at least one decade. But in Syria and Tunisia signs of internal strife have been mounting in the last two years. Similarly, Morocco has increasingly been involved in a protracted conflict with its neighbor Algeria over the Sahara Desert. Much of Jordan's political stability in the short and medium runs hinges on the modalities now entertained by others (e.g., Egypt, Israel, and the U.S.) for settling the Palestinian question. Thus, while factors of potential political instability are present in almost all Arab countries, their relative impact in changing the stratification position of a country would be more immediately felt among members of the Struggling Middle Stratum.

The Poor Arab States

The bottom of the Arab stratification pyramid is broadly based, containing six countries: The two Yemens, Egypt, Sudan, Mauritania, and

Figure 6.5

Inter-Arab Stratification: Inverted Pyramids of Wealth & Population
in Mid-1970s

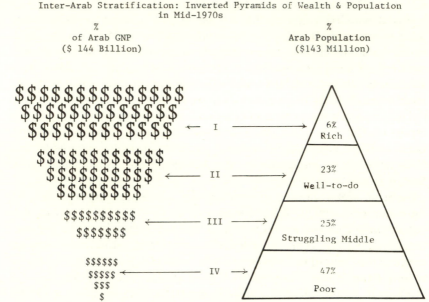

Somalia. Together they have over 47 percent of the Arab World's total population, yet they account for only 15 percent of its GNP. In terms of income they truly represent the poor of the Arab World. The per capita annual average income in 1977 was $319 for the six countries combined. This is less than half of its counterpart in Stratum III, less than one third of Stratum II, and less than one twentieth of Stratum I.

Among this stratum, there are countries that are poorer than others. The per capita GNP in Arab Yemen, for example, is four times that of Somalia across the Red Sea ($430 vs $110; see Table 6.1). If Kuwait represents the super-rich among the Arab states, Somalia has the unfortunate honor of being the poorest of the poor Arab states.

One of the poor in Stratum IV, Egypt, is the most populous Arab state. On most socioeconomic indicators other than income per capita, Egypt would more naturally belong in The Struggling Middle. Egypt has one of the most developed infrastructures and a sizable and well-trained work force. It is also the most industrialized among the Arab states. Its economic base is the most diversified, having a developed agricultural sector, tourism, the Suez Canal, and even enough oil for its needs with a little extra for export. Egypt's perennial population problems and its heavy defense burdens, however, have been among the factors that have stunted its steady development. Before the advent of oil in the region,

Egypt was at the top of the Arab stratification pyramid. Even well into the early 1960s it was still ranking high among the non-oil Arab states in terms of per capita income.[31] It was from the mid-1960s on that its relative standing in this regard began to deteriorate. Its most pressing economic problems at present are finding enough capital to finance its developmental programs, pay its heavy debts, and balance its trading sheet with the outside world. Servicing its external debts alone in the late 1970s used as much as 40 percent of its export earnings.[32]

Unlike Egypt, the other five countries of Stratum IV, the poor of the Arab World, are quite underdeveloped on most socioeconomic indicators. They have little, if anything, in the way of infrastructure. They have high illiteracy rates and no diversified economic base to speak of. Sudan is the only country in this stratum that possesses tremendous growth potential. Several million acres of its land can be cultivable if only enough capital and know-how are made available. Unlike Egypt, whose ability to expand its arable land has nearly reached the upper limit, Sudan's economic future lies in agriculture above all else. Experts contend that should Sudan's agricultural potential be exploited, not only would it thrust the country out of poverty, but it could also make the Arab World "self-sufficient" in food, especially grain.[33]

Stratum IV countries, being the most populous and the poorest, are cast in the economic role of labor exporters to their sister-states in Stratum I. In the mid-1970s they supplied 63 percent of all exported Arab labor to countries of Stratum I. Egypt and the two Yemens alone accounted for more than 60 percent of total inter-Arab migration (see Table 3.4). By the late 1970s, the share of the poor countries in the total export of Arab labor is believed to have increased to more than 70 percent. This Arab economic division of labor linking the countries of Strata I and IV is one of the most salient features of the new Arab social order.

Other Indicators of Inter-Arab Stratification: Incongruencies of the System

Income distribution is a crucial indicator of stratification in any society, but it is by no means the only indicator. Treating the Arab states as if they were actors or subgroups of one single pan-Arab society showed the sharp stratification by income as measured in terms of GNP per capita within each state or subgroup. To complete the picture, we now look at other indicators of stratification. In the case of a single society, sociologists usually identify education, occupation, "life-style," and sometimes "power" as components of "socioeconomic status" (SES) besides income.[34] In other words, the SES of an individual or group in a given society is a combined function of ranking on these dimensions vis-à-vis others.

Western sociologists of the subject have evolved elaborate techniques for the operationalization and measurement of SES. Marxist sociologists, on the other hand, have concentrated on the measurement and analysis of "class" rather than "stratum" in terms of modes and relations of production.[35] Neither approach is particularly appropriate to inter-Arab stratification. Without getting too involved in a technical discussion of this point, suffice it to note a few considerations that render the categories of both approaches inapplicable. The Marxist orientation usually assumes a linear succession of modes and states of production (primitive communism, slavery, feudalism, capitalism, etc.). Ownership of means of production in a given state determines the relationships of production, and therefore, the class structure of society in that stage.[36] In the Arab World we do not encounter a linear succession, but often a co-existence of more than one mode of production (e.g., quasicommunal or tribal, quasifeudalist, quasisocialist). Furthermore, we encounter in almost all Arab countries "state control" of the most important means of production (the oil industry). In brief, some of the Marxist conceptual categories, while clear and consistent in their own theoretical context, postulate a neatness and historical orderliness to which Arab social-historical realities do not conform. By the same token, functionalistic criteria of performance and rationality determine the allocation of material and nonmaterial rewards in society. As such, one's share of these rewards is a function of achievement, i.e., education, training, skill, occupation, etc.[37] It should be clear from the ongoing analysis that such a premise is itself seriously questionable, at least in the present Arab societal context.

Both approaches, nevertheless, contain brilliant insights that I have implicitly utilized in the present analysis. Above all, each has at least one built-in "saving grace." If the evolution of a society does not proceed according to "theory," neo-Marxists would describe it as "distorted development"; thanks to a continous proliferation of conceptual categories, we now encounter not just simply "bourgeoisie" and "proletariat" in a "capitalist society," but several subcategories of each.[38] By the same token, proponents of the functional theory of stratification are constrained by notions of "equilibrium" or consistency among components of SES. If such consistency does not exist, then there would be "status incongruency," a situation assumed to be "abnormal" and generating strain for individuals or societies involved.[39]

In examining other components of inter-Arab stratification, the concept of "status incongruency" is quite useful (as we shall equally find the concept of "distorted development"). In Table 6.2 we compare the Arab states on a number of indicators that roughly correspond to occupation, education, life-style, and power in intrasocietal studies of stratification. In the first column of the table is the ranking of countries of each stratum on the GNP dimension discussed above. It is readily observed that Arab countries that ranked high on per capita GNP do not, in general, rank high on other indicators of SES. Brief comments on each indicator are in order.

Labor Participation

The ratio of participation of each Arab country's population in the work force has been discussed (Chapter 3). Here we are using it as a rough indicator of social potential for gainful employment and productivity. It is obvious that Stratum I on GNP does not fare well at all. The combined ranking of the five rich countries of that stratum in fact puts them at the lower end of native population participation ratio in the work force. Such low participation rate may be a function of more children in school, fewer entries by women into the labor force, or high birth rates that increase the proportion of underage population. No doubt some or all of these factors apply in the case of the rich Arab countries (Stratum I). As a component of country status, however, a low economic participation rate is a "depressant." It means a high rate of "dependency" on native population who are gainfully employed or, worse still, on expatriate work force. If "power" is defined in inverse terms to "dependence" (e.g., power of A over B = the dependence of B on A), then a low participation rate is reflective of high vulnerability in some respects.

In contrast to Stratum I, we note from Table 6.2 that the highest participation rates are among the poor Arab countries. This may be a function of women and children participation (although the ratio is usually computed for population above the 10–15-year-old category). Strata III and II follow respectively on this indicator. In other words, it looks as if the higher the per capita GNP the lower the participation rate, and vice versa. Of course there are some exceptions here and there, but the observation holds in general. I have reiterated the contention that it is precisely this inverse relationship (between GNP and participation rate within and between Arab countries) that has a) triggered the inter-Arab migratory system, and b) shaped the present inter-Arab stratification system with all its incongruencies. In other words, the poor countries (Stratum IV) who are dependent on the flow of money (remittances or outright aid) from the rich, do have a balancing mechanism that makes such dependency a two-way street.

TABLE 6.2
Inter-Arab Stratification: Selected Indicators of Status 1977

Country	1 Per Capita GNP (Rank)	2 Labor Partic-ipation Rate % (Rank)	3 Literacy Rate % (Rank)	4 Death Rate % (Rank)	5 Life Expectancy % (Rank)	6 Armed Forces % (Rank)
Stratum I (The Rich)						
Kuwait	(1)	19.4 (16)	60 (2)	0.5 (1)	69 (1)	10 (17)
U.A.E.	(2)	22.5 (11)	18 (14)	1.9 (7)	49 (9)	26 (12)
Libya	(3)	20.2 (15)	45 (7)	1.4 (5)	55 (6)	29 (11)
Qatar	(4)	18.4 (17)	35 (9)	2.0 (8)	50 (8)	4 (18)
Saudi Arabia	(5)	22.4 (12)	18 (14)	1.8 (6)	48 (10)	62 (7)
Combined Ranking	(1)	(4)	(3)	(3)	(3)	(4)
Stratum II (The Well-to-do)						
Oman	(6)	24.9 (8)	20 (13)	2.0 (8)	49 (9)	13 (16)
Bahrain	(7)	21.4 (13)	50 (6)	1.3 (4)	55 (6)	2 (19)
Iraq	(8)	24.0 (10)	26 (12)	1.3 (4)	55 (6)	188 (3)
Lebanon	(9)	28.0 (3)	88 (1)	0.8 (2)	65 (2)	17 (14)
Algeria	(10)	25.0 (7)	35 (9)	1.3 (4)	56 (5)	76 (5)
Combined Ranking	(2)	(3)	(2)	(2)	(2)	296 (3)

Stratum III (The Struggling Middle)

Syria	(11)	25.1 (6)	53 (5)	1.3 (4)	57 (4)	228 (2)
Tunisia	(12)	26.0 (4)	55 (4)	1.2 (3)	58 (3)	30 (10)
Jordan	(13)	20.4 (14)	59 (3)	1.3 (4)	56 (5)	68 (6)
Morocco	(14)	25.0 (7)	28 (10)	1.3 (4)	55 (6)	85 (4)
Combined Ranking	(3)	(2)	(1)	(1)	(1)	411 (2)

Stratum IV (The Poor)

Arab Yemen	(15)	28.3 (2)	13 (16)	1.9 (7)	47 (11)	40 (9)
Democratic Yemen	(16)	25.9 (5)	27 (11)	1.9 (7)	50 (8)	22 (13)
Egypt	(17)	33.5 (1)	44 (8)	1.3 (4)	54 (7)	345 (1)
Sudan	(18)	24.6 (9)	20 (13)	1.9 (7)	46 (12)	52 (8)
Mauritania	(19)	24.0 (10)	17 (15)	2.2 (9)	46 (12)	15 (15)
Somalia	(20)	25.0 (7)	50 (6)	2.0 (8)	43 (13)	40 (9)
Combined Ranking	(4)	(1)	(1)	(4)	(4)	514 (1)

Source: World Development Report, Washington D.C.: The World Bank, 1979, pp.128-171; The Military Balance 1977-1978, London: Institute of Strategic Studies, 1979, pp.34-42; other scattered Arab and foreign sources.

If I have accentuated the incongruencies of inter-Arab stratification, this should not imply the absence of elements of status consistency in several cases. Although there are glaring negative correlations between the wealth component and other components of country status in the Arab World, such incongruencies are most preponderant at the uppermost and the lowest layers of the stratification system.

In the middle of the system, however, there are more congruencies among most if not all components of status. This is particularly the case with The Struggling Middle. If all dimensions of status (GNP, economic rate of participation, education, living opportunities, and power) are given equal weight, members of this stratum would have the highest overall ranking. Their combined ranking was first on three of the six indicators.

Stratification of Education

Literacy rate has been used as an indicator of the educational component of country status; with better and more reliable data a more refined indicator could be used. But crude as they may be, literacy rates still reflect marked incongruency in the inter-Arab stratification system. With the exception of Kuwait, which ranked second among all twenty Arab countries, other members of the rich stratum did not fare well on this indicator of education. Saudi Arabia and the United Arab Emirates (U.A.E.), for example, were tied in the fourteenth rank in literacy despite their high per capita GNP. The highest on educational ranking was Lebanon (Stratum II), followed by Kuwait (Stratum I), Jordan, Tunisia, and Syria (Stratum III). Even some members of Stratum IV ranked higher than most members of Stratum I. Somalia, the poorest of the poor, ranked sixth, better than four of the richest countries. Egypt, also among the poor, ranked eighth on literacy, higher than three of the richest Arab countries.

All in all, the combined educational ranking of Stratum III (The Struggling Middle) puts it on top, followed by Stratum II (The Well-to-do), Stratum I (The Rich), then Stratum IV (The Poor). In other words, while being rich is no guarantee of educational achievement, poverty does have a depressing effect in this regard. It is worth noting, however, that the richest country, Kuwait, with its second highest rank on education, demonstrates what wealth can do over time with regard to achievement in other areas of human endeavor. By the same token, the poorest Arab country, Somalia, with its relatively high ranking on the educational indicator, demonstrates that much can be achieved despite poverty. Libya, among the rich, and Democratic Yemen, among the poor, seem to be following the Kuwaiti and Somali paths, respectively.

Stratification of Life Opportunity

One measure of well-being is the reduction of human misery. Sickness and premature death are among such universally defined miseries. Wealth loses an essential part of its meaning if it does not reduce human suffering. Therefore, two indicators are selected to correlate with wealth: crude death rate and life expectancy. In columns 4 and 5 of Table 6.2, the twenty Arab countries are ranked on the two indicators. Again, Kuwait is the only country among members of Stratum I in which there is perfect congruency between its wealth and the two indicators of life opportunity. It is the only case so far in which wealth from "wellhead" (oil) has been almost completely translated into human "well-being" for its own citizens. The others may follow suit in life opportunity but Stratum I in wealth, as a whole, ranks third among the four strata of Arab countries. For the time being this is one of the glaring incongruencies of the inter-Arab stratification system.

As in education, the stratum that fares best on life opportunity indicators is not the rich or the well-to-do, but the struggling middle: Syria, Tunisia, Jordan, and Morocco. They are followed in this respect by countries of the well-to-do stratum.

Again, as in education, if wealth is no guarantee of achievement, poverty has a more depressing effect on life opportunities. Members of Stratum IV ranked the lowest as a group, even though Egypt is a noted exception. In other words, there is more congruency between poverty and other indicators of well-being than there is between wealth and these indicators in the Arab World. Of course poverty itself is one of the universally defined human miseries.

Stratification of Military Power

The questions of wealth and security are by necessity interlinked, as seen in our discussion of one of the Saudi dilemmas in Chapter 5. The incongruency between the two is a source of fear for the countries involved, and a source of potential tension in the overall Arab order as well as in the entire regional Middle Eastern system (which includes non-Arab actors, e.g., Iran and Israel, and a presence of the superpowers). The fact that the region has for a number of years been number one in the purchase of arms reflects the high saliency of the interlink between wealth and security.[40]

I have roughly operationalized "military power" by the size of the armed forces of each Arab country. This of course does not take into account the types of weapon systems, quality of training, military doctrines used, or morale of the armed forces in each country. But as in other components of country status, I am opting here for a general simple indicator. The last column of Table 6.2 shows the stratification of Arab countries on military power. Countries of Stratum I in wealth are the weakest in this regard. As a group they display a perfect negative correlation between money power and military power, a cause for serious concern. Their military weakness maximizes their vulnerability and the potential threat to their wealth. Their dependence in this regard is only matched by their dependence on expatriate labor. Both types of vulnerability, of course, derive from the same structural weakness: a small demographic base.

Stratum IV (The Poor), because Egypt is in its midst, ranks highest in this dimension of inter-Arab stratification. It is followed by Stratum III and Stratum II. This means an inverse correlation between money-wealth and military power in the Arab system. The high military ranking of the two lower strata (in terms of GNP) reflects in part the nature of the indicator "power," which is the size of armed forces. These two groups are the most populous, comprising more than 71 percent of total Arab population, in contrast to the two upper strata with less than 30 percent. The differential demographic bases have a direct bearing on the country's ability to raise a sizable army. The fact remains, however, that the rich of the Arab World are vulnerable to the poor in terms of manpower both at work and at war, just as the poor are dependent on the rich for financial aid and remittances from their workers employed by the rich.

Stratum III ranked first on three indicators, second on two, and third on one. In other words, there is no disparate ranking among various indicators for the stratum as a whole. The growth indicators in countries of this group seem to go more hand in hand economically, socially, and militarily; development is relatively more balanced. Given the fact that none of the countries in this stratum (Syria, Tunisia, Jordan, and Morocco) is a major producer or exporter of oil, their ability to slip out of "poverty" is indicative of the prevalence of indigenous dynamic forces of development. This observation suggests neither problem-free development nor the absence of external factors from the developmental equation of the four countries. All of them have a work force abroad and have been recipients of Arab and foreign aid. But the fact that on most indicators of status they have done better than some of their sister-states in Stratum IV, where the same external factors are at play, should be noted. Some of their developmental bottlenecks lie in the social-political arena. Recent strifes in the struggling middle countries have to do either with the slower pace of democratization or with issues of socioeconomic equity. But these two problems, as we shall see later, are common in nearly all Arab countries.

Elements of status congruency are also present in Stratum II. The combined rankings of all five countries in this stratum was second or third on all six indicators. Internal variations within the countries involved are much wider than those of Stratum III, however. But all in all they showed less of the incongruency typical of both Stratum I above and Stratum IV at the bottom. Four of the five countries (Oman, Bahrain, Iraq, and Algeria) are oil producers and exporters. But they seem to have harnessed this comparative advantage for a more diversified and balanced development. All five countries have a leadership legitimacy problem. Three of them (Oman, Iraq, and Lebanon) have in fact already witnessed serious internal strifes. The extended one-party rule in Algeria and the abortion of the democratic experiment in Bahrain threaten these two with some internal unrest. But as we have seen, this is more of a general problem to all Arab countries at present.

The fact that Strata III and II contain less incongruencies and more consistency among various dimensions of country status should have significant implications for the new Arab order. Together the two groups comprise nine countries with a combined population of 67 million, a combined GNP of $67 billion annually, and a combined military force of 707,000. These represent 77 percent of the Arab World's total population, 46 percent of its GNP, and 52 percent of its total armed forces. In other words, on all the vital indicators, the two strata hold the balance of the entire Arab order. They outmatch the rich in terms of GNP and the poor in terms of population and military power. For members of these two strata to keep the Arab order on an even keel assumes, of course, that they are able to concert their policies—a tenuous assumption for any observer to venture in the present state of Arab and Middle Eastern affairs.

The last caveat does not exclude the balancing role that single Arab countries may play in their subregions of the Arab World. Because of the prevalence of more congruencies in Strata II and III, some members of the two strata are potential candidates for being regional powers. Iraq and Algeria from Stratum II and Syria and Morocco from Stratum III are already on their way to playing such roles. The other two candidates, Egypt and Saudi Arabia, are plagued by status inconsistencies, as we have clearly seen. Only if they combine their human and financial resources, a condition that seemed possible for a short period in the 1970s, could the two provide the badly needed "maestro" for the Arab social order. Iraq, Syria, Algeria, and Morocco all have sizable populations, diversified economic bases, developed civilian and military manpower, and more overall status congruency. But their role as effective regional powers requires other necessary conditions. One such condition is for them to settle their own "dyadic" conflicts (Syria vs Iraq and Algeria vs Morocco). The other is to complement their socioeconomic developmental efforts by a credible drive toward more political development as well. The latter at present would simply mean greater participation in the political process by the newly emerging social formations (e.g., the new middle class and the urban working class) as well as some of the older but hitherto deprived groups (e.g., ethnic minorities).

Intra-Arab Stratification

So far in this chapter I have treated the Arab countries as if each is a member of a socioeconomic class or stratum. The emphasis has been on aspects of differentiation among various states or groups of states. Little has been said explicitly about social differentiation within each state. The reader ought not to be left with the impression that there are no poor within rich Arab countries or that there are no rich people within poor countries. Naturally, as there is sharp inter-Arab regional stratification, there is a stratification system, often as sharp, within each Arab country. As there are sources of tension in the pan-Arab stratification system of states, there are as many sources within each country. The two orders of stratification, the inter-Arab and the intra-Arab, are closely linked. The dynamics and ramifications of one affect the other, and vice versa.

Unfortunately, data on income distribution within each Arab country is virtually nonexistent. What is available in a few cases does not go beyond family budget surveys, which only reflect the relative share of consumption by various population percentiles.[41] Despite their severe limitations, and in the absence of anything better, such surveys were used on occasion as rough indicators of income stratification. Instead of reviewing these studies (some of which are by this author) we refer the interested reader to them.[42] We shall only give a brief overview, partly historical and partly impressionistic, of the evolution of social formations within various Arab countries.[43]

From the ninth century to the nineteenth century, the Arab society as a whole and in most of its parts was broadly differentiated into two strata. The upper stratum, made up of a small percentage of the population, comprised a central elite (a Caliphate, a Sultanate, or a Monarchy), its provincial representatives or allies (Wali, Viceroy, Hakem, Bay, Day, etc.), army officers, the religious ulama and judges, the upper echelon of a bureaucracy (diwans and scribes), and big merchants. The lower stratum, the vast majority of the population, was comprised of city craftsmen and rural peasants. Nomadic tribes lived on the margin of this stratification system but often without completely submitting to central authority.[44] During those ten centuries, the upper stratum changed its human makeup (e.g., from Arab Muslim to non-Arab Muslim) and territorial jurisdiction (from central to provincial, to local, to central again, etc.) several times. The rise and fall of dynasties had a cyclical regularity that inspired Ibn Khaldun to come up with his famous theory of history in the fourteenth century.[45] But despite the constant change of the human makeup and jurisdiction, the social-political functions of the upper stratum had remained the same, as had its relationship with the lower stratum.

With the advent of the nineteenth century, that class structure began to change organically as a result of several factors, among them Western penetration in the Arab World and attempts to ward it off by local forces. Here it may be important to note a time lag in the ensuing change of class structures from one part of the Arab World to another. Arab countries of the north, mostly bordering the Mediterranean, experienced the change at least fifty to one hundred years before countries of the Arab south. Therefore, we shall examine each group separately.

The Arab North

The most important change in class structure of the northern Arab countries was the gradual emergence of a "middle class" and an urban "working class." Both remained small in size, together not exceeding 15 percent of the population in any Arab country during the period between the mid-nineteenth and mid-twentieth centuries. The "new middle class" (NMC), as some authors call it,[46] began to play an increasingly significant role socially and politically despite its small size. Its members descended from the old merchants and rural notables. What distinguished members of the NMC from their parents and ancestors was their modern secular education, their occupations, and their outlook. By virtue of their modern education, they were professionals (doctors and businessmen). Some have even tried to be industrialists like their counterparts in the West (e.g., Talaat Harb in Egypt and al-Sharikah Al-Khumasiyya in Syria). In outlook the NMC, again as a result of modern ideas, harbored nationalist and progressive tendencies. They were disenchanted with foreign domination and critical of the native traditional elite (the old upper stratum) for having succumbed to, failed to resist, or allied itself with the foreign colonialists. Equally, they began to entertain amorphous ideas about liberalism, social reform, and democracy. It was this class that formed nationalist and patriotic political parties, led the struggle against Western colonialism, and agitated the social reform throughout the first part of this century in most Arab countries of the northern tier (Egypt, Syria, Lebanon, Iraq, Palestine, Morocco, Tunisia, and Algeria). Using nonviolent, quasiviolent, or armed-struggle methods, and enlisting the support of other classes below them, the NMC managed to get some kind of political independence for their respective countries. In the few years following that independence, civilian elements of the NMC assumed the helm of leadership. But as social and economic problems kept mounting, junior officers of the newly formed Arab armies began to stage coups d'etat in one country after another. At present, ruling elite in Iraq, Syria, Arab Yemen, Somalia, Sudan, Egypt, Libya, Algeria, and Mauritania are the direct results or heirs of such military coups. Some have acted on behalf of ideological parties already in existence (e.g., the Baath in Syria and Iraq); some have tried to establish their own parties after the fact (e.g., Somalia, Egypt, Sudan, and Libya); and some have turned their initial coup d'etat into nearly full-fledged revolutions (e.g., Egypt under Nasser).

Variations among countries of the northern tier notwithstanding, there has been a steady growth in the size and role of the NMC over the last hundred years. Similarly, a new working class (NWC) has formed and grown. Its earlier human elements came from the ranks of urban craftsmen who could no longer compete with mass-produced goods flooding Arab markets on the heels of Western occupation armies. The demographic transition and land tenure system coalesced to drive an increasing number of landless ruralites to Arab cities, thus adding to the NWC in urban areas. The growth of the NWC leaped three times in countries of the northern tier: during the two World Wars and in the 1960s as a result of ambitious industrial programs by eager modernizing elite. At present the NWC ranges between 10 and 20 percent of the population in most countries of the northern tier.

The relationship between the ruling elements of the NMC on one hand and the NWC and peasantry on the other hand has oscillated between alliance, pacification, and repression. In the early stages of power of the military wing of NMC there is usually an alliance and some marked economic gains for the classes below, but hardly any real political participation. At a later stage in some countries (e.g., Egypt, Sudan), the ruling elite shifts alliance to surviving elements of the former upper class and either ignores or begins to repress the working class.

The thing to remember from this overview of northern Arab countries is: a) there has been a steady growth of a new middle class and a new urban working class; b) their growth has been a long historical process; c) the relationship between the two new classes has been tenuous; and d) those who make up the ruling elite represent a small part of the military wing of the new middle class, with little circulation. As long as the ruling elite keeps its enthusiasm for industrial expansion and service institutions there is usually room for social upward mobility for the children of the lower middle, working, and peasant classes, at least economically and technocratically. Thus the society as a whole would be moving toward greater socioeconomic equity, even if political participation continues to be restricted. But as enthusiasm for industrialization wanes or serious development is hampered or set back for any reason, there is usually a hardening of social arteries within the country. Both the incidence of upward mobility and the drive toward greater equity gradually diminsh. I discussed this point with regard to Egypt in Chapter 4, but the same applies to most countries of the northern tier (with the possible exception of Iraq and Algeria).

The Southern Tier

Most of the oil-rich countries are located in the southern half of the Arab World; they are thinly populated and abundantly rich in financial resources. Except for the Holy Places in Hijaz and strictly military or trading outposts, the bulk of the population in the southern-tier countries did not come into contact with the outside world in a sociologically significant way until the middle of this century. None of the social and economic processes that Western penetration triggered in the north a century earlier took place in the southern tier. As a result of this time lag, their social formations remained less differentiated and mostly tribalistic well into this century.

The typical pattern of their sociopolitical evolution revolved around the conquest or domination by one tribe over the others. The ability of a given tribe to do so was mainly a function of its size and/or its daring, and shrewd leadership. In one case this was further achieved through an alliance with a rising revivalist religious movement (the Saudi clan of the ʿAnza Tribe in central Najd). The tribal clan from which leadership emerged in this process of domination over other tribes established itself as a dynasty in the latter part of the nineteenth and through the twentieth centuries.[47] The consolidation of such dynasties was further helped by Western colonial connections, and later by the discovery and exploitation of oil. This pattern holds for the tribal clans of Al-Saud (Saudi Arabia), Al-Sabbah (Kuwait), Al-Nuhian (Abu Dhabi), Al-Khalifa (Qatar), and Al-Thani (Bahrain).

Until the 1940s, the economic base in countries of the southern tier consisted of subsistence agriculture, pastoralism, hunting, fishing, and pearl-diving. Aside from the social prestige that some tribes enjoyed because of military prowess, political influence, or historical lineage, there was not much economic differentiation among or within these tribal formations. Categories of "class" or "strata" would hardly apply in that context at the time.

In the last three decades, however, these subsistence economic bases have been swiftly undermined. Abandonment of fishing, diving, grazing, and subsistence agriculture occurred on a large scale within one generation. Oil replaced most of the above activities as the new economic substructure. Despite the narrow-based work force in the oil industry itself, the financial spillovers enticed an increasing number of the native population to live in rapidly growing urban areas and to engage in trade, the military, and government services.[48]

The transition from one economic stage to another within such a short period of time has not allowed a process of crystallization and maturation of social formations similar to that in countries of the northern tier. Thus, from subsistence economy the natives of oil countries found themselves dealing in billions of dollars and "controlling" an energy source on which a far more complex and industrial world depends.

This sudden transition has led to, among other things, the emergence of what may be called a "society-class" (as distinct from class societies in the Arab north and elsewhere in the world). The small size of native population in these countries, their tribal and historical ties with the ruling tribal clan, and expedient requirements of internal security have all coalesced and inspired a marked measure of spreading the new oil wealth. Direct and indirect policies have enabled most of the natives to be financially well-to-do or outright rich. Land grants, real estate speculation, banking, trading in stocks, currency and gold speculation, imports, and investments abroad have become favorite activities of most natives.[49] From secondary school students to members of the ruling elite, such activities verge on being "national sports." Some pockets of the native population have been left out of this process, namely the nomads and those in some backwater regions (e.g., southwest Saudi Arabia).

But all in all natives of these countries have become a distinct class that enjoys high incomes from salaries, profits, rents, returns on investments abroad, and commissions. Some economists have labeled these countries as "rentier societies."[50] In terms of income alone, the stratification of these rentier societies is more of a diamond shape than a pyramid, as shown in Figure 6.6. The majority are well-to-do, with a small number of rich and super-rich at the top, and a relatively small number of poor at the bottom. This situation may superficially resemble income stratification in the U.S. or the Scandinavian societies. One crucial difference, however, is that in the "rentier" or "society-class," the diamond-shaped stratification is not the result of a long historical process of industrial

Figure 6.6
Income Stratification Among Natives
of Oil-Rich Countries

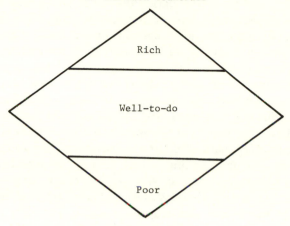

Figure 6.7
Income Stratification Among Natives
and Expatriates in Oil-Rich Countries

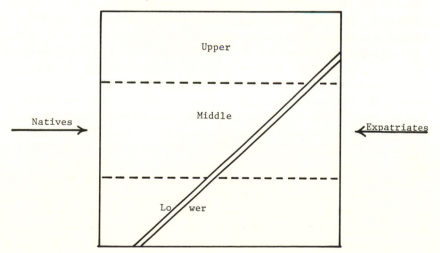

capitalist evolution (roughly 200 years in the U.S. and Western Europe), nor of any indigenous development of productive forces; instead it has formed quickly and artificially during the life of one generation.

There are productive forces in the society-class countries of the southern tier. But these are not indigenous or sociopolitically integrated with the original natives. As we have seen, they are an important expatriate work force with no equal civil or political rights. In terms of income stratification, their percentage at the upper level is quite small (e.g., expatriate professionals and high level manpower), somewhat bigger at the middle, but quite broad and overrepresented at the bottom. As Figure 6.7 shows, the natives as a whole form a "society-class" superimposed and distinctly separate from the expatriates (Arabs and non-Arabs alike). The double dividing line is indicative of an apartheid-like socioeconomic coexistence, i.e., separate and unequal. This situation is understandably replete with resentment and dormant class hostility on the part of the expatriates, especially if they are Arabs. The resentment reaches its maximum among the highly educated expatriates, who often feel better qualified than their native superiors and yet are receiving much less material (e.g., salaries and wages) and non-material (e.g., civil and political rights) rewards.

Growing Arab Interdependence

It is clear by now how closely linked the Arab countries have become as a result of oil and its multitudinal spillovers. Of course cultural, religious, and political links always existed, and long before oil. But oil has turned the stratification of the Arab World nearly upside down. Many of the formerly poverty-stricken countries, with small populations, tribal formations, and undifferentiated social structures, have emerged almost overnight as financial giants by both regional and world standards. Several of the formerly well-to-do countries have become, in relative terms, the poor stratum of the Arab World.[51]

The links among the rich, the well-to-do, the middle, and the poor Arab countries have locked the Arab World into a new social order with a sharp division not only of wealth but also of socioeconomic labor. Figure 6.8 shows the salient features and directions of "inputs" in the new order.

Some Arab nationalists have been lamenting the lack of progress in Arab economic integration recently, a step deemed necessary by them for ultimate political unification. Several have even pointed at regression in this regard over the last decade as indicated by the diminishing percentage of, say, inter-Arab trade, or the contradictory and competitive

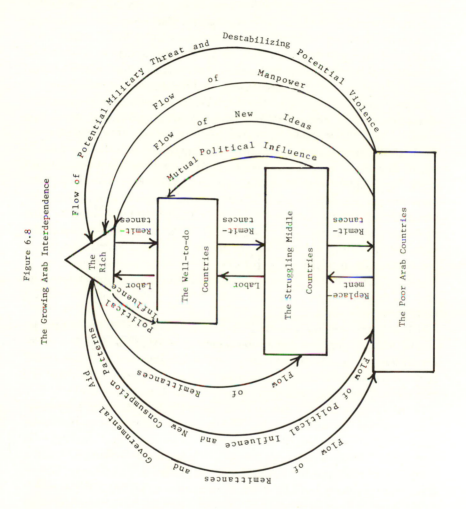

Figure 6.8

The Growing Arab Interdependence

economic policies of Arab states.[52] Using these indicators, the lamentation may be quite warranted. There is a conceptual problem in these assessments, however. They are based on a vision of what Arab socioeconomic integration "ought to be." Such idealized vision was written about extensively in the 1950s and 1960s, and its literature is still flowing in popular books as well as academic textbooks. The vision was even articulated and formalized in numerous inter-Arab treaties and charters of all varieties: bilaterally, multilaterally, under the auspices of the League of Arab States, and outside the league.[53] But little has come out of all this intellectual, ideological, and institutional commotion.

Nevertheless, I suggest that the Arab World is more closely linked socioeconomically at present than at any time in its modern history. The linkage, as I have tried to substantiate throughout this book, is dramatically manifested in the flow of manpower and money (in opposite directions) across Arab state borders at levels and magnitudes never precedented in the last few centuries. With such two-way flow, there are more subtle flows of ideas, attitudes, new consumption patterns, and attempts at intergovernmental political influence; and the flow of fears, potential military threats, upheavals, and socio-political destabilization. These subtle flows are also at levels and magnitudes never precedented in modern Arab history. Observers may debate what is "negative" and what is "positive" in these intense interactions within the new Arab order, but they can deny neither their reality nor their magnitude.

We call this reality a new Arab social order, and we assess its magnitude as a growing Arab interdependence. Both the reality and the magnitude are gradually assuming a self-propelling power of their own to the extent of rendering the whims of political leaders increasingly unrealizable. Two major examples may illustrate this contention.

In the summer of 1977, relations between the Egyptian and Libyan regimes reached an all-time low. The spiral of deterioration had been marked by an escalation of mass media attacks and acts of sabotage on both sides. Threats and counterthreats were heatedly exchanged. Then a border war broke out between the two neighbors in July. Army, naval, and air forces were used by both sides in that brief but intense war.[54] Arab blood was spilled between the two regimes, who only six years earlier had signed a political unity agreement. In fact "unity with Libya" was President Sadat's rallying cry in his showdown with his rivals (the Ali Sabry-Shaarawy Gouma-Sami Sharaf group) in May 1971. Sadat, at the time, accused them of turning their backs on sister Libya and of betraying the cause of Arab unity for which the late President Nasser had worked so hard.[55] But by July 1977 much had changed, and Sadat's new battle cry was to punish the "madman of Libya."

These ups and downs of inter-Arab regime relations are not exactly new. Malcolm Kerr documented them and analyzed their patterns in his *Arab Cold War* for the period of the 1950s and 1960s.[56] What is new, however, is the inability or unwillingness of either Sadat or Qaddafi to tamper seriously with the manpower link between the two countries. Thus while diplomatic relations were severed and angry words and bullets and bombs were exchanged, the bulk of the Egyptian work force in Libya continued to function with business almost as usual. There were minor incidents here and there (or at least accusations to that effect), but by and large the 400,000 Egyptians in Libya were not asked to leave; nor did they want to leave. If anything, the Libyan regime, out of idealism, expediency, or both, made a point of assuring "the Egyptian brothers" in Libya that they were in one part of the "Arab homeland."[57] Sadat did not call on the Egyptians working in Libya to come home either. We suspect that had he done so many would have ignored his call. In brief, despite the passionate hate between the two leaders and their mutual desire to inflict pain on each other, there was still a cool realization that tampering with the manpower question would be of greater self-inflicting pain. For Qaddafi, deporting the Egyptian work force would have meant then (and probably now) courting an economic collapse. For Sadat, asking the 400,000 Egyptians to come home would have created as much of a serious economic problem for his regime, at least in the short run. Egypt would have lost about $500 million in remittances annually, badly needed for its ailing economy. The regime would have been hard pressed to reabsorb that many Egyptians in the national labor force at a time when it had frozen the public sector and when the private sector had opted for capital-intensive (rather than labor-intensive) schemes.

The second example that illustrates the growing Arab interdependence also involves Egypt and its rich sister Arab states. This time the occasion was President Sadat's "Peace Initiative" toward Israel, his subsequent trip to Jerusalem (November 1977), the signing of the Camp David Accords (September 1978), and the Peace Treaty between Egypt and Israel (March 1979). Most of the Arab regimes, including those of the oil-rich states, deplored Sadat's actions and denounced his agreements with Israel as betrayal of the Arab Nation and the Palestinian Cause. Several official Arab meetings, including three summits, were held to deliberate Sadat's moves and to come up with appropriate policy responses.[58] The latter involved a "carrot and stick" approach. The amount of official Arab aid to Egypt was to be raised substantially and to be sustained for five years (totaling $15 billion at $3 billion annually) if Sadat stopped his moves toward Israel.[59] When that did not entice him to come back to the Arab fold, severe penalties were to be imposed: severing diplomatic relations, cutting off all bilateral and multilateral aid (averaging then about

$1.5 billion annually), withdrawing Arab governments' deposits in Egyptian banks, and a ban on trade with Egypt.[60] These and other measures were thought to be severe deterrence to the Egyptian regime. As events unfolded, many of the penalty measures were indeed enforced. While they may in fact have hurt the Sadat regime and isolated him morally and diplomatically in Arab, Islamic, and Third World circles, Egypt under Sadat has so far managed to muddle its way through them. The one thing that could have had a much greater damaging effect on Egypt and the regime would have been a manpower boycott. This may have been contemplated by both sides, but obviously neither one has dared so far to tamper with it. Even Iraq's regime, one of the most vehement in the Arab crusade against Sadat, which sits in a country more endowed with diverse human and natural resources and therefore relatively less dependent on Egyptian imported labor, has steadily increased rather than decreased its importation of Egyptian manpower since Camp David.

In brief, the Arab states are no longer willing to "cut off their noses to spite their faces," as they often did in the 1950s and 1960s. In the 1970s, and probably through the 1980s, such action would involve much more than deforming "a face." It risks deforming the whole "body economic." This does not apply only to the relationship between Egypt and the rich Arab states; it applies as much to that between the latter and the Palestinian work force. Some rulers in the Gulf may toy with the idea of reducing the Palestinian presence in their sheikdoms as a way of reducing the potential of internal unrest, but they must also realize that the socioeconomic (if not also political) risks are much greater.

Gone are the days when one Arab ruler could send home the citizens of another wholesale, or for one to withdraw his citizens wholesale in retaliation. The Saudi regime could do so in the early 1960s as a protest against Egypt's involvement in Yemen; the Nasser regime could afford repatriating its work force in Saudi Arabia by absorbing them in its expanding public sector and ambitious developmental programs. The order of magnitude was then much different than it is at present. Feuding regimes may go all the way to shooting wars before seriously acting on manpower boycotts.

This is the new calculus of Arab interdependence. It may be replete with all kinds of unequal exchange between the poor Arab states and the rich Arab states, i.e., the labor exporters and the labor importers. It may entail distortions in the evolution of Arab socioeconomic structures, generate and spread new but "undesirable" values, attitudes, and behavioral patterns; and it is definitely a far cry from the kind of Arab interdependence idealistically envisioned by the romantics and practitioners of Arab political unification. But it is an interdependence woven by millions and millions of their dependents on both sides of the wealth divide in the Arab World. It is an interdependence that far exceeds in level and magnitude anything the several thousand Arab nationalist intellectuals and practitioners were able to produce between 1945 (the birth date of the Arab League) and 1973, the date of the October War, which accelerated the birth of the new Arab order.

The Challenge

The inter-Arab stratification system with all its incongruencies is replete with overt and covert sources of tension. But these are by no means the only strains in the new Arab order. Other major sources of tension stem from imbalanced socioeconomic growth, and from the increasing dependence of the Arab World on the outside.

Uneven growth is sometimes mistaken for "development," and dependence may be mistaken for "interdependence." Their perpetuation is enhanced by interest groups that most stand to benefit from them. But as often happens in complex societies, countertendencies gather social force from below and clash with such interest groups at the top. This dialectical interplay is now unfolding in the Arab World, as it has in neighboring Iran. The scale, the form, and the chronological script may be different, but the dynamics are basically the same. In this concluding chapter we shall elaborate on these contentions.

Growth vs. Development

The Arab World has achieved impressive growth rates in the 1970s. Starting with population, it grew from 120 million at the beginning of the decade to about 160 million in 1979 (33 percent). The gross domestic product (GDP) rose from $40 billion to $214 billion (435 percent). In the region as a whole, school enrollment on all levels increased from 16.3 to 25.6 million in the first seven years of the decade (57 percent), and the teaching staff from 566,000 to 1,014,000 (79 percent). The number of doctors doubled in seven years (from 31,369 to 62,852); that of dentists more than doubled (from 4,365 to 10,900); that of pharmacists more than tripled (from 9,634 to 31,067); and the number of hospitals nearly tripled (from 2,344 to 6,451).[1]

These and other socioeconomic indicators reflect growth rates that are indeed quite high by Third World standards. They no doubt are having a tangible impact as far as improving living conditions in the Arab World. Nevertheless, the growth has been disproportionate among Arab countries and in many cases within each country. A closer look at the growth indicators of the Arab World reveals a further imbalance among these indicators themselves. Although wealth quadrupled, education (as measured by school enrollment) expanded by less than 80 percent. Other growth indicators only doubled. Such imbalances create gaps and bottlenecks of their own.

Economic growth is the most spectacular. But because most of it is financial (due to oil revenues), the diversification of the economic base of the Arab World has been much slower. The growth of productive forces outside the oil sector has been quite modest, and in some cases has declined. Wheat production, for example, has declined in the Arab World from its 1970 volume of 7.5 million tons to 7 million in 1977, a 6.5 percent decrease. The contribution of the manufacturing sector to total Arab GDP remained at its low level of 10 percent between 1960 and 1977. Cultivable land has equally remained unchanged in size (13.47 million hectares in 1970 and 13.51 million in 1977).[2]

Despite the much-publicized growth of Arab wealth because of the quadrupling of oil prices in the 1970s, the Arab World as a whole registered a GDP about one half of the combined sales of the top 20 U.S. corporations in 1977 ($214 billion vs $403 billion).[3] The average GNP per capita for the Arab World was slightly over $1,000 per annum, about one eighth of its counterpart in the U.S. The "rich Arabs," whose per capita income comes close to that of the U.S. (namely Kuwait, U.A.E., Libya, Qatar, and Saudi Arabia), represent no more than 6 percent of the total population of the Arab World. The poorest Arab countries (Yemen, Egypt, Sudan, Mauritania, and Somalia) represent 50 percent of all Arab population; as a group they had an income per capita of $320 per annum in the late 1970s.

This brief overview of growth indicators of the Arab World in recent decades suggests a number of conclusions. First, there is an inter-Arab stratification system with steep differentiation in financial wealth among the "super-rich," the "struggling middle," and the poor Arab countries, as elaborated in the previous chapter.

Second, the growth indicators of the Arab World in the last two decades have yielded tremendous incongruencies among countries and within each country. As we saw in the preceding chapter, on the pan-Arab level the rich in wealth are poor in almost everything else: manpower, social development, economic diversification, and military capabilities. The middle-level countries and Egypt have, despite their modest wealth and severe economic problems, much more viable manpower, socioeconomic formations, economic diversification, and military capabilities. These incongruencies are giving rise to an Arab order replete with overt and potential sources of tension.

The Many Faces of Dependence

The last decade witnessed a growing Arab dependence on the outside world. The quests for Arab unity, political independence, internal socioeconomic development, and assertion of cultural authenticity have all been set back since the Arab military defeat of 1967. Here I will briefly sketch some aspects of growing Arab dependence in the world capitalist system.

The volume of trade between the Arab region and the outside world has steadily increased in the last two decades. It grew from $12.4 billion in 1960 to $151 billion in 1977, a twelvefold increase. Inter-Arab trade, on the other hand, increased roughly six times, from $1.3 to $7.7 billion. Thus, while the volume among Arab countries was 10.5 percent of their international trade in 1960, that percentage declined to 5.1 percent in 1977.[4]

The composition of trade between the Arabs and the outside world is no less significant. The Arabs export raw material, especially oil, and they import food, arms, and other manufactured goods. This trend has intensified in the last two decades. In 1960, raw materials made up 83 percent of all the exports of the Arab World, with oil accounting for 52 percent of the total. In 1977 the share of raw materials increased to 95 percent, with oil accounting for over 87 percent of total export. In 1960, manufactured goods and food made up 77.4 percent of the Arab World's total imports (55.3 and 19.2 percent, respectively). Nearly two decades later, Arab imports of the same items made up 85 percent of the total (with manufactured goods accounting for 69 percent and food 15.3 percent).[5]

Most of the Arab World's external trade has been with capitalist industrial nations. In 1978, 69 percent of all Arab exports went to the U.S., Western Europe, and Japan, and 74 percent of total imports came from the same countries.[6] This pattern has existed since 1950, with a brief drop in the late 1960s.

Two additional remarks are relevant to the question of trade linkages between the Arabs and Western powers. The percentage of external trade of various Arab countries is quite excessive when compared with that of industrialized countries. Thus, while the value of such trade (both imports and exports) represents no more than 20 percent of the GDP in the U.S., Britain, France, or Japan, it has averaged anywhere between 50 and 225 percent of the GDP of most Arab countries.[7] This indicates that the nature of the Arab World's integration in the international economic system is one of dependency and vulnerability.

The second remark has to do with arms trade. The Middle East has been the world's leading region in arms importation for the last ten years.

In 1977, for example, out of the U.S. total sales of arms ($11.2 billion), the Middle East imported more than 75 percent, valued at $8.4 billion. Likewise, the Soviet Union, the second leading arms exporter, sold 70 percent of its world total to the Middle East and North Africa. This same region appropriated 49 percent of Britain's and 47 percent of France's total arms sales.[8]

The volume, composition, and direction of external trade in the last two decades suggest some conclusions. First, there is a steady decline in intra-Arab trade despite all the rhetoric, pan-Arab pacts, charters, and bilateral and multilateral treaties aimed at forging functional organic unification. Second, the Arab World is still specialized in producing and exporting raw materials in the international division of labor. Third, the Arabs are still heavily dependent on the industrialized nations of the First World for food, manufactured goods, and arms. Fourth, the Arab World is fully integrated in the world capitalist economic system. These conclusions apply not only to the Arab World as a whole but also to most of its countries singularly, including those that have or claim to have centrally planned socialist economies and whose regimes may espouse anti-Western ideologies (Algeria, Libya, Syria, and Iraq). These conclusions likewise apply to both rich and poor Arab countries, despite Western alarm over dependence on Arab oil.

The superpowers' impact on Arab modes of development displays itself not only in terms of trade but also in the transfer of capital, technology, and managerial know-how. The transfer of capital has been a two-way affair. The major powers transfer some capital in the form of loans and grants to some of the poor Arab countries. On the other hand, most of the oil-rich Arab countries transfer capital to the U.S. and Western Europe in the form of bank deposits and the buying of stocks and real estate (estimated at $35 billion in 1978).[9] However, the movement of industrial commodities, technology, and managerial know-how has been a one-way stream from the big powers to various Arab countries. Again, Egypt and Saudi Arabia illustrate the point.

Egypt is a prime example of an Arab country recipient of all such forms of transfer: financial and technical aid, commodities, and managerial know-how. The history of aid to Egypt in the past three decades illustrates the differential impact of linkages with both superpowers on its mode of development. For fifteen years (1958–1973), Egypt was a recipient of uninterrupted Soviet aid. Likewise, Egypt has received American aid on and off during the last three decades, with a ten-year interruption from 1965 to 1974.

Whenever aid from either external source increased, it tended to distort Egyptian socioeconomic development and diminish Egypt's independence in formulating domestic, Arab, and international policies. Thus, Soviet aid to Egypt coincided with the new orientation of Nasser's Egypt from the mid-1950s to 1970. Internationally, the leadership espoused "nonalignment" and anti-colonial (anti-Western) policies. Regionally, it championed the cause of Arab nationalism and anti-Zionism, and attacked conservative and pro-Western regimes. Domestically, Nasser's Egypt adopted quasisocialist policies and central planning, with a strong drive toward industrialization and social equity.

As the aid from Soviet and Arab sources dwindled, U.S. aid to Egypt mushroomed in the 1970s. The bulk of this aid ($6.8 billion) was given in the late 1970s.[10] This was hardly accidental. The sudden increase in American generosity has coincided with a new policy orientation of Sadat's Egypt. Internationally, Egypt has been moving away from the Soviets and also away from nonalignment policies. Regionally, it has counseled moderation in Arab affairs. President Sadat has been moving boldly and singularly toward a peaceful accommodation with Israel. Domestically, he has launched a steady de-Nasserization drive, officially known as the Open Door Policy, which aims at encouraging domestic, regional, and international investors to develop Egypt's economy. Much could be said by way of explaining the Sadat regime's new policy orientation. Accounts range from the very subjective (Sadat's personal motivations and idiosyncrasies) to the objective (structural forces on the national, regional, and global levels). But the fact remains that heavy dependence on U.S. aid is profoundly influencing Egypt's internal development.

The overall impact of present U.S. aid on the growth of the Egyptian economy has been marked. Growth rates for the late 1970s have averaged 7 to 8 percent annually. Urban areas, on balance, have had greater net gains. This may have been intended by both donor and receiver, since major cities were the scene of serious food riots in 1977. And while the urban poor have benefited from American aid more than have rural poor, the most substantial gains have gone to sprouting Egyptian capitalism. Construction firms have flourished as a result of the infusion of large investments in infrastructure projects. Private banks, import-export businesses, and other commercial concerns have equally flourished.[11] Consumer goods, including durable and luxury items, are widely available in urban centers and free zones. These thriving economic activities are not solely a function of U.S. aid. Remittances from Egyptians working abroad (averaging $2 billion a year in the late 1970s) have contributed their share.

Two overall negative consequences must be noted. First, there has been marked inflationary pressure in the Egyptian economy. The inflation rate is estimated to run between 20 and 30 percent annually. As elsewhere, such high inflation hits the poor, the lower middle class, and those on fixed incomes more than other categories of the Egyptian population. The impact of a state subsidy is more than wiped out by price inflation of nonsubsidized items. The second negative effect is the apparent increase in income differentials among various strata. According to a World Bank report, the share of national income received by the lowest 20 percent of the Egyptian population has dropped from 6.6 percent in 1960 to 5.1 percent in the late 1970s. In contrast, the share of the top 5 percent of the population has increased from 17.5 to 22 percent of national income.[12] This widening gap is accompanied by provocative displays of conspicuous consumption on the part of Egypt's upper class, especially the nouveau riche, created by open door policies.

Saudi Arabia's link with the U.S. represents a different modality, but in many ways is similar in outcome to that of Egypt. Here is an Arab country with abundant oil, surplus financial resources, but faced with underpopulation, an undiversified economic base, and underdeveloped modern institutions. The linkage with the U.S. is not one of aid but of exchange—its oil for American goods, technology, management, arms, and military security.

The American presence in Saudi Arabia is probably the longest of any Arab country, dating back to the 1930s. Until the late 1950s, it was largely confined to ARAMCO's oil activities in the Eastern Province. In the last two decades, however, American presence in various forms has spread horizontally and vertically all over the desert kingdom. This has been induced by the vast oil revenues of Saudi Arabia, especially since the 1973 War. The Saudi ruling elite has willfully chosen the American economic mode of development, partly because of the long "special relationship," partly because of fascination, but mostly because of class interest and security imperatives. Due to the absence of many indigenous prerequisites for capitalist development and because of the fragile socioeconomic structure of Saudi Arabia, the ruling elite is facing several dilemmas, elaborated in Chapter 5.

Our emphasis on Egypt and Saudi Arabia and the impact of superpower linkages on their respective modes of development was for obvious reasons. The two countries are the central actors in the Arab regional system—Egypt because of its demographic weight, military strength, and cultural dominance; Saudi Arabia because of its vast oil resources and spiritual status in the Arab-Islamic sphere. Their structural differences epitomize the wide spectrum of Arab diversity and internal contradiction. Yet in recent Arab history, when in tacit alliance or collaboration, the two countries have held the region in relative stability. In periods of discord, the level of stability drops markedly.

Ironically, the two countries at present (early 1980s) are more strongly linked to the U.S. than ever before. Nevertheless, relations between Egypt and Saudi Arabia have soured since Sadat's peace initiatives toward Israel, and regional stability has suffered. Discord between the two central Arab countries, however, is by no means the only cause for regional concern. Their modes of internal development have been heavily impacted by their linkages to the U.S. in recent years. In different ways, both Egypt and Saudi Arabia are becoming increasingly dependent on the United States. Their modes of development display marked distortions and sociopolitical incongruencies, despite steady economic growth. Part of the blame for that is placed by their citizens on the American connection. The resulting social discontent directed against the two regimes naturally spills over to their superpower "partner."

The Crisis of Legitimacy: New Cleavages, New Quests

The impressive socioeconomic growth of the Arab World has been neither evenly distributed nor accompanied by increased political participation. At the end of the 1970s, an observer would be hard pressed to name a single country out of the twenty sovereign Arab states with a viable democracy at work. In the two preceding decades one could argue that revolutionary ideologies, charisma, or customary authority were major sources of a legitimacy of sorts for most Arab countries.

The Arab defeat of 1967 was a shattering experience. Regimes deriving their legitimacy from one or more of the above ideologies were substantially discredited. Nasser's charismatic authority was as much bruised as the Baathist Syrian regime with its proclaimed revolutionary ideology. The monarchical Jordanian regime with its traditional authority was similarly shaken. Even regimes that were not directly humiliated on the battlefield hardly escaped the process of eroding legitimacy, for most of these regimes were similar in structure and orientation, and were politically allied to one of the three principal losers of the June War. The regimes in Iraq, Yemen, and Algeria had strong affinities to those of Egypt and Syria. The Arab monarchies in Saudi Arabia, the Gulf, Libya, and Morocco were linked ideologically to Jordan.

Of course it would be an oversimplification to attribute all problems of legitimacy to the 1967 Arab defeat. But it is fair to assert that the traumatic event dramatically exposed the hitherto unfulfilled tasks of modern nation-building. Major sectors of Arab society had foregone the quest for political participation, itself an important component of development, in the belief that some of these ruling regimes were effectively fulfilling other major tasks of nation-building: eradicating leftovers of colonialism, seeking Arab unification, asserting economic-political independence in the world system, industrializing, establishing social equity, building strong national armies to liberate Palestine and defend the Arab homeland. Substantial progress in all these was in fact being accomplished, especially in Nasser's Egypt, but the defeat of 1967 revealed that such progress fell far short of what Arab masses had been led to believe at the time.

Nasser's Egypt was the bulwark of a revolutionary Arab order that was severely undermined by the defeat. Nasser's charisma and the ideology he espoused had been the major legitimizing force for his regime and others like it in the Arab World. Nasser's design all but collapsed in 1967. The building blocks were all there, albeit scattered in several directions. The Arab masses clung to a dream that the man would be able to put the blocks together again. Nasser tried relentlessly for three years. But he departed from the Arab landscape with the task undone. The true believers still hoped Nasser's spirit would triumph at the end. Their dream had a momentary lease on life in October 1973: The creditable performance of Arab armies and diplomacy was matched by effective use of the "oil weapon" in the fourth Arab-Israeli war.

Ironically, it was that last element, the oil weapon, that hastened the end of the revolutionary Arab order erected by Nasser's Egypt. The quadrupling of oil prices, meant at the time as a pressure tactic on the West to expedite an honorable resolution of the Arab-Israeli conflict, triggered instead the birth of a new Arab order. The march of sociopolitical events during the remainder of the 1970s compounded a crisis of legitimacy in this emerging order.

Petrodollars spoke louder than revolutionary ideologies. Pragmatism gained precedence over idealism. Arab dreams of national unification gave way to vigorous country-state building by ruling elite. Assertion of economic-political independence in the world system, while ritually observed, has in fact been eclipsed in favor of integration in the international capitalist system. Socialist measures and central planning to ensure equitable development have been brushed aside in favor of growth policies and market mechanisms, with an implicit assumption that the "trickle-down effect" would take care of the masses below.

Significant as these changes may be, they are not altogether new on the Arab scene. Similar institutions and policy orientations had once existed, either during the colonial era or during the short liberal experiments immediately following political independence of several Arab states (e.g., Egypt and Iraq between the 1920s and the 1950s; Syria and Sudan in the

1940s and 1950s; Jordan, Morocco, Saudi Arabia, and the Gulf States throughout). Their earlier introduction coincided with either liberal-type democracy or primordial traditional authority. When such policies were challenged in the 1950s and 1960s and were replaced by radically different ones in central Arab countries, the political authority officiating over them derived its legitimacy from revolutionary ideologies. Nasser's charisma at the center stage of Arab politics at the time sealed the approval of Arab masses for socialist transformation, liberation, Arab unity, and nonalignment.

The swing back to prerevolutionary policies—domestically, regionally, and internationally—was gradual and quite subtle in Egypt, Syria, Iraq, the Sudan, Somalia, and Algeria. Echoes of revolutionary rhetoric have even been retained in some of these countries. In Egypt and Sudan, slogans such as "socialism" and "struggle of working classes" have finally been dropped from official use in favor of "social peace," "drive toward prosperity," and "open door policy." The realignment with the West is now veiled under slogans of "friendship" and "full partnership." Conservative monarchies were not only pleased with their change of course, but were also spared the effort of verbal gymnastics because they have continued the business of ruling as usual.

The swing of most Arab regimes back to prerevolutionary politics has not been accompanied by a solid base of legitimacy. The present regimes derive their legitimacy neither from a liberal-type democracy similar to that of post-independence years nor from the charisma and revolutionary ideology characteristic of Nasserism. Periodically there are engineered plebiscites, referenda, and elections. Very few Arabs take them seriously, for the outcome invariably hovers around 99 percent in favor of regime policies. But aside from such transparent political machinations, the longevity of present Arab regimes has relied on one or more of the following: legitimacy by default, oppression, effective problem-solving, dream selling, and crisis politics.

Legitimacy by default is predicated on fear arousal regarding alternative contenders for power. The ruling elite's near-monopoly of the mass media in most Arab countries has made this possible for some time. The typical case of legitimacy by default would suggest that alternatives to the present regime are either "bloody communist rule" directed from Moscow (like Afghanistan and South Yemen), "fanatic Islamic dictatorship" (like Khomeini's Iran), or chaos (like the civil strife in Lebanon). No other viable alternatives are acknowledged or allowed to evolve. Built into legitimacy by default is also a sustained smearing of previous regimes by exaggerating their faults. In brief, it is suggested to the citizenry in one thousand and one ways that they are much better off with the present regime; things could have never been better; to consider any alternative amounts to courting a calamity.

Oppression by any name has the same ugly content. It is resorted to in varying degrees by most regimes in the Arab World to contain, frighten, or wipe out both collective opposition and individual dissidents. Even among members of the same ruling elite, ruthless physical liquidation has been used to settle policy and personal differences. The regimes of Iraq, Syria, and Libya have been only the most notorious in this regard. Other regimes in the area have developed more sophisticated and subtle means of oppression. Periodic announcements of plots to overthrow the regime often serve as a pretext for public trials, heavy sentences, and an overkill strategy toward would-be conspirators and "enemies of the people." Sustained oppression keeps organized opposition off-balance, intimidates potential dissidents, and buys time for the ruling elite.

Effective problem-solving is probably closest to what may pass in Western social science as a reasonable ground for legitimacy. Some of the ruling elite in the Arab World have used their country's wealth and/or efficient bureaucracies to deal with chronic problems of illiteracy, housing, unemployment, and infrastructure. Success, no matter how modest, is heralded out of all proportion, and is invariably used as a pretext for selling more dreams of national grandeur and prosperity. A variant of such dreams may even be the promise of "true democracy" at some time in the foreseeable future.

Politics of crisis is neither unique nor new in the Arab World. Grounds for real crises, domestic and regional, are abundant. Border incidents, however, substantially increased in the 1970s. In the height of the Arab nationalist drive for unification, border issues were largely contained. The tacit assumption was that all borders among Arab states were after all a mere colonial artifact, and therefore temporary and bound to be done away with. With the waning of an active drive toward unification, border issues have become magnified and repeatedly pushed to a crisis level. Ruling elite with diminishing legitimacy have used them as a pretext for political mobilization in support of their regimes. Morocco-Algeria; Libya with Tunisia, Egypt, Sudan, and Chad; Sudan-Ethiopia; Somalia-Ethiopia; Syria with Jordan, Iraq, and Lebanon; Iraq-Iran; and the People's Democratic Yemen with Arab Yemen, Saudi Arabia, and Oman are all cases in point. To that, of course, must be added the real and ever present Arab-Israeli conflict, which could be heated up to a crisis situation at any time by ruling elite of countries bordering the Jewish state.

The above legitimacy substitutes have carried most Arab regimes through the 1970s. It is indeed striking that with the exception of three marginal Arab states (Mauritania and the two Yemens), all other Arab states have been under the control of their present regimes for an entire decade or more: Bourgiba in Tunisia, Gaddafi in Libya, Sadat in Egypt, Numairy in Sudan, Siadberry in Somalia, Asad in Syria, and Saddam Hussain in Iraq. In Algeria, Kuwait, and Saudi Arabia the change of rulers was caused by death and followed smoothly within the framework of the existing regime. Other Arab monarchies have remained intact through the 1970s. This is all the more striking because the Arab region has not been known for the stability of its ruling elite. The 1970s, in this regard, are in sharp contrast with the previous two decades (Syria alone used to have a coup d'etat every year and a half on the average).

The legitimacy substitutes of the 1970s, however, appear to be quickly losing their effectiveness. Structural and psychological changes within most Arab countries are converging with regional and international forces in discrediting present ruling elites.

Of central importance is the fact that some of the major historical quests of all Arabs have remained unfulfilled—mainly Arab unification, liberation of Palestine, and consolidating national independence. The average Arab feels that whatever progress had been achieved regarding these objectives in earlier decades has been eroded during the last ten years at the hands of present ruling elite. One Arab regime has already signed a peace treaty with Israel; others are flirting with the idea. Not only has the active drive toward unification nearly ceased, but Arab fragmentation and disunity is on the increase. Not only has the march of nonalignment nearly stopped, but even worse is the inviting of foreign influence and the granting of military facilities and bases for troops of both superpowers. The abject failure of Arab regimes to effectively address major historical concerns of the Arab masses has diminished their legitimacy, which was weak to begin with.

Secondly, impressive growth indicators in the Arab World may not add up to real development. Nevertheless, such growth has effected several structural changes and triggered immense social forces, which ruling elite have neither experience nor know-how to deal with.

In 1980 the number enrolled in schools of the Arab World was over 30 million students, about 20 percent of the total Arab population. Of these there were roughly 1.5 million university students. This fact alone means a growing constituency of highly educated Arabs. The continued absence of democratic participation makes such a constituency increasingly alienated from the ruling elite. Signs of its discontent abound; and its desertion is rapidly growing. Millions of college-educated Arabs constitute what Manfred Halpern called the new middle class.[13] Country data and data for the Arab World as a whole show the NMC to be the fastest growing class in the region in both relative and absolute terms.

Of equal importance, though growing only in absolute numbers, is the industrial working class (IWC). Of an estimated 30 million Arabs in the labor force, 25 percent, or over 7 million, are industrial workers. Along with another 8 million service workers, they are mainly concentrated in urban centers. Most of them are recent migrants from rural areas. The transformation of their sociopolitical consciousness may be slow but it is steady. While bread and butter issues are usually their major concern, these millions of workers, along with others who are underemployed, comprise a potentially manipulable urban mass that the alienated NMC could ignite in political protest. The food riots in Egypt (January 1977) and widespread demonstrations in Tunisia (1978 and 1980) were led by an alliance of students and workers. In other words, questions of equity for the working class and political participation for the middle class show signs of converging into a single protest movement challenging the legitimacy of Arab ruling elite.

At the same time, other structural factors are undermining political legitimacy. Transformation of ethnic consciousness is one such factor. So long as the Arab World was gripped in an anticolonial battle to throw off overt foreign domination, the whole region responded to broad cultural-historical "unifiers" against regional outsiders. Nasser skillfully invoked and mobilized these unifiers. But with his departure, the coming of windfall oil money, and the death of authentic visions capable of galvanizing the masses, there has been a loss of direction. Parochialism and small traditions, i.e., societal "dividers" that had always existed but remained temporarily dormant, have again been triggered. Ethnic groups in the Arab World are launching a quest for self-assertion within their respective countries. The civil war in Lebanon, persisting since 1975, is only one dramatic case in point. Similar flare-ups have been on and off in Iraq (the Kurds and Shiʿa), the Sudan (southern and western provinces), the Gulf States and Saudi Arabia (the Shiʿa), Syria (Sunnis vs Alawites), Egypt (the Copts), and Algeria and Morocco (the Berbers). Invariably such a challenge to ruling elite is more complex than the mere question of ethnicity. It often represents an intersection of a multitude of factors: class or relative socioeconomic deprivation in the midst of general economic growth, absence of political participation, ethnic repression, and regional and international manipulation.

All in all, the new Arab social order, of which oil was a prime mover, has generated new tensions, revived old but hitherto dormant ones, and exposed the ineptness of the ruling elite in dealing with both. Furthermore, the great historical aspirations of the Arabs (unification, liberation of Palestine, and real independence) have remained unfulfilled. Emerging concerns of new classes and groups for political participation and social equity are equally unfulfilled. In brief there is no solid *raison d'être* for continued legitimacy of most Arab ruling elite.

To make things worse, these elite are now in the grip of an intermural conflict. Their respective state-controlled propaganda machines are constantly discrediting one another. The foreign links, corruption, repressive measures, and failures of each are dramatically exposed by the mass media of rivals. Opposition groups of one region are given shelter, money, arms, and a media platform by other regimes. A striking case in point is the Baathist Syrian regime's support of Iraqi Muslim organizations opposing the Baathist ruling elite of Iraq. The Jordanian and Iraqi regimes, in turn, are supporting the Syrian Muslim Brotherhood against the Syrian ruling elite. The irony speaks for itself.

Among Arab masses, cynicism, apathy, and social discontent have become rampant. The popular discontent take various forms: periodic riots and demonstrations, civil strife, and the mushrooming of opposition groups abroad. But the most organized of these forms in the last few years is Islamic militant groups. When stripped down to the bare bones, the bulk of Islamic militants are from lower-middle and middle class backgrounds, well-educated, high achievers, and intensely nationalistic. Their quests are for a greater share in power and wealth, for independence, and for cultural authenticity. Revolutionary Islam of the present generation of the Arab lower-middle class is the functional equivalent of Arab nationalism a generation ago, and of anticolonial patriotism two generations earlier. The choice of Islam as a banner for these quests is not accidental. It is a cultural-political shield against accusations of being "communists" or importers of "foreign ideologies," charges that autocratic rulers in the area have often used to suppress protest movements.

Islamic militancy gives the disaffected a cultural legitimacy over and against Arab regimes of various political colors, from the supposedly Islamic fundamentalist Saudi elite, to the secular socialist Baathists in Syria and Iraq, to the supposedly middle-of-the-road regimes in Egypt, Sudan, and Tunisia. Whichever superpower happens to be linked with any of these regimes receives its proportionate share of the Islamic militants' wrath, whether it is the U.S. or the Soviet Union.

The sociological irony in all this is that the economic growth of the Arab World has made possible expansion of the ranks of the lower-middle class and the lumpen urban proletariat. But this growth has not been accompanied by marked social equity, political democratization, or assertion of cultural authenticity. These very classes are, therefore, increasingly disposed to bring the present Arab social order down.

Notes

Chapter 1

1. For an elaboration of these great waves of social change see S. Ibrahim and N. Hopkins (eds.), *Arab Society in Transition* (Cairo: American University in Cairo Press, 1977), pp. 179–182, 299–322, 409–417, 515–587. Also Frantz Fanon, *A Dying Colonialism* (New York: Monthly Review Press, 1965); Michael Hudson, *Arab Politics: The Search for Legitimacy* (New Haven: Yale University Press, 1977), pp. 107–162.

2. Some social scientists have noted a corresponding emergence of new regional and political orders in the area. See Jamil Matter and Ali Eddin Hillal, *The Arab Regional System: A Study of Arab Political Relations* [Arabic] (Beirut: Centre for Arabic Studies, 1979); John Waterbury and Ragei El Mallakh, *The Middle East in the Coming Decades: From Wellhead to Well-being?* (New York: McGraw Hill, 1978); Michael Hudson, *Arab Politics, op. cit.*, pp. 389–404.

Chapter 2

1. On the concept of "structural change" see Lincoln Gordon, *The Growth Policies and the International Order* (New York: McGraw Hill, 1979), pp. 7–11; Fred Hirsch, *Social Limits to Growth* (Cambridge: Harvard University Press, 1976).

2. This account of the mechanized Bedouin is based primarily on the author's field work on the Saudi nomads in 1976 and 1977. Some of the findings of this field work were reported in S. E. Ibrahim and D. P. Cole, *Saudi Arabian Bedouin* (Cairo: AUC's *Cairo Papers in Social Science* Vol. One, Monograph Five, April 1978). See also D. Cole, *Nomads of the Nomads* (Chicago: Aldine, 1975).

3. D. Cole, "Bedouins of the Oil Fields," in *Natural History* magazine (November 1973).

4. Additional enticements include land grants and loans to build permanent housing, better and periodic veterinary services for their herds. But such incentives are by no means universal all over the kingdom. They have been tried on a limited scale in the Haradh Project in the southwestern part of the kingdom.

5. The Saudi National Guard is a full-fledged military organization, equipped with artillery and armored tanks, as well as light arms. It is distinct from and believed to be a counterweight of the regular Saudi armed forces. The size of the

National Guard was estimated at 35,000 and the army at 45,000 in 1978. See the *Military Balance 1977/78* (London: Inst. for Strategic Studies); J. T. Cummings et al., "Military Expenditure and Manpower Requirements in the Arabian Peninsula," *Arab Studies Quarterly* Vol. 2, No. 1 (1980), pp. 38–49.

6. This section is based on in-depth interviews and field observations conducted by the author during 1977 and 1978.

7. All proper names in this account are fictitious.

8. For an empathetic view of the new Saudi entrepreneur see Marwan Ghandour, "The Leader-Entrepreneur in the Private Sector," in the proceedings of a conference on Leadership and Development in the Arab World sponsored by the Faculty of Arts, American University of Beirut, (10–14 Dec. 1979).

9. We owe the coining of this term to a discussion with Professor Charles Issawi of Princeton University.

10. M. Ghandour, "The Leader-Entrepreneur," *op. cit.*, p. 10.

11. This account is based on the author's field observations in Saudi Arabia in 1977 and 1978.

12. These include the Arab Economic Unity Agreement (1957) and the Arab Common Market Agreement (1964), both of which call for freedom of capital and labor movements across Arab boundaries.

13. All proper names are fictitious.

14. This account is based on the author's field observations in the course of his research on income distribution and social mobility, the findings of which are reported in a forthcoming volume: see Robert Tignor and Gouda Abdel-Khalek (eds.), *Income Distribution in Egypt*.

15. For more details on this relationship see Ibrahm ʿAmer, *The Land and Peasant* [Arabic] (Cairo: 1964); Ahmed Ezzat ʿAbdul-Karim et al., *Land and Peasant in Egypt Through the Ages* [Arabic] (Cairo: The Egyptian Historical Society, 1974); Muhammed Shafique Ghourbal, *The Formation of Egypt* [Arabic] (Cairo: Al-Nahdha al-Misriyya Book Co., 1957); Nazih N. M. Ayubi, *Bureaucracy and Politics in Contemporary Egypt* (London: Ithaca Press, 1980), pp. 77–156; and Talcott Parsons, *Societies: An Evolutionary and Comparative Perspective* (Englewood Cliffs, N.J.: Prentice-Hall, 1966).

16. Because of inter-Arab strains following the Camp David Accords, air travel between Egypt and most rejectionist Arab states (Iraq, Syria, Libya, and Algeria) was disrupted. Egyptians going to those countries had to detour via Lebanon, Jordan, or Greece. Some ended up staying as transients, especially in Jordan and Lebanon.

17. For more details on this pioneer movement see Lois Beck and Nikki Keddie (eds.), *Women in the Muslim World* (Cambridge: Harvard University Press, 1979), especially the selections by Afaf Lutfi al-Sayyid Marsot, "The Revolutionary Gentlewomen in Egypt," and Thomas Philips, "Feminism and Nationalist Politics in Egypt."

18. The first woman cabinet member was appointed in 1960, but the first woman deputy was elected four years earlier (1956).

19. Proper names are fictitious. The account of this role-model is based on the author's field research on Islamic Revivalist Movements (1977–1979), which was

sponsored by Egypt's National Centre for Sociological and Criminological Research.

20. Unlike the American college system, students are assigned to their majors—including professional schools such as medicine, law, engineering, and business—in their first (freshman) year. Their assignment depends strictly on their grades rather than on their own wishes. Of course, a student with very high grades can choose any major requiring his grade level or less. This system was instituted in the early days of the Revolution to ensure universal justice in college admissions, whereas previously they had depended in part on connections (*wasta*).

21. For a discussion on this issue of the reappearance of the veil in Egypt, see John A. Williams, "A Return to the Veil in Egypt," *Middle East Review* Vol. XI, No. 3 (Spring 1978).

22. Here the situation may be analogous to that described by Frantz Fanon of the Algerian women to whom veiling was an integral part of their assertion of national and cultural identity. When they were encouraged by the colonialist French to unveil, Algerian women clung to the veil as a symbol of resistance. However, when the national struggle required that they unveil to infiltrate French quarters and plant explosives, they readily unveiled. See Frantz Fanon, *A Dying Colonialism* (New York: Monthly Review Press, 1965), pp. 35–67.

23. Note for example the mass hysteria among Muslims and Copts alike over the appearance of the Virgin Mary as a pure light above a small Coptic church in the Cairo suburb of Zeitoun, just a few months after the 1967 defeat. The Arab Socialist Union and Egypt's major newspaper *Al-Ahram* jumped in and proceeded to drum up a religious frenzy among the population.

24. When President Nasser, who was an avowed secularist, said in a major speech after the defeat of 1967 "that religion should play a more important role in the society," the broken hero was greeted by an exceptionally enthusiastic roar of applause. See Nazih Ayubi, "The Political Revival of Islam: The Case of Egypt," *memo.*, 1980, p. 17. President Sadat, in his turn, upon taking power, declared that he was committed to building a society based on Science and Faith (*al-cIlm w al-Iman*). He made a point of being photographed by the media every Friday saying his prayers.

25. For details on this group see Saad E. Ibrahim, "Anatomy of Egypt's Militant Islamic Groups," *International Journal of Middle East Studies* (November 1980), pp. 423–453.

26. For details see Note 25 above.

27. For factual details of these events see *Al-Ahram*, 15–19 July 1977.

28. For details about this group in terms of ideology, organization, leadership, and strategy see Saad E. Ibrahim, "Anatomy of Egypt's Militant Groups," *op. cit.*

29. The 1978 student elections at Alexandria University illustrate this point. "Candidates of Islamic associations won on the various faculties as follows: 60 out of 60 in Medical School; 60 out of 60 in Engineering; 47 out of 48 in Agriculture; 42 out of 48 in Pharmacy; 43 out of 60 in the College of Science, and 44 out of 48 in Law School." See Ali Dessouki, "The Resurgence of Islamic Movements in Egypt," *memo.*, 1979, p. 4.

30. See for example: Bernard Lewis, "The Return of Islam," *Commentary* (January 1976), pp. 34–49; John Williams, "A Return to the Veil in Egypt," *op. cit.*; R. S. Humphreys, "Islam and Political Values in Saudi Arabia, Egypt and Syria," *Middle East Journal* Vol. 33, No. 1 (Winter 1979); Israel Altman, "Islamic Movements in Egypt," *The Jerusalem Quarterly* Vol. 3, No. 10 (Winter 1979); Ali Dessouki, "The Resurgence of Islamic Movements," *op. cit.*; Nazih Ayubi, "The Political Revival of Islam," *op. cit.*; Hrair Dekmejian, "The Anatomy of Islamic Revival and the Search for Islamic Alternatives," *Middle East Journal* Vol. 34, No. 1 (Winter 1980), pp. 1–12.

31. Proper names are fictitious. The account of this role-model is based on the author's research on Islamic revivalist movements in Egypt.

32. For more militants' ideology see Saad E. Ibrahim, "Anatomy of Egypt's Militant," *op. cit.*

33. The reference here is to the fighting between King Hussein's armed forces and the Palestinian Resistance in September 1970, known usually as Black September.

34. The reference is to the assassination of Jordan's Prime Minister in the Cairo Sheraton on 28 November 1971. The assassins were two young Palestinians, said to be members of the clandestine Black September Organization. The Prime Minister, Wasfi al-Tal, was assassinated for his role in massacring Palestinians in the 1970 fighting in Jordan. See *Arab Reports and Records* (henceforth ARR), 16–30 November 1971, p. 600.

35. The attack by members of the Black September took place on 5 September 1972 in Munich; 11 Israeli athletes, 5 Palestinian guerillas and one West German policeman were killed. *ARR*, 1–15 September 1972, p. 437.

36. The reference is to the UN invitation to Yasser Arafat (chief of the PLO) to address the General Assembly on 13 November 1974. This was the first time ever for a representative of the Palestinian Resistance to be recognized by and invited to speak to a UN organization.

37. The Lebanese Civil War flared up in April 1975 when right-wing armed militia attacked a bus carrying Palestinians and killed and wounded about 40 of them. The war went on and off throughout the rest of 1975, 1976, and part of 1977. Syrian troops became involved in 1976, ostensibly to put an end to the fighting, but ending up in clashes with the Palestinian Resistance, which by that time had been fully committed on the side of the Lebanese Leftists and patriotic forces.

38. The reference is to Yasser Arafat's historic visit to Ayatollah Khomeini in February 1979, only a few days after the latter's triumphant return to his country as the leader of the Islamic Iranian Revolution. See *ARR*, 28 February 1979, p. 1.

39. In Syria, the government of President Assad has been attacked on grounds that it is lopsidedly an Alawite minority regime controlling and oppressing the Sunni majority (80 percent) of the population. See *ARR*, 1978–80, for details of violent clashes, bombings, and assassinations. The Syrian government in its turn blamed these incidents on the Muslim Brotherhood and described that organization as right-wing fanatics. In Egypt, rising tension between some Coptic and Muslim groups in the last three years has prompted the government and the Peo-

ple's Assembly to form several investigating committees, the last of which was in May 1980. President Sadat himself was obliged to address the issue of religious strife publicly for the first time in a major speech on 15 May 1980. See *Al-Ahram*, 16 May 1980.

40. This fact was revealed during the interrogation and trials of the Technical Military Academy Group in 1974 and the Repentance and Holy Flight Group in 1977. See *ARR*, 11–16 July and 1–15 Aug. 1977.

41. The Saudi authorities announced that among those arrested, tried and executed were five Egyptians.

Chapter 3

1. This label is coined by J. S. Birks and C. A. Sinclair in their pioneering work *International Migration and Development in the Arab Region* (Geneva: International Labor Organization [ILO], 1980), which is a culmination of a series of studies undertaken by Durham University under the auspices of ILO since 1976. We find the term capital-rich especially appropriate not only because it states the most salient fact about these countries, but also because this is about the only aspect of richness that they have at present. As the text argues, these countries have a shortage (i.e., poverty) in almost all other resources (manpower, agriculture, etc.).

2. These include J. S. Birks and C. A. Sinclair, *International Migration, op. cit.*; Nazli Choucri, N. Eckaus and A. Mohie El-Din, *Migration and Employment in the Construction Sector: Critical Factors in Egyptian Development* (MIT: Technology Adaptation Program, 1978); N. Choucri, "Migration Among Developing Countries: The Middle East," presented to the American Political Science Association Meeting, Washington, D.C., Sept. 1977; Joan Clarke, "Jordan: A Labor Receiver—a Labor Supplier," prepared for the AID/Near East and presented to the Seminar on Labor Migration in the Middle East, Washington, D.C., 1977. Another paper by the same author was presented at the same seminar, entitled "Yemen in Profile." See also Muhammad Amin Faris, "Movement of Arab Labor Force among Arab States" [Arabic], presented to the National Conference on Strategy for Joint Arab Economic Action, Baghdad, 2–5 May 1978; Mahmoud Abdul Fadil, *Oil and Arab Unity* [Arabic] (Beirut: Centre for Arab Unity Studies, 1979); and Naim Sherbiny, "Flow of Labor and Capital in the Arab Homeland" [Arabic], in *Oil and Arab Cooperation* [Arabic] Vol. 3–4, 1977, pp. 44–64.

3. Our main sources included the *Preliminary Results of Egypt's 1976 Census* (Cairo: CAPMAS, 1977); "Possibilities of Agricultural Arab Labor Force Movement During the 1975–85 Period" [Arabic], prepared by The Arab Labor Organization, Dec. 1977; Lee Ann Ross, "Yemen, Migration: Blessing and Dilemma," presented to AID/Near East Bureau Seminar on Labor and Migration in the Middle East, Washington, D.C., 2 September 1977; Joan Clarke, "Jordan," *op. cit.*, in which she relied on reports published by Jordan's Ministry of Labor.

4. Birks and Sinclair, *International Migration, op. cit.*, pp. 20–21.

5. See Saad E. Ibrahim, "Population of the Arab World: An Overview," in Ibrahim and Hopkins (eds.), *Arab Society in Transition, op. cit.*

6. For more on this point see Saad E. Ibrahim and Donald Cole, *Saudi Arabian Bedouin, op. cit.*

7. It is believed that the actual participation ratio is even higher in labor-exporting countries like Egypt and Yemen, where a sizable number of women are often engaged in agricultural labor on family farms, but are not counted as gainfully employed when in fact they are.

8. M. A. Faris, "Regional Cooperation and Integration of Arab Manpower Resources: A Migration Strategy," presented to the Seminar on Population, Labor and Migration in the Arab Gulf States, Kuwait, 16–18 December 1978.

9. M.A. Fadil, *Oil and Arab Unity, op. cit.*, p. 40.

10. M.A. Ramadan, "Status of Egyptians in Kuwait" [Arabic], a diploma paper for the Arab Institute of National Planning, Kuwait, June 1978, and cited in Fadil, *Ibid.*, p. 41.

11. For a treatment of migration replacement see the two studies by Joan Clarke, "Jordan: A Labor Receiver—A Labor Giver" and "Yemen in Profile," *op. cit.*

12. M. A. Fadil, *Oil and Arab Unity, op. cit.*, p. 33.

13. *Ibid.*, p. 33.

14. Birks and Sinclair, *International Migration, op. cit.*, pp. 49–50.

15. *Ibid.*, p. 50.

16. See e.g., Muhammad al-Rumaihy, "Arab Migration to the Gulf: Economic Causes and Social Consequences" [Arabic], in *Al-ʿAraby* (an Arabic monthly) March 1979.

17. "The World Bank's Research Project on Labor Migration and Manpower in the Middle East and North Africa: Interim Report" (mimeo.) (Washington, D.C.: Dec. 1979).

18. *Ibid.*, p. 95.

Chapter 4

1. See Birks and Sinclair, *International Migration, op. cit.*, pp. 43–46.

2. See M. A. Fadil, *Oil and Arab Unity, op. cit.*, pp. 28–30.

3. *Ibid.*, p. 21.

4. For a comparative analysis of Arab migrant groups in oil-rich countries see the World Bank's report on "International Labor Migration and Manpower in the Middle East and North Africa," mimeographed (Washington, D.C.: September 1980).

5. Egypt's Foreign Ministry declared in 1978 that there were 1,365,000 Egyptians abroad distributed as follows: 500,000 in Libya, 500,000 in Saudi Arabia, 150,000 in Kuwait, 150,000 in the U.A.E., 5,000 in Iraq, and 15,000 in Qatar. *Al-Ahram* 18 Sept. 1978.

6. See Ali E. Hillal Dessouki, "Development of Egypt's Migration Policy 1952–1978," a mimeographed paper prepared for the project on Egyptian Labor

Migration, Cairo University-MIT Technology Adaptation Program, Cairo, 1978.

7. All figures in this paragraph are derived from *Egypt's 1976 Census*, Central Agency for Public Mobilization and Statistics (Cairo: September 1978), pp. 15–22.

8. For an elaborate discussion on over- and underpopulation in the Arab World see S. E. Ibrahim, "Population of the Arab World," in Ibrahim and Hopkins (eds.), *Arab Society in Transition, op. cit.*, pp. 303–322.

9. J. S. Birks and C. A. Sinclair, "Egypt: A Frustrated Labor Exporter," in *The Middle East Journal*, Vol. 33, No. 3 (Summer 1979), pp. 289–290.

10. For an elaboration see S. E. Ibrahim, "Income Distribution and Social Mobility in Egypt" in a forthcoming volume by R. Tignor and G. Abdel-Khalek (eds.), *Income Distribution in Egypt*.

11. The share of agricultural labor declined from 69 percent in 1938 to 50 percent by the end of the sixties; the share of manufacturing rose from 6 percent to 15 percent during the same period. See footnote 7 above for sources of these figures.

12. For an elaborate description of these restrictions see Dessouki, *Development of Egypt's Migration Policy, op. cit.*

13. For a full economic treatment of this period see Robert E. Mabro, *The Egyptian Economy 1952–1972* (London: Oxford University Press, 1974).

14. See S. Ibrahim, "Income Distribution and Social Mobility in Egypt," *op. cit.*

15. Some discussion of this point is to be found in Gouda Abdel-Khalek, "The Open Door Policy in Egypt: A Search for Meaning, Interpretation and Implication," in Herbert Thompson (ed.), *Studies in the Egyptian Political Economy* (Cairo: The American University in Cairo, *Cairo Papers in Social Science* Vol. Two, Monograph 3, 1979), pp. 74–100.

16. The reference here is to the marriages of President Sadat's three daughters (by his second wife) respectively to the sons of a pre-revolutionary Pasha (Ahmed Abdul-Ghaffar), a big landlord (Sayed Marʿei) and a new contractor-businessman (Osman Ahmed Osman).

17. The following account is summarized from Dessouki's *Development of Egypt's Migration Policy, op. cit.*, pp. 8–15.

18. Spokesmen for these ministries voiced their objection on several occasions in the mass media. See for example *Al-Ahram*, 27 Nov. 1968, 5 July 1969, 9 Sept. 1969; and *Al-Ahram al Iqtisadi* [Al-Ahram Economist], No. 308 (15 June 1968), pp. 36–37, and No. 401 (1 May 1972), pp. 6–7.

19. Dessouki, *Development of Egypt's Migration Policy, op. cit.*, pp. 15–16.

20. The slowdown of upward social mobility is documented and discussed in S. E. Ibrahim, "Income Distribution and Social Mobility," *op. cit.*

21. Amr Mohie El-Din, *The Emigration of University Academic Staff* (Cairo Univ.-MIT Project on Egyptian Labor Migration, 1980), mimeo.

22. Suzanne Messeiha, "Export of Egyptian Teachers." Cairo: MA Thesis in Economics, submitted to the American University in Cairo, 1979. Mimeo. Also appeared as Monograph 4, April 1980, of *Cairo Papers in Social Science*.

23. Amr Mohie El-Din, *The Emigration of University Academic Staff, op. cit.*, p. 48.

24. *Al-Ahram al-Iqtisadi* [Al-Ahram Economist], special supplement, "Financial and Economic Policy: 1980" (1 January 1980).

25. M. A. Fadil, *Oil and Arab Unity, op. cit.*, p. 51.

26. *IMF Consolidated Balance of Payments Report* (Washington D.C., 1979).

27. *Ibid.*

28. Declaration by Egypt's Minister of Economy (Dr. Hamed al-Saieh), published in *Al-Ahram al-Iqtisadi, op. cit.*, p. 94.

29. From a statement made by Egypt's Deputy Prime Minister for Economic Affairs (Dr. A. A. Magid), *Al-Ahram* daily newspaper (9 January 1981).

30. *Ibid.*

31. *Al-Ahram al-Iqtisadi* (1 January 1980), pp. 83–84.

32. See Fadil, *Oil and Arab Unity, op. cit.*

33. *Al-Ahram al-Iqtisadi* (15 January 1980), p. 30.

34. *Ibid.*

35. For a discussion on this point see the World Bank's report on *International Labor Migration, op. cit.*, p. 202.

36. For a discussion on this point see M. A. Fadil, "Impact of Egyptian Labor Migration to the Oil Countries on the Inflationary Process, the Future of Development, and Social Justice in the Egyptian Economy" [Arabic], a paper submitted to the Fifth Conference of Egyptian Economists, Cairo, March 1980.

37. Choucri, Eckaus, and Mohie El-Din, *Migration and Development, op. cit.*

38. Birks and Sinclair, *International Migration, op. cit.*, p. 94.

39. *Ibid.*, p. 94.

40. See their argument in "Egypt: A Frustrated Labor Exporter," *op. cit.*, pp. 288–303.

41. See S. E. Ibrahim, "Negative Effects of Income Differentials Among Arab Countries on the Lower Income Countries: the Case of Egypt" [Arabic], in *Oil and Arab Cooperation* [Arabic] Vol. III, No. 4 (1977), pp. 22–40; Adel Hussain, "Oil Money: An Obstacle for Integration and Unification" [Arabic], in *Arab Future* [Arabic] Vol. II, No. 5 (January 1979), pp. 16–32; M. A. Fadil, *Oil and Arab Unity, op. cit.*, pp. 53–58.

42. Dessouki, *Evolution of Egypt's Migration Policy, op. cit.*, p. 17.

43. Amr Mohie El-Din, *The Emigration of University Academic Staff, op. cit.*

44. Abdel Fattah Kandil, "Commitment of Arab Capital Toward the Arab Region" [Arabic], paper submitted to the Fifth Congress of Arab Economists, Baghdad, 12–15 April 1975, p. 26.

45. Isam Montaser, "The Arab Economic Order and Strategy of Development" [Arabic], paper submitted to the National Conference for Strategic Joint Economic Arab Action, Baghdad, 6–12 May 1978, pp. 7–8.

46. For more on this point, see Suzanne Paine, *Exporting Workers: The Turkish Case* (Cambridge: Cambridge University Press, 1974).

47. M. A. Fadil, *Oil and Arab Unity, op. cit.*, p. 58.

48. This observation was conveyed to the author by the Egyptian sociologist Muhammed al-Gawhary while on secondment to Saudi Arabia (1975–79). He was describing himself and others like him.

49. M. A. Fadil, *Oil and Arab Unity, op. cit.*, p. 58.

50. Suzanne Messeiha, *Export of Egyptian Schoolteachers, op. cit.*, pp. 33–39.

51. Amr Mohie El-Din, *Emigration of University, op. cit.*, pp. 48–54.

52. Statements to that effect have been made on several occasions by President Sadat. See for example the scripts of his two-hour interviews televised on Egyptian Television on 25 December 1979, and 1980, and published each in its entirety in *Al-Ahram* (Cairo daily) 26 December 1979 and 26 December 1980, respectively.

53. Dessouki, *Development of Egypt's Migration Policy, op. cit.*, pp. 17–25.

54. This is the law that allows citizens to use their hard currency in importing goods from abroad without obtaining the usual "import permit" which used to be required. For more details see G. Abdel-Khalek, "The Open Door Economic Policy in Egypt," *op. cit.*, pp. 74–100.

55. Up to 1975 the figures are from the *UN Yearbook of Internation Trade Statistics*, Vol. I. The figure for 1979 is from the Minister of Economy's Report to the People's Assembly in *Al-Ahram*, 1 Jan. 1980, p. 92.

56. See the *Minister of Economy's Report, op. cit.*, pp. 89–92.

57. See a discussion on the impact of oil wealth on work attitudes in Adel Hussain, "Oil Money, an Obstacle," *op. cit.*, pp. 27–28.

58. *Al-Ahram al-Iqtisadi* (15 January 1980, p. 30) reproduced an announcement to that effect advertised in all daily newspapers by Egypt Electric Distribution Company, a public-sector state corporation.

59. This point was stated by the Turkish Sociologist Deniz Kondioyoti in "Rural Transformation and Sex Roles in Turkey," a public lecture at UCLA's G. E. Von Grunebaum Center for Near Eastern Studies, Los Angeles, 2 June 1980.

60. These figures are from data presented in *Saudi Arabia's Ministry of the Interior Annual Statistical Book: 1979* (Riyadh, 1980), p. 238.

61. Saad E. Ibrahim, "Social Mobility and Income Distribution," *op. cit.*

62. Saad E. Ibrahim, "Anatomy of Egypt's Militant Islamic Groups," presented at the Middle East Studies Association Meeting, Washington, D.C., 6–9 Nov. 1980.

63. *Ibid.*, pp. 26–36.

64. Among these are Drs. Hikmat Abu-Zeid (former minister of social affairs under Nasser), Abdel-Aziz Kamel (former deputy prime minister), A. Kamal Abu El-Magd (former minister of information), General Saad El-Shazly (chief of staff of the Egyptian Army during the 1973 Arab-Israeli War, and later ambassador to London and Lisbon), and Ahmed Bahaa El-Din (journalist and former editor in chief of *Al-Ahram*).

Chapter 5

1. Fred Halliday, "Labor Migration in the Middle East" in *MERIP* Reports, No. 59, p. 6.

2. *Ibid.*, pp. 6–7.

3. Birks and Sinclair, *International Migration, op. cit.*, pp. 76–77.

4. *Ibid.*, p. 131; Halliday, "Labor Migration," *op. cit.*, p. 4; David Long, *Saudi Arabia* (Beverly Hills: Sage Publications and the Center for Strategic and International Studies of Georgetown University's *Washington Papers*, No. 39, 1976), p. 65; Alvin Cottrell and Frank Bray, *Military Forces in the Persian Gulf* (Beverly Hills: Sage Publications and the Center for Strategic and International Studies of Georgetown University's *Washington Papers*, No. 60, 1978), pp. 15–27.

5. This is the figure released by the Saudi Ministry of Finance and National Economy, Central Department of Statistics in its official publication of the *Saudi Population Census, 1974*, Vol. I, 1978. It is also quoted in the World Bank's *World Development Report, 1979* (Washington, D.C.: August 1979), p. 127.

6. In 1964, following the Yemeni Revolution, the late King Faisal, upon ascendance to power, launched sweeping political and social reforms. One of these was abolishing slavery, a system already in decline.

7. Birks and Sinclair, *International Migration, op. cit.*, p. 77.

8. See Chapter 2.

9. Birks and Sinclair, *International Migration, op. cit.*, p. 77.

10. The figures in this paragraph are from *The World Tables*, published for the World Bank by the Johns Hopkins University Press (Baltimore: 1980) p. 458.

11. For a discussion of this point see Halliday, "Labor Migration," *op. cit.*, pp. 3–4.

12. Ghazi Al-Gosaibi, "Saudi Development—a Unique Experiment," in *Middle East Business Exchange*, June 1980, p. 37.

13. *Ibid.*, p. 37.

14. "Saudi Arabia—Steady Growth in Economy" in *The Arab Economist* Vol. XII, May 1980, pp. 24–27.

15. The Wahhabi movement began in the later decades of the eighteenth century. Its founder, Muhammad Ibn Abdul Wahhab, a puritanical fundamentalist, allied himself politically with the house of Al-Saud of Najd in Central Arabia. Together they began a drive to unite Arabia and to institute fundamentalist Islamic institutions. Despite the ups and downs of this alliance vis-à-vis the outside world, it has persisted, and finally triumphed politically in the early decades of the twentieth century. Saudi Arabia as constituted today is a culmination of this effort. For more details on the Wahhabis, see John S. Habib, *The Ikhwan Movement in the Najd: Its Rise, Development and Decline* (Ann Arbor: University of Michigan, 1970); Harry S. Philiby, *Saudi Arabia* (Beirut: Libraire du Liban, 1968).

16. For a brief and concise account of sociopolitical development of Saudi Arabia in the last fifty years, see David Long, *Saudi Arabia, op. cit.*; also M. Hudson, *Arab Politics, op. cit.*, pp. 168–182.

17. *Al-Ahram* (Cairo daily), 9 January 1981, p. 5; *Egypt's Annual Statistical Abstract 1957–1978* (Cairo: CAPMAS, 1979), p. 212.

18. "Saudi Arabia: Slowdown in Development Eases Social Pressure," in *The Arab Economist* Vol. XI, No. 117, June 1979, pp. 22–25.

19. These figures are compiled from the *Saudi Prison Department's Yearbook 1396 H* [Arabic] (Riyadh: 1976), pp. 88–98.

20. An eyewitness account of upper class Saudi life style is to be found in Linda Blanford, *Oil Sheikhs* (London: Weindenfeld & Nicholson, 1976).

21. It is even alleged that the Saudi Prince who assassinated King Faisal in 1975 was identified with a family faction that had violently opposed the introduction of television to the kingdom several years earlier. See Hudson, *Arab Politics, op. cit.*, p. 173.

22. *The Middle East Monitor* Vol. IX, No. 22, 1 December 1979.

23. On this point see Yousef Sayegh, "The Social Cost of Oil Revenues," a paper submitted to the First Energy Conference, Abu Dhabi, U.A.E., 4–8 March 1979.

24. Central Department of Statistics, Ministry of Finance and National Economy, *National Accounts of Saudi Arabia 1970 through 1978 and 1979 Preliminary Estimates* (Riyadh: 1979).

25. "Hidden Commissions on Saudi Deals," in *The Arab Economist* Vol. XII, p. 42. The Saudi government had, by 1979, legalized commissions under the polite term of *"Sa'ai"* (expediting) fee.

26. See a lucid analysis of this attitude in Youssef Sayegh, "The Social Cost of Oil Revenues," *op. cit.*, pp. 11–12.

27. This account was reported in the *Manchester Guardian*, 17 July 1977.

28. Fred Halliday, "Labor Migration," *op. cit.*, pp. 12–13.

29. For a background on the major tribal federations and groupings and their rivalries, see H. St. John Philiby, *The Heart of Arabia*, 2 volumes (London: Constable, 1922); and the tribal map of Arabia in Roy Lebkicher et al., *ARAMCO Handbook* (Netherlands: Arabian-American Oil Company, 1960).

30. This limited circulation of the elite was noted some twenty years ago by Manfred Halpern, in *The Politics of Social Change in the Middle East and North Africa* (Princeton: Princeton University Press 1963), pp. 41–50. It is still applicable today, as Michael Hudson asserts in his *Arab Politics, op. cit.*, pp. 165–167.

31. Several of these attempted coups d'etat were admitted by the Saudi authorities in the 1960s and 1970s. See an account of some of these in the London *Daily Telegraph* (8 August 1969) and *Newsweek* (5 May 1978).

32. Some accounts of this discrimination are given in F. Halliday, "Labor Migration," *op. cit.*, pp. 9–13.

33. *Ibid.*, p. 12.

34. "Threat to Society with Everything," *The Guardian* (Manchester), 17 July 1977.

35. *Ibid.*

36. *Ibid.*

37. F. Halliday, "Labor Migration," *op. cit.*, pp. 12–13.

38. "Saudi Arabia: Slowdown in Development," *The Arab Economist, op. cit.*, p. 23.

39. "Kuwait: Expatriate Workers Outnumber Nationals," in *The Arab Economist* Vol. XI, No. 115, p. 32.

40. "Saudi Arabia: Slowdown in Development," *op. cit.*, p. 23.

41. This account is based on various media reports as summarized in *The Middle East Monitor* Vol. IX, No. 22, 1 December 1979, and No. 23. 15 December 1979.

42. Significantly, *Al-Ikhwan* was the name of the earlier Wahhabi fundamentalist movement that allied itself with the Al-Saud family and was instrumental in bringing about the present political order in Saudi Arabia (see footnote 15 above). The same name, Al Ikhwan, has been used in Egypt's Islamic militant mass movement, The Muslim Brotherhood, from 1978 on.

43. The reference here is to the storming of Egypt's Technical Military Academy in April 1974 by a militant Muslim group calling itself the *Islamic Liberation Organization*, and to the seizure of the Tunisian government building by a group of militant dissidents in the city of Gafsa on 28 January 1980. It took several days before Tunisian government forces backed by French warships and military supplies were able to take back the town of Gafsa, according to *The New York Times* of 28, 30, and 31 January 1980. Curiously enough, it was also rumored that French advisors were instrumental in the Saudi forces' counterattack on the Grand Mosque of Mecca two months earlier.

44. *The Middle East Monitor* Vol. IX, No. 24, 30 December 1979.

45. "Can Inflation be Slowed Without Recession?" in *The Arab Economist* Vol. XI, No. 114, 1979, p. 34.

46. The author's own observation during field work in Saudi Arabia in 1977.

47. For more on this point, see Saad E. Ibrahim, "Arab Cities: Present Situation and Future Prospects," proceedings of the U.N. Second Regional Population Conference of ECWA, Damascus, 1–6 December 1979.

48. This pattern prevails in most oil-rich countries of the Gulf. See Ishaq Y. al-Koutb, "Socioeconomic Consequences of Migration in Arab Gulf Societies" [Arabic], proceedings of the Third International Seminar of the Arab Gulf Studies (Basrah, Iraq, 29–31 March 1979), pp. 37–38.

49. *Ibid.*, p. 37; and S. E. Ibrahim, "Arab Cities," *op. cit.*, p. 37.

50. "Saudi Arabia: Slowdown in Development," *op. cit.*, p. 22.

51. A. Cottrell and F. Bray, *Military Forces in the Persian Gulf, op. cit.*, p. 18; Ali Mahmoud, "Arms Purchases Outpace Reconstruction and Economic Development," in *The Arab Economist* Vol. XI, No. 113, Feb. 1979, p. 22.

52. *Ibid.*, p. 22.

53. Cottrell and Bray, *Military Forces, op. cit.*, p. 16.

54. *Ibid.*, p. 19.

55. *Ibid.*, p. 21.

56. D. R. Tahtinen, *National Security Challenge to Saudi Arabia* (Washington, D.C.: American Enterprise Institute for Public Policy Research 1978), p. 17.

57. "$285 Billion Saudi Arabia Third Five-Year Development Plan Spending," in *Mid-East Business Exchange*, June 1980, p. 34.

58. Birks and Sinclair, *International Migration, op. cit.*, pp. 110–111.

59. "Kuwait: Expatriate Workers," *op. cit.*, p. 32.

60. This assessment is confirmed by the *World Bank Research Project on*

Labor Migration in the Middle East and North Africa: Interim Report, op. cit.
  61. Birks and Sinclair, *International Migration, op. cit.*, p. 110.

Chapter 6

1. Most of the constitutions and political charters of Arab states explicitly state the people of these respective countries are integral parts of the "Greater Arab Nation." Several make a point of putting the adjective "Arab" in the official name of the state (Egypt as the Arab Republic of Egypt, the same with Saudi Arabia, Yemen, Iraq, Syria, the United Arab Emirates, Libya, etc.).

2. See for example the preamble of the Labor Force Agreement signed in 1975 by fifteen Arab states, which states that the governments of these countries are signing it "as part of its relentless efforts in achieving comprehensive unity which makes the Arab homeland an integrated socioeconomic unit."

3. The findings of this survey are published in Saad Eddin Ibrahim, *Trends of Arab Public Opinion Toward the Issue of Unity* [Arabic] (Beirut: Center for Arab Unity Studies, 1980).

4. *Ibid.*, pp. 83–84.

5. *Ibid.*, pp. 139–144.

6. *Ibid.*, pp. 119–138.

7. For a survey of these pan-Arab organizations and their roles, see Jamil Matter and Ali Dessouki, *The Arab Regional System* [Arabic] (Beirut: Center for Arab Unity Studies, 1979).

8. For a historical account and assessment of the present role of Arab funds, see Soliman Demir, *Arab Development Funds in the Middle East* (New York: Pergamon Press for UNITAR, 1979).

9. See critical reviews of pan-Arab efforts for economic integration in Abdel Hamid Ibrahim, *Arab Economic Integration* [Arabic] (Beirut: Center for Arab Unity Studies, 1980); Mahmoud Al-Himsey, *Arab Development Plans: Convergence and Divergence* [Arabic] (Beirut: Center for Arab Unity Studies, 1980); Samir Al-Tanir, *Arab Economic Integration and the Issue of Unity* [Arabic] (Beirut: Arab Development Institute, 1978); A. H. Yammout, *Arab Economic Cooperation and the Necessity of Integration for Development* [Arabic] (Beirut: Arab Development Institute, 1976).

10. An example is the Lebanese complaint to the UN against alleged interference in its affairs by the United Arab Republic (Egypt and Syria) in 1958. Another is Tunisia's complaint to the Arab League against Libya, alleging Libya's intervention in Tunisian affairs by aiding the rebels in the Gafsa incident in January 1980.

11. An example is the Libyan and Egyptian intervention in helping President G. Numairy of the Sudan put down a Marxist coup d'etat in 1971.

12. Examples of armed interventions include Iraq-Kuwait incidents in 1960–1961; Egyptian involvement in Yemen and border forays against Saudi Arabia in 1962–1964; periodic border clashes between the two Yemens (1972, 1973, 1976, 1977); Egyptian-Libyan border war and mutual acts of sabotage

(1977); Algeria's and Morocco's entanglement over the Sahara. For a detailed account and analysis of the 1950s and 1960s in this regard see Malcom Kerr, *The Arab Cold War: Gamal Abd al Nasir and His Rivals 1958–1970* (London: Oxford University Press for Royal Institute of International Affairs, 1971); Jamil Matter and Ali Dessouki, *Arab Regional System, op. cit.*

13. Since 1977 especially, President Sadat has been quite blunt about the matter; see his annual review of internal, Arab, and world affairs on Egyptian television interviews with Himmat Mustafa, 25 December 1977, 1978, and 1979, published the following day (26 December) in those respective years in *Al-Ahram.*

14. Examples of this debate to be found in: M.A. Fadil, *Oil and Arab Unity, op. cit.*, pp. 143–157; Mohamed Sayed Ahmed, "Oil Surplus and its Role in Changing the Features of the Arab Homeland" [Arabic], in *Arab Future* Vol. 1, No. 3 (September 1978); Saad Eddin Ibrahim, "Negative Effects of Income Differentials Among Arab Countries" [Arabic], in *Oil and Arab Cooperation* Vol. 3, No. 4, 1977; Hazim al-Biblawi, "Toward a New Arab Economic Order" [Arabic], paper submitted to the Symposium on the New World Economic Order and the Arab World, Kuwait, 27–30 March 1976; Adel Hussain, "Oil Money is an Obstacle of Unification and Integration" [Arabic], in *Arab Future* Vol. 1, No. 5 (January 1979); Mohammed Al-Rumaihi, "Arab Migration to the Gulf: Economic Causes and Social Consequences" [Arabic], in *Al-Arabi*, No. 244, March 1979.

15. For example, A. Sakban, "The Arabs and the Reality of their Economic Unit" [Arabic],*Al-Ahram al-Iqtisadi*, 15 July 1975; Mahmud Riad, "Before the Opportunity is Lost" [Arabic], *Al-Ahram*, 12 Dec. 1975; Sayyid Marʿei and Saad Hagras, *If the Arabs Want it* [Arabic] (Cairo: Dar Al-Taʿawon, 1975); Loutfial-Kholi, "Petro-dollars and Petro-blood" [Arabic], *Al-Ahram*, 30 January 1975.

16. For the arguments on the side of oil-rich countries see, for example, a statement by Sheikh Ahmed Zaki Yamani, quoted in John Waterbury and Ragaei El-Mallakh, *The Middle East in the Coming Decade: From Wellhead to Well-being* (New York: McGraw Hill, 1978), pp. 75–76, and Abdulatif Al-Hamad, *Multilateral Investment and Arab Economic Integration* (Kuwait: Publications of the Kuwaiti Fund for Arab Economic Development, 1975); "Fifteen Years of International Development: The Kuwaiti Fund for Arab Development" [Arabic], in *Oil and Arab Cooperation* Vol. 3, No. 1, 1977.

17. The most extensive and sustained debate on the side of the poor countries, namely Egypt, was carried on in the Egyptian press in the winter and spring of 1978. It commenced with an article by the renowned author Tawfik Al-Hakim calling in essence for Egyptian "neutrality" in Middle Eastern affairs because its Arab sisters get her involved in wars but not in the sharing of their wealth. He followed that by four more articles arguing and amplifying the same point. One quotation is illustrative: "The Arab States to-day are divided into those concerned about doubling their wealth and others concerned about their bankruptcy. The first are enjoying their economic security, the latter are licking the wounds of their wars. Some are thinking of peace conferences, the others of oil conferences," *Al-Ahram*, 21 April 1978. The debate, in which most of Egypt's prominent thinkers took part, is documented and analyzed in S. E. Ibrahim (ed.) *Arabism of*

Egypt: The Debate of the Seventies [Arabic] (Cairo: Center for Political and Strategic Studies of Al-Ahram, 1978). Most of the arguments presented in the following pages of the text are abstracted from that debate.

18. On the question of risks, see Hisham Sadeq, "The Arab System of Guaranteeing Investment Against Non-Commerical Risks" [Arabic], in *Studies on Investment Guarantees in the Laws of Arab Countries* (Cairo: Institute of Arab Research and Studies, 1978), pp. 132–156.

19. On this point see Youssef A. Sayegh, "Arab Integration and the Pretext of Sovereignty" [Arabic], in *Arab Future*, No. 6, March 1979, pp. 23–41.

20. This has particularly been the case in Kuwait, where a greater measure of freedom of the press exists. See for example M. al-Rumaihy, *Obstacles of Socio-economic Development in the Contemporary Arab Gulf Societies* (Kuwait: Dar al-Syasa, 1977), p. 4, p. 32. He argues that oil-rich countries cannot have a meaningful development (as distinct from growth) in isolation from their broader Arab (and poor) surroundings.

21. This and other figures mentioned below are from the findings of the survey referred to in footnote 3 above, S. E. Ibrahim, *Trends of Arab Public Opinion, op. cit.*, pp. 183–205.

22. One hardly encounters an Arab professor working in Kuwait or Saudi Arabia without hearing endless accounts of discriminatory treatment especially in salaries and freedom of movement. Despite such complaints, very few would pass up the opportunity of working there for an additional year or two. In other words, their attitudes are quite ambivalent.

23. These averages are computed from the World Development Indicators Annex of the *World Development Report, 1979, op. cit.*, pp. 126–127.

24. *Ibid.*, p. 127. (Japan, New Zealand, and Australia are included in that average.)

25. The next highest worldwide is Switzerland, with $9,970 per capita GNP per annum. *Ibid.*, p. 127.

26. See, for example, Galal Amin, *The Modernization of Poverty: A Study in the Political Economy of Growth in Nine Arab Countries* (Leidin: E. J. Brill, 1974); J. Waterbury and R. E. Mallakh, *The Middle East, op. cit.*, p. 35.

27. F. Halliday, "Labor Migration in the Middle East," *op. cit.*, p. 5.

28. For a discussion of the nature of these "city-states" see S. E. Ibrahim, "Present and Future of Arab Cities," *op. cit.*

29. F. Halliday, "Labor Migration in the Middle East," *op. cit.*, p. 4.

30. The guerrilla war against the regimes of Sultan Qabus and his father was waged by the People's Front for the Liberation of Oman (PFLO). The war began in the early 1960s (by what was then called the Dhofar Liberation Front). It was aided by the neighboring radical Marxist regime of People's Democratic Yemen, while the Sultan's regime was aided by troops from the Shah of Iran. The guerrilla operations seemed to cease by 1976–1977.

31. Egypt's Gross Domestic Production (GDP) in 1960 represented 20.3 percent of the combined total of the 21 Arab states' GDPs. In 1965 its share rose to 21 percent, but by 1977 it declined to 16.2 percent of the Arab total. See M. al-Himsey, *Arab Development Plans, op. cit.*, p. 176.

32. J. Waterbury and R. E. Mallakh, *The Middle East, op. cit.*, p. 36.

33. Sudan at present has about ten million acres under cultivation. It could, without much technical difficulty, bring thirty million more acres under cultivation (both rainfed and river irrigated). Experts estimate that this would make the Arab World self-sufficient in grain and sugar. See Sayyid Mar'ei and S. Hagras, *If the Arabs Want It, op. cit.*, pp. 137–155.

34. An excellent account of major theories and methods of studying stratification is to be found in Reinhard Bendix and Seymour Lipset (eds.), *Class, Status, and Power: Social Stratification in Comparative Perspective* (New York: The Free Press, 1966, 2nd ed.).

35. A concise account of the two approaches and their respective methodologies is to be found in Frank Parkin, *Class in Equality and Political Order: Social Stratification in Capitalist and Communist Societies* (New York: Praeger, 1971).

36. For an original statement on the Marxist conception of class, see Karl Marx, *Capital: A Critique of Political Economy* Vol III (unfinished chapter) (Moscow: Foreign Language Publishing House, 1962), p. 862.

37. For an original statement of functionalism, see Kingsley Davis and Wilbert Moore, "Some Principles of Stratification," *The American Sociological Review* Vol. 10, No. 2, pp. 242–249.

38. Thus there are "commercial bourgeoisie," "compradore bourgeoisie" (local agents of foreign companies), and besides the "lumpen proletariat" (one of the original Marxist categories) there are "rural proletariat" and "urban proletariat," etc. See an attempt to apply the Marxist framework to Egypt in Mahmoud Hussain, *Class Conflict in Egypt 1945–1970* (New York: Monthly Review Press, 1973).

39. For a discussion of "status incongruency" see the sources cited in footnotes 34 and 35 above.

40. On arms systems and military expenditure in the region, see A. Cottrell and F. Bray, *Military Forces in the Persian Gulf, op. cit.*; Mahmoud Azmy "Facing Change in the Arab-Israeli Military Balance" [Arabic], in *Arab Future* Vol 3, No. 18, September 1980, pp. 88–114; J. T. Cummings, H. G. Askari, and M. Skinner, "Military Expenditures and Manpower Requirements in the Arabian Peninsula," *Arab Studies Quarterly* Vol. 2, No. 1, pp. 38–49.

41. Such family budget surveys exist for Egypt, Jordan, Iraq, and Sudan.

42. Used, for example, by G. Amin in his *Modernization of Poverty, op. cit.*; and by this author in his "Social Mobility and Income Distribution," in R. Tignor and G. Adel-Khalek (eds.), *Income Distribution in Egypt, op. cit.*

43. This overview is based on a previous study by the author. See S. E. Ibrahim, "Social Dimensions of Arab Economic Unity," in Labib Shukair (ed.), *Arab Economic Unity* [Arabic], forthcoming (Beirut: Center for Arab Unity Studies); part of the same study appeared under the same title in *Arab Thought* [Arabic], September 1979.

44. Variations within this broad categorization often existed. For more on this point see M. Halpern, *The Politics of Social Change, op. cit.*, and for the Maghrabe (Algeria, Tunisia, and Morocco), see Elbaki Hermassi, *Leadership and*

National Development in North Africa: A Comparative Study (Berkeley and Los Angeles: University of California Press, 1972).

45. Ibn Khaldun postulated the cycle as beginning with a conquering tribe that has a strong esprit de corps (*asabiyah*) marching from a hinterland to the urban seat of power, bringing down its decadent elite, and taking over. The first generation of consequences retains the *asabiyah* and the hinterland toughness. The second generation of this dynastic tribe consolidates and builds, but with less of the *asabiyah* cohesion. The third generation patronizes the arts and higher forms of culture and begins to enjoy luxurious living, with its *asabiyah* steadily declining. The fourth generation is born into luxury and fully indulges itself, with weakling rulers and hardly any *asabiyah* left. It is at this point that another tribe marches from the hinterland with strong *asabiyah*, brings down that fourth generation, takes over, and thus ushers in a new cycle. For a full account see Ibn Khaldun, *Prolegomenon: An Introduction to History*, translated by Franz Rosenthal (Princeton: Princeton University Press, 1967).

46. The term "new middle class" (NMC) was first coined by Manfred Halpern in 1951, and he later developed it fully in his *Politics of Change, op. cit.*, pp. 40–55.

47. For a concise account of this process, see Michael Hudson, *Arab Politics, op. cit.*, pp. 165–229.

48. For more on the social formations of the oil-rich countries, see M. Al-Rumaihy, *Obstacles of Socio-Economic Development, op. cit.*, pp. 23–26.

49. *Ibid.*, p. 24.

50. Yousef Sayegh, "The Social Cost of Oil Revenues," *op. cit.*; Mahmoud Abdel-Fadil, "The Pure Oil-Rentier States: Problems and Prospects of Development" [Arabic], in *Oil and Arab Cooperation* Vol. 5, No. 3, 1979.

51. For a view over time of the distribution of Arab countries on several socioeconomic indicators see M. Al-Himsey, *Arab Development Plans, op. cit.*, pp. 195–215, which presents valuable statistical data on the period between 1960 and 1977.

52. See, for example, *Ibid.*, pp. 216–243; M. A. Fadil, *Oil and Arab Unity, op. cit.*, pp. 143–165; Adel Hussain, "Arab Oil: An Obstacle to Unity and Integration" *op. cit.*; Y. Sayegh, "Arab Economic Integration and the Pretext of State Sovereignty," *op. cit.*

53. See, for example, Nadim al-Bitar, *Economic Theory and the Road to Arab Unity* [Arabic] (Beirut: Arab Development Institute, 1978); Samir al-Tanir, "Economic Integration and the Issue of Arab Unity," *op. cit.*; A. Yammout, *Arab Economic Cooperation, op. cit.*; J. Matter and Ali Dessouki, *Arab Regional System, op. cit.* The last three sources contain appendixes of various inter-Arab treaties on socioeconomic cooperation, as well as lists of various pan-Arab agencies within and outside the framework of the League of Arab States.

54. For a detailed account of the events of this border war see *Arab Reports and Records*, the issues of 1–15 July, 16–31 July, and 1–15 August 1977.

55. *Arab Reports and Records*, 15–31 May 1971.

56. Malcom Kerr, *The Arab Cold War, op. cit.*

57. *Arab Reports and Records*, 16–31 July 1977.

58. For an account of diverse Arab reactions to President Sadat's peace initiative, see *Arab Reports and Records*, issues of 15–30 November 1977, 16–30 September 1978, 1–15 October 1978; 1–15 April 1979, 16–30 April 1979.

59. *Arab Reports and Records*, 16–31 October 1978.

60. An account of these penalties and the broader economic issues of Sadat's peace initiatives are discussed in Fouad Morsy, "Economic Consequences of the Egyptian-Israeli Treaty" [Arabic], in *Arab Future* Vol. 3, No. 18, August 1980, pp. 28–53.

Chapter 7

1. The figures on these growth indicators are derived from *Statistical Indicators of the Arab World for the Period 1970-1978*, U.N. Economic Commission for West Asia—League of Arab States, 1980, pp. ix–xiv.

2. *Ibid.*, pp. ix–xiv, and *World Development Report, 1980*, published for the World Bank by Oxford University Press, pp. 110–121.

3. From data compiled from *Information Please Almanac Atlas and Yearbook, 1979* (33rd ed.) (New York: Information Please Publishing Inc., 1978), p. 48.

4. These figures on Arab trade are derived or computed from *The U.N. Statistical Yearbook, 1978* (New York, 1979), pp. 446–449; *OPEC Annual Statistical Bulletin, 1977* (Vienna: OPEC, 1978), pp. 1–5.

5. These figures are derived or computed from *World Development Report, op. cit.*, pp. 124–133; various issues of *United Nations Yearbook of International Trade Statistics*; and various issues of *Direction of Trade* (Washington, D.C.: International Monetary Fund, 1970–1979).

6. *Ibid.*, and *World Tables 1980*, published for the World Bank (Washington, D.C.: Johns Hopkins University Press, 1980), pp. 396–407.

7. M. Al-Himsey, *Arab Development Plans: Trends of its Complementarity and Divergence* [Arabic] (Beirut: Center for Arab Unity Studies, 1980), pp. 54–55.

8. These figures are compiled from various sources and cited in Sami Mansour, *Arms Trade and the Third World* [Arabic] (Cairo: Center for Political and Strategic Studies, 1979), pp. 30–34.

9. *World Development Report, op. cit.*, p. 139.

10. *Agency for International Development (AID) Congressional Presentation, Fiscal Year 1981, Annex IV: Near East*, p. 15.

11. For a full treatment of the subject see Gouda A. Khalek, "Development Assistance and its Impact on Income Distribution in Egypt," in R. Tignor and G. A. Khalek (eds.), *Income Distribution in Egypt*, forthcoming (New York: Holms and Meier, 1981).

12. *World Tables, op. cit.*, p. 463.

13. Manfred Halpern, *The Politics of Social Change in the Middle East and North Africa* (Princeton: Princeton University Press, 1963).

Bibliography

Abdel-Khalek, Gouda. "The Open Door Policy in Egypt: A Search for Meaning, Interpretation," in Herbert Thompson (ed.), *Studies in the Egyptian Political Economy* (Cairo: The American University in Cairo, *Cairo Papers in Social Science* Vol. II, Monograph 3, 1979).

Abdul-Fadil, Mahmoud. "Impact of Egyptian Labor Migration to the Oil Countries on the Inflationary Process, the Future of Development, and Social Justice in the Egyptian Economy" [Arabic]. A paper submitted to the Fifth Conference of Egyptian Economists, Cairo, March 1980.

_____.*Oil and Arab Unity* [Arabic] (Beirut: Center for Arab Unity Studies, 1979.

_____."The Pure Oil-Rentier States: Problems and Prospects of Development" [Arabic], in *Oil and Arab Cooperation* Vol. 5, No. 3, 1979.

Abdul-Karim, Ahmed Ezzat, et al. *Land and Peasant in Egypt Through the Ages* [Arabic] (Cairo: The Egyptian Historical Society, 1974).

Ahmed, Mohamed Sayed. "Oil Surplus and its Role in Changing the Features of the Arab Homeland" [Arabic], in *Arab Future* Vol. 1, No. 3 (Sept. 1978).

Al-Ahram al-Iqtisadi (Al-Ahram Economist). No. 308, June 15, 1968; No. 401, May 1, 1972. Special Supplement "Financial and Economic Policy: 1980," Jan. 1, 1980; Jan. 15, 1980.

Al-Ahram Daily Newspaper. Nov. 27, 1968; July 5, 1969; Sept. 9, 1969; July 15-19, 1977; April 21, 1978; Sept. 18, 1978; Dec. 26, 1979; Jan. 1, 1980; May 16, 1980; Dec. 26, 1980; Jan. 9, 1981.

Agency for International Development (AID) Congressional Presentation, Fiscal Year 1981, Annex IV: Near East.

Al-Biblaivi, Hazim. "Toward a New Arab Economic Order" [Arabic]. A paper submitted to the Symposium on the New World Economic Order and the Arab World, Kuwait, 27-30 March 1976.

Al-Bitar, Nadim. *Economic Theory and the Road to Arab Unity* [Arabic] (Beirut: Arab Development Institute, 1978).

Al-Gasaibi, Ghazi. "Saudi Development—A Unique Experiment," in *Middle East Business Exchange* (June 1980).

Al-Himsey, Mahmoud. *Arab Development Plans: Convergence and Divergence* [Arabic] (Beirut: Center for Arab Unity Studies, 1980).

Al-Koutb, Ishaq U. "Socioeconomic Consequences of Migration in Arab Gulf Societies" [Arabic]. Proceedings of the Third International Seminar of the Arab Gulf Studies, Basrah, Iraq, 29–31 March 1979.

Al-Rumaihy, Muhammad. "Arab Migration to the Gulf: Economic Causes and Social Consequences" [Arabic], in Al-ᶜAraby (an Arabic monthly), March 1979.

Al-Tanir, Samir. Arab Economic Integration and the Issue of Unity [Arabic] (Beirut: Arab Development Institute, 1978).

Altman, Israel. "Islamic Movements in Egypt," The Jerusalem Quarterly Vol. 3, No. 10 (Winter 1979).

ᶜAmer, Ibrahim. The Land and Peasant [Arabic] (Cairo: 1964).

Amin, Galal. The Modernization of Poverty: A Study in the Political Economy of Growth in Nine Arab Countries (Leiden: E. J. Brill, 1974).

The Arab Labor Organization. "Possibilities of Agricultural Arab Labor Force Movement During the 1975–85 Period" [Arabic]. Dec. 1977.

Arab Reports and Records. 16–30 Nov. 1971; 1–15 Sept. 1972; 11–16 July 1977; 1–15 Aug. 1977; 28 Feb. 1979; all issues of 1978–1980.

Arab Reports and Records. 15–31 May 1971; 15–31 July 1977; 1–15 Aug. 1977; 15–30 Nov. 1977; 16–30 Sept. 1978; 1–15 Oct. 1978; 16–31 Oct. 1978; 1–15 April 1979; 16–30 April 1979.

Ayubi, Nazih H.M. Bureaucracy and Politics in Contemporary Egypt (London: Ithaca Press, 1980).

_____. "The Political Revival of Islam: The Case of Egypt," memo., 1980.

Azmy, Mahmoud. "Facing Change in the Arab-Israeli Military Balance" [Arabic], in Arab Future, Vol. 3, No. 18 (Sept. 1980).

Beck, Lois and Nikki Keddie (eds.). Women in the Muslim World (Cambridge: Harvard University Press, 1979).

Bendix, Reinhard and Seymour Lipset (eds.). Class, Status, and Power: Social Stratification in Comparative Perspective, 2nd edition (New York: The Free Press, 1966).

"$285 Billion Saudi Arabia Third Five-Year Development Plan Spending," in Mid-East Business Exchange, June 1980.

Birks, J. S. and C. A. Sinclair. "Egypt: A Frustrated Labor Exporter," in the Middle East Journal Vol. 33, No. 3 (Summer 1979).

_____. International Migration and Development in the Arab Region (Geneva: International Labor Organization [ILO], 1980).

Blanford, Linda. Oil Sheikhs (London: Weindenfeld and Nicholson, 1976).

Bray, Frank. Military Forces in the Persian Gulf (Beverly Hills: Sage Publications and the Center for Strategic and International Studies of Georgetown University's Washington Papers, No. 60, 1978).

Choucri, N. "Migration Among Developing Countries: The Middle East," presented to the American Political Science Association Meeting, Washington, D.C., Sept. 1977.

Choucri, Nazli, N. Eckaus, and A. Mohie El-Din. Migration and Employment in the Construction Sector: Critical Factors in Egyptian Development (MIT: Technology Adaptation Program, 1978).

Clarke, Joan. "Jordan: A Labor Receiver—A Labor Supplier," prepared for AID/Near East, presented to the Seminar on Labor Migration in the Middle East, Washington, D.C., 1977.

Cole, Donald. "Bedouins of the Oil Fields," in *Natural History* (Nov. 1973).

———. *Nomads of the Nomads* (Chicago: Aldine, 1975).

Cummings, J. T., H. G. Askari, and M. Skinner. "Military Expenditures and Manpower Requirements in the Arabian Peninsula," *Arab Studies Quarterly* Vol. 2, No. 1 (1980).

Daily Telegraph of London (Aug. 8, 1969).

Davis, Kingsley, and Wilbert Moore. "Some Principles of Stratification," *The American Sociological Review* Vol. 10, No. 2.

DeKmejian, R. Hrair. "The Anatomy of Islamic Revival and the Search for Islamic Alternatives," *Middle East Journal* Vol. 34, No. 1 (Winter 1980).

Demir, Soliman. *Arab Development Funds in the Middle East* (New York: Pergamon Press for UNITAR, 1979).

Dessouki, Ali Eddin Hillal. *Development of Egypt's Migrant Policy 1952–1978* (Cairo: Cairo University—MIT Technology Adaptation Program, 1978).

———. "The Resurgence of Islamic Movements in Egypt," memo., 1979.

Direction of Trade (Washington D.C.: International Monetary Fund, 1970–1979).

Egypt's Annual Statistical Abstract 1957–1978 (Cairo: CAPMAS, 1979).

Egypt's 1976 Census (Cairo: Central Agency for Public Mobilization and Statistics, September 1978).

Fadil, Mahmoud Abdul. *Oil and Arab Unity* [Arabic] (Beirut: Center for Arab Unity Studies, 1979).

Fanon, Frantz. *A Dying Colonialism* (New York: Monthly Review Press, 1965).

Faris, Muhammad Amin. "Movement of Arab Labor Force among Arab States" [Arabic]. Presented to National Conference on Strategy for Joint Arab Economic Action, Baghdad, 2–5 May 1978.

———. "Regional Cooperation and Integration of Arab Man-power Resources: A Migration Strategy." Presented to the Seminar on Population, Labor and Migration in the Arab Gulf States, Kuwait, 16–18 December 1978.

"Fifteen years of International Development: The Kuwaiti Fund for Arab Development" [Arabic], in *Oil and Arab Cooperation* Vol. 3, No. 1 (1977).

Ghandour, Marwan. "The Leader-Entrepreneur in the Private Sector," in proceedings of conference on Leadership and Development in the Arab World, American University of Beirut, 10–14 Dec. 1979.

Ghorbal, Muhammed Shafique. *The Formation of Egypt* [Arabic] (Cairo: Al-Nahdha al-Mis-miyya Book Co., 1957).

Gordon, Lincoln. *The Growth Policies and the International Order* (New York: McGraw-Hill, 1979).

Habib, John S. *The Ikhwan Movement in the Najd: Its Rise, Development and Decline* (Ann Arbor: University of Michigan, 1970).

Halliday, Fred. "Labor Migration in the Middle East," in *MERIP* Reports, No. 59.

Halpern, Manfred. *The Politics of Social Change in the Middle East and North Africa* (Princeton: Princeton University Press, 1963).

Al-Hamad, Abdulatif. *Multilateral Investment and Arab Economic Integration* (Kuwait: Publications of the Kuwaiti Fund for Arab Economic Development, 1975).

Hermassi, Elbaki. *Leadership and National Development in North Africa: A Comparative Study* (Berkeley and Los Angeles: University of California Press, 1972).

"Hidden Commissions on Saudi Deals," in the *Arab Economist* Vol. XII, p. 42.

Hirsch, Fred. *Social Limits to Growth* (Cambridge: Harvard University Press, 1976).

Hudson, Michael. *Arab Politics: The Search for Legitimacy* (New Haven: Yale University Press, 1977).

Hussain, Adel. "Oil Money: An Obstacle for Integration and Unification" [Arabic], in *Arab Future* [Arabic] Vol. II, No. 5 (January 1979).

Hussain, Mahmoud. *Class Conflict in Egypt 1945-1970* (New York: Monthly Review Press, 1973).

Humphreys, R. S. "Islam and Political Values in Saudi Arabia, Egypt and Syria," *Middle East Journal* Vol. 33, No. 1 (Winter 1979).

Ibn Khaldun. *Prolegomenon: An Introduction to History*, translated by Franz Rosenthal (Princeton: Princeton University Press, 1967).

Ibrahim, Abdel Hamid. *Arab Economic Integration* [Arabic] (Beirut: Center for Arab Unity Studies, 1980).

Ibrahim, Saad Eddin. "Anatomy of Egypt's Militant Islamic Groups" (forthcoming), in *International Journal of Middle East Studies* (November 1980).

_____. "Arab Cities: Present Situation and Future Prospects." Proceedings of the U.N. Second Regional Population Conference of ECWA, Damascus, 1–6 Dec. 1979.

_____ (ed.). *Arabism of Egypt: The Debate of the Seventies* [Arabic] (Cairo: Center for Political and Strategic Studies of Al-Ahram, 1978).

_____. "Income Distribution and Social Mobility in Egypt," in Robert Tignor and Gouda Abdel-Khalek (eds.), *Income Distribution in Egypt* (forthcoming).

_____. "Negative Effects of Income Differentials Among Arab Countries on the Lower Income Countries: the Case of Egypt" [Arabic], in *Oil and Arab Cooperation* [Arabic] Vol. III, No. 4 (1979).

_____. "Social Dimensions of Arab Economic Unity," in Labib Shukair (ed.), *Arab Economic Unity* [Arabic] (forthcoming) (Beirut: Center for Arab Unity Studies).

_____. *Trends of Arab Public Opinion Toward the Issue of Unity* [Arabic] (Beirut: Center of Arab Unity Studies, 1980).

Ibrahim, S. E., and D. P. Cole. *Saudi Arabian Bedouin* (Cairo: AUC's *Cairo Papers in Social Science*, Vol. I., Monograph V., April 1978).

Ibrahim, Saad E. and Nicholas S. Hopkins (eds.), *Arab Society in Transition* (Cairo: American University in Cairo Press, 1977).

IMF Consolidated Balance of Payments Report (Washington, D.C.: 1969).

Information Please Almanac Atlas and Yearbook, 1979, 33rd. edition (New York: Information Please Publishing Inc., 1978).

Kandil, Abdel Fattah. "Commitment of Arab Capital Toward the Arab Region"

[Arabic]. A paper submitted to the Fifth Congress of Arab Economists, Baghdad, 12–15 April 1975.

Kerr, Malcolm. *The Arab Cold War: Gamal Abd al-Nasir and His Rivals 1958–1970* (London: Oxford University Press for Royal Institute of International Affairs, 1971).

Al Kholi-Loutfia. "Petro-dollars and Petro-blood" [Arabic], *Al-Ahram* (30 January 1975).

"Kuwait: Expatriate Workers Outnumber Nationals," in *The Arab Economist* Vol. XI, No. 115.

Lebkicher, Roy, et al. *ARAMCO Handbook* (Netherlands: Arabian American Oil Company, 1960).

Lewis, Bernard. "The Return of Islam," *Commentary* (January 1976).

Long, David. *Saudi Arabia* (Beverly Hills: Sage Publications and the Center for Strategic and International Studies of Georgetown University's Washington Papers, No. 39, 1976).

Mabro, Robert E. *The Egyptian Economy 1952–1972* (London: Oxford University Press, 1974).

Mahmoud, Ali. "Arms Purchases Outpace Reconstruction and Economic Development," in the *Arab Economist* Vol. XI, No. 113 (Feb. 1979).

The *Manchester Guardian* (Manchester: 17 July 1977).

Mansour, Sami. *Arms Trade and the Third World* [Arabic] (Cairo: Center for Political and Strategic Studies, 1979).

Marᶜei, Sayyid, and Saad Hagras. *If the Arabs Want It* [Arabic] (Cairo: Dar Al Taᶜawon, 1975).

Marx, Karl. *Capital: A Critique of Political Economy*, Vol. III (Moscow: Foreign Language Publishing House, 1962).

Matter, Jamil, and Ali Eddin Hillal. *The Arab Regional System: A Study of Arab Political Relations* [Arabic] (Beirut: Center for Arabic Studies, 1979).

Messeiha, Suzanne. *Export of Egyptian Teachers* (mimeo). M.A. Thesis in Economics, submitted to the American University in Cairo, 1979. Also in *Cairo Papers in Social Science*, Monograph 4, April 1980.

The *Middle East Monitor* Vol. IX, No. 22 (Dec. 1, 1979).

The *Middle East Monitor* Vol. IX, No. 24 (Dec. 30, 1979).

Military Balance 1977/1978 (London: Institute for Strategic Studies).

Mohie El-Din, Amr. *The Emigration of University Academic Staff* (mimeo). (Cairo University—MIT Project on Egyptian Labor Migration, 1980).

Montaser, Isam. "The Arab Economic Order and Strategy of Development" [Arabic]. A paper submitted to the National Conference for Strategic Joint Economic Arab Action, Baghdad, 6–12 May 1978.

Morsy, Fouad. "Economic Consequences of the Egyptian-Israeli Treaty" [Arabic], in *Arab Future* Vol. 3, No. 18 (Aug. 1980).

National Accounts of Saudi Arabia 1970 through 1978 and 1979 Preliminary Estimates (Riyadh: Ministry of Finance and National Economy, 1979).

Newsweek (May 5, 1978).

New York Times (Jan. 28, 30, 31, 1980).

OPEC Annual Statistical Bulletin 1977 (Vienna: OPEC, 1978).

Paine, Suzanne. *Exporting Workers: The Turkish Case* (Cambridge: Cambridge University Press, 1974).

Parkin, Frank. *Class in Equality and Political Order: Social Stratification in Capitalist and Communist Societies* (New York: Praeger, 1971).

Parsons, Talcott. *Societies: An Evolutionary and Comparative Perspective* (New Jersey: Prentice-Hall, 1966).

Philiby, Harry S. *Saudi Arabia* (Beirut: Libraire du Liban, 1968).

Philiby, John. *The Heart of Arabia* (2 volumes) (London: Constable, 1922).

Preliminary Results of Egypt's 1976 Census (Cairo: CAPMAS, 1977).

Ramadan, M. A. "Status of Egyptians in Kuwait" [Arabic], the Arab Institute of National Planning (Kuwait: June 1978).

Riad, Mahmud. "Before the Opportunity is Lost" [Arabic] *Al-Ahram* (Dec. 12, 1975).

Ross, Lee Ann. "Yemen Migration: Blessing and Dilemma," presented to AID/ Near East Bureau Seminar on Labor and Migration in the Middle East, Washington, D.C., 2 September 1977.

Al-Rumaihi, Muhammad. *Obstacles of Socio-economic Development in the Contemporary Arab Gulf Societies* (Kuwait: Dar al-Syasa, 1977).

Sadeq, Hisham. "The Arab System of Guaranteeing Investment Against Non-Commercial Risks" [Arabic], in *Studies on Investment Guarantees in the Laws of Arab Countries* (Cairo: Institute of Arab Research and Studies, 1978).

Sakban, A. "The Arabs and the Reality of their Economic Unit" [Arabic], *Al-Ahram al-Iqtisadi*, July 15, 1975.

Saudi Arabia's Ministry of the Interior Annual Statistical Book: 1979 (Riyadh, 1980).

"Saudi Arabia: Slowdown in Development Eases Social Pressure," in *The Arab Economist* Vol. XI, No. 117 (June 1979).

"Saudi Arabia—Steady Growth in Economy," in *The Arab Economist* Vol. XII (May 1980).

Saudi Population Census, 1974 Vol. I (1978).

Saudi Prison Department's Yearbook 1396H [Arabic] (Riyadh: 1976).

Sayegh, Yousef A. "Arab Integration and the Pretext of Sovereignty" [Arabic], in *Arab Future* No. 6 (March 1979).

_____. "The Social Cost of Oil Revenues." A paper submitted to the First Energy Conference (Abu-Dhabi, U.A.E., 4–8 March 1979).

Sherbiny, Naim. "Flow of Labor and Capital in the Arab Homeland" [Arabic], in *Oil and Arab Cooperation* [Arabic] Vol. 3-4, 1977.

Statistical Indicators of the Arab World for the Period 1970–1978, U.N. Commission for West Asia—League of Arab States, 1980.

Tahtinen, D. R. *National Security Challenge to Saudi Arabia* (Washington, D.C.: American Enterprise Institute for Public Policy Research, 1978).

Tignor, Robert, and Gouda Abdel-Khalek (eds.). *Income Distribution in Egypt* (forthcoming) (New York: Holms and Meier, 1981).

The U.N. Statistical Yearbook 1978 (New York: 1979).

U.N. Yearbook of International Trade Statistics Vol. I.

Waterbury, John, and Ragaei El-Mallakh. *The Middle East in the Coming Decades: From Wellhead to Well-being?* (New York: McGraw-Hill, 1978).

Williams, John A. "A Return to the Veil in Egypt," *Middle East Review* Vol. XI, No. 3 (Spring 1978).

The World Bank's Research Project on Labor Migration and Manpower in the Middle East and North Africa (mimeo.) (Washington, D.C.: Dec. 1979).

World Bank's report on *International Labor Migration and Manpower in the Middle East and North Africa* (mimeo) (Washington, D.C.: Sept. 1980).

World Bank's *World Development Report, 1975* (Washington, D.C.: August 1979).

The World Tables. Published for the World Bank (Baltimore: Johns Hopkins University Press, 1980).

Yammout, A. H. *Arab Economic Cooperation and the Necessity of Integration for Development* [Arabic] (Beirut: Arab Development Institute, 1976).

Index

D5